CURRICULUM MANAGEMENT
FOR EDUCATIONAL AND
SOCIAL SERVICE ORGANIZATIONS

ABOUT THE AUTHORS

Fenwick W. English is Vice Chancellor for Academic Affairs at Indiana University-Purdue University at Fort Wayne, Indiana. Formerly he was Dean of the School of Education at IPFW. He served as Department Head of Educational Administration in the College of Education at the University of Cincinnati, and as a professor at the University of Kentucky and Lehigh University in Bethlehem, Pennsylvania.

Dr. English's practitioner experience includes that of a classroom teacher and middle school principal in California, project director in Arizona, assistant superintendent in Florida, and a superintendent of schools in New York. He has been an associate director of the American Association of School Administrators (AASA) in Arlington, Virginia, and a partner in the consulting division of Peat, Marwick, Main (KMPG). He is the author or co-author of sixteen previous books in education. He has worked in 49 of the 50 states, the U.S. Virgin Islands and Puerto Rico, as well as nine foreign countries including Saudi Arabia and Japan.

Dr. English received his B.S. and M.S. from the University of Southern California, and his Ph.D. from Arizona State University.

Robert L. Larson is a Professor of Education in the College of Education and Social Services at The University of Vermont. He teaches courses in curriculum management, effecting and managing change, leadership, research methods, supervision, and staff evaluation and development.

Dr. Larson has been a high school teacher, an administrative intern with the National Assocation of Secondary School Principals Ford Foundation Program, and a faculty member at The University of Vermont since 1968. During his years in Vermont he has served on committees of the Vermont Principals' Assocation, and the National Association of Secondary School Principals. He is an active member of the American Association of School Adminstrators, and has been a presenter for national AASA and Phi Delta Kappa institutes.

Currently, he is writng the second edition of his book, *Changing Schools from the Inside Out*, based on field research in secondary schools, and has completed a study of restructuring in two Vermont high schools.

Second Edition

CURRICULUM MANAGEMENT FOR EDUCATIONAL AND SOCIAL SERVICE ORGANIZATIONS

By

FENWICK W. ENGLISH

Vice Chancellor for Academic Affairs
Indiana University-Purdue University
at Fort Wayne, Indiana

and

ROBERT L. LARSON

Professor of Education
College of Education and Social Services
The University of Vermont
Burlington, Vermont

CHARLES C THOMAS • PUBLISHER, LTD.
Springfield • Illinois • U.S.A.

Published and Distributed Throughout the World by

CHARLES C THOMAS • PUBLISHER, LTD.
2600 South First Street
Springfield, Illinois 62794-9265

© *1996 by* CHARLES C THOMAS • PUBLISHER, LTD.
ISBN 0-398-06667-1 (cloth)
ISBN 0-398-06668-X (paper)

Library of Congress Catalog Card Number: 96-20320

First Edition, 1987
Second Edition, 1996

With THOMAS BOOKS *careful attention is given to all details of manufacturing
and design. It is the Publisher's desire to present books that are satisfactory as to
their physical qualities and artistic possibilities and appropriate for their particular
use.* THOMAS BOOKS *will be true to those laws of quality that assure a good
name and good will.*

Printed in the United States of America
SC-R-3

Library of Congress Cataloging-in-Publication Data

English, Fenwick W.
  Curriculum management for educational and social service
organizations / by Fenwick W. English and Robert L. Larson. — 2nd
ed.
      p.   cm.
  Rev. ed. of: Curriculum management for schools, colleges,
business. c1987.
  Includes bibliographical references (p.   ) and index.
  ISBN 0-398-06667-1 (cloth). — ISBN 0-398-06668-X (paper)
  1. Curriculum planning—United States. 2. School management and
organization—United States. I. Larson, Robert L. (Robert Lowell),
1936–   . II. English, Fenwick W. Curriculum management for
schools, colleges, business. III. Title.
LB2806.15.E53   1996
375'.001—dc20   96-20320
                                                             CIP

INTRODUCTION

This is the second and revised edition of the original book released by Charles C Thomas in 1987. It remains true to the thrust of the first edition, but much new content has been added and old content modified, resulting mainly from interactions with students and the culling of their questions and responses through a course taught by one of the coauthors at The University of Vermont. Everything in the first edition was put up against the yardstick of student feedback. Nearly ten years of student papers, projects, and solicited feedback after completion of the course, have rounded out and polished the principles, concepts, processes, and practices presented in 1987. In addition to the classroom laboratory, most of the material has also been tested by participant feedback in national in-service programs focusing on curriculum auditing and the development of curriculum guides.

All organizations have a curriculum. Look around in schools, colleges, businesses, and in human service and government agencies; there will be pieces of paper with varying labels but which will bear upon the tasks which comprise the roles and jobs people *do* in those organizations. *Curriculum* is the descriptor for defining the tasks which comprise human work. Sometimes the work is incomplete. Most often the curriculum lacks a full delineation of the assumptions which lie behind the words, but the collectivity of paper defining work *is the curriculum.* Curriculum is the work plan(s).

Although schools (and implicitly colleges and other higher education institutions) are the target of the book, we have been pleasantly surprised, since the first edition was published, that most of the content, with some adaptation by the consumer, is also highly relevant to social service organizations. Students employed as administrators or staff developers in United Way agencies, hospitals, and agencies of state government (e.g., Departments of Corrections, Education, and Social and Rehabilitation Services) have applied curriculum management ideas to their internal needs.

In schools, curriculum represents all the paper that a teacher may use to guide her/his instruction. That collectivity includes lesson plans, textbooks, board policies, student work and feedback, parental input, colleague reviews, locally produced guides, state prescriptions, and even national standards where they exist. All of this paper represents an attempt *to influence* the act of teaching in the classroom.

Teachers make choices. From one perspective a curriculum spreads out the choices, enriches them, defines them. From another the paper *controls* them. In the former view curriculum promises diversity. In the latter view it may be a form of oppression. In some situations both may be occurring simultaneously.

Curriculum development in the United States has been a peculiar blend of national task forces, state initiatives, and local prerogatives. This strange amalgam has produced a patchwork of curricula with occasional spots of brilliance popping up in a sea of mediocrity. Local curriculum too often is anchored to the lowest common denominator of teacher interest and local board and administrator support. The American penchant for resisting external governmental controls has consistently failed to produce continuity of improved curricula and student expectations for high achievement, particularly on international comparisons. It has allowed textbook publishers and test makers to dominate local curriculum development practices.

We do have a national curriculum. That is the "textbook collectivity" of six or seven publishers who control much of the marketplace. In turn, the national curriculum has been established by textbook adoptions in California, Texas, and recently Florida. This curriculum is the set of expectations that exist for the greatest number of potential school systems in these three states. This situation hardly represents "quality" or "the highest ceiling of expectations for student learning." In other words, as long as curriculum practices are driven by textbook adoptions in a handful of states, the occasional "local spot of brilliance" will be drowned in the sea of low level, minimal expectations for student learning. Trying to improve achievement by bootstrapping local expectations never gets beyond the boots.

The sad fact is that too many Americans do not expect enough from our students. Local politics have produced both educational and political compromises that have left huge holes in systematic instruction unaddressed for long periods of time. The empirical base for these judgments is from interactions with students who are employed in a wide spectrum of schools and school systems, from our experiences for four decades each in the field, and from national curriculum audits that show again and again the pitfalls and potholes of local politics combined with state agencies failing to intervene effectively to improve pupil learning via a focused and connected curriculum.

Curriculum design in the United States is much like baking a layer cake. Each layer rests on the other and has its own set of problems. Imagine the top layer being the state government, the second layer being the local board, the third layer being the local school, and the fourth layer being the classroom. State pronouncements are part of the cake, but they don't affect the bottom layer, in most instances, in a substantive way. Board policies are part of the whole, but they don't impact what really happens in the classroom.

Some of the critics think that the problem of the layer cake can be solved by giving all the authority to the bottom two layers, schools and administrators and teachers. We disagree. The problem is with the structure. Uncoordinated "bottom-up" approaches will not improve student achievement, particularly if achievement, as measured by tests, is seen as cumulative, focused learning. Rather, assessment (to use a broader term than "testing") requires connectivity between classrooms in schools. This is produced by a *managed curriculum*. A managed curriculum requires coordination and articulation. These are the results of *control*.

We believe that what is required is a *marble cake,* a true mixture of the elements which consist of a high level of interactivity and influence across and between the layers. These, in turn, must be geared to the highest levels of expectations for students on the *international* scene, and not the lowest common levels of the bulk of the school systems in California, Texas, and Florida. High expectations are *uncommon*. We raise averages by raising ceilings, not adopting minimal expectations for the majority. In this sense, improving educational attainment is not a democratic enterprise. It lies, rather, in the relentless pursuit of excellence for the largest number of students. It is democratic in that we believe nearly all students are capable of learning more than they do now in the nation's classrooms, whether they be located in the public, private, or home arenas.

A long time ago, a scholar of teacher behavior and student achievement explained that all of the research could be effectively summarized by the idea, "You get what you teach for." The concept of "what you teach for" is contained *in the curriculum.* This second edition still aims to define, clarify, and provide examples which respond to the queries "for what?", "for whom?", and "by what means?" In this sense, the book is eminently *practical.*

In another sense it is practical, too. What is in these pages revolves around the *common, everyday activities, events, and infrastructure of organizations.* Rarely does anything new have to be created to utilize the principles, concepts, processes, and practices contained in these chapters. Thus, curriculum management promotes organizational *efficiency as well as effectiveness.*

In concluding this introduction, we want to express our appreciation to several people for their encouragement and support for our tackling a second edition, or for their assistance in developing it. At the risk of skipping someone, here they are: the students in our courses who provided feedback in class, responded to mail questionnaires, and who gave permission for their words to be quoted; Doctor Robert Henry of Campbell University; Doctor Albert Pautler of the University of Buffalo; Doctor Betty Steffy of Indiana University-Purdue University at Fort Wayne; Michael Dooley for demonstrating time and again how curriculum management principles and practices could be applied to the field of human services; Wayne Kenyon for his editorial critique of the first edition; George Voland for his editorial work on this edition; Christa Greaney for several new illustrations; and Joyce Keeler for typing the final manuscript within a short time frame.

F.W.E.
R.L.L.

CONTENTS

CURRICULUM MANAGEMENT
FOR EDUCATIONAL AND
SOCIAL SERVICE ORGANIZATIONS

Chapter 1

CURRICULUM MANAGEMENT

Nearly all complex organizations have a curriculum. For some like industrial work organizations, human services agencies, government bureaus, the military, and religious organizations it may be in the form of operational manuals, work guides, procedure and policies, program descriptions, job descriptions, and historic documents.

For educational organizations, curriculum may exist in the form of course catalogs, curriculum guides, lesson plans, scope and sequence charts, and textbooks. Human work in complex organizations is defined, shaped, coordinated, evaluated and regulated by a vast array of expectations cast into documents that provide purpose, content, and structure to it. Such documents are both a result of top-down and bottom-up development.

Work in complex organizations cannot be improved unless it can be sufficiently defined, described, discussed, assessed, and made intelligible to the people who must perform it. In the larger society, organizations delineate their purposes and create boundaries around their societal functions. Schools educate and train the young and old. Factories make things. Hospitals restore health. Prisons punish and reform criminals. Governments provide services to their peoples from collecting and redistributing money to national defense. Churches, temples and synagogues provide meaning and structure to human spiritual life.

It can be seen that more than one organization educates and trains people. For example, religious organizations, military organizations and industrial organizations are all involved in education and training. But their education and training is specific to their purposes. Certain skills are redundant across many types of human organizations such as calculation, analysis, and communication. Curriculum is the name of an interrelated set of codified expectations that define and provide the regulatory framework for different types of work in the organizations where it is located. The key to improving work in organizations lies in shaping it so that it is consistent, i.e., *repeatable.* This does not mean that

3

the work is exactly the same, though it may be. For example, in factories the creation of products usually involves a series of repetitious acts, though workers doing the production may not always do exactly the same thing.

In medical, educational, legal, and religious organizations the scope and content of the work may be structured differently according to the needs of the clients served, but there is a certain consistency to it. If this were not so, it would be impossible to separate good from poor performance for the clients, or good from poor practice on the part of the people doing the work. The only way judgments can be made about the quality and nature of human work is that there is some consistency to it. Work is, therefore, not random acts which once seen occur no more. What makes work peculiar to other kinds of human activity is its quality of being reproducible and the results obtained from it.

For instance, "going to work" indicates a certain predictability, and economic remuneration is present even though the work itself may be quite different in application. A medical doctor "going to work" is quite different from an auto worker "going to work." Both occupations involve repetition, but the nature of the repetition is different in scope, content, and application. Even play has a certain repetitious quality. One may play golf, i.e., the game (the rules which define what golf is and isn't) provides the consistency. The golfer may be playing, but the caddie is working. One may go to see a play as entertainment. The audience is playing; the actors, ushers and stage hands are working.

Curriculum in the broadest sense is therefore the codification of expectations of work around: (1) what is to be done, produced or performed, or work content and process, and (2) the expected result or outcome of the production of an object or the rendering of a service. In educational organizations the work to be performed is called *teaching*. The expected result is *learning*. Curriculum spans both the definition of teaching and the production of knowledge as manifested in learning. Curriculum is profoundly influenced by culture, politics, class, and economics as well as by conceptions of the nature of teaching and learning. None of these are neutral activities. They all involve decisions about the nature of the good life and even the afterlife, the purpose of human society and its responsibilities to its citizenry, conceptions of wealth and class, economic activity, and decisions about acceptable and unacceptable human responses to moral, ethical, economic, political and spiritual situations which specific people confront, cope, and resolve during their individual lives and the life of their civilization or tribal or communal activity.

Curriculum Development Is Not a Neutral Activity

There was a time when curriculum development was considered similar to engineering, relying on a set of principles that resulted in the creation and definition of work content in educational organizations. This view no longer prevails. It was naive. Since schools are not neutral or apolitical places, neither can the curriculum that defines the work teachers do in them or defines what learners are to learn in them be considered neutral or apolitical. The "value free" curriculum is an oxymoron. All human work and its results represent value-laden decisions, i.e., *choices.*

Curriculum in schools and colleges is both a process and a product. It encompasses choices made about what is considered appropriate teaching and desired outcomes or results from that teaching. The two are interrelated. The desired result or outcome often determines what the teacher does and how the teacher does it.

For example, if the desired outcome is that students learn how to make decisions derived from a consideration of alternatives, the teacher may decide to establish certain conditions in an environment which represents those alternatives and structure activities so that students practice confronting them and discerning how they engage in a process of deciding which ones are most desirable. The conditions may be in a special location (classroom, gymnasium, laboratory, library, auditorium) within a work organization devoted to such activities typically called a school or college, or it may be outside such a place on a field trip, athletic field, and the like.

Curriculum is integral to making decisions about the work to be done; it should have an impact on it. Improving the effectiveness and efficiency of any organization requires searching for what determines how the work being done *gets done.* An absence of written documents having utility, such as those described above, leads to work decisions being made largely by individual employees whose personal "curriculum" may or may not mesh with the organization's mission and goals. What makes a school system possible is its *commonality* of purpose and content. Otherwise the opposite occurs, a system of *individual* schools. Complex learning requires focus and connectivity (not uniformity) within and across grades or other significant learning-related grouping criteria. For this reason a curriculum cannot be simply a series of unrelated "exposures" to what teachers feel comfortable doing.

A school does not have a curriculum simply to have one, but most teachers' experiences with curriculum are that they are "shelf" documents, hauled out only to prepare for a state department or accreditation visit. A functional curriculum provides the means for work to be restructured and renewed to improve total organizational performance, *despite* faculty and administrative turnover. Without a curriculum, educators would have to resort to exhortation and good intentions to improve pupil learning.

Curriculum also provides a boundary for the organization in terms of the services it does or ought to provide, and gives consistency to activities. Curriculum also serves as a sort of institutionalized memory to perpetuate the best of what has been accomplished, what has been taught and learned, and what needs to be changed in the future. It provides a data base upon which to alter teaching and learning. Curriculum represents the sum total of decisions reached over time.

The Matter of Organizational Focus and Control

When looking at schools or school systems it is assumed that their collective performance can be improved. What makes this assumption workable is that it is taken for granted that the school or system is in control of itself, that is, it could pursue a different course of action if it chose to do so. Schools and school systems are collectivities, i.e., wholes. The whole is more than the sum of its parts, just as a team should be more than individual players. The idea behind this assumption is *synergy.* When a team plays like a team it is better than any of its individual members, no matter how good they might be.

What makes *synergy* possible is *control.* Control can take many forms. It can be imposed externally and/or developed internally by consent of its members. In schools control works both ways. Public schools function within a state framework which has usually been imposed by legislative mandate. Within that framework schools and school systems may have initiatives to create responses and alternatives. Control is both *top down* and *bottom up.* Control is central to the idea of the existence of a synergistic organization.

Control means that there is some regulation and guiding tasks, activities and overarching goals (Cartwright, 1965) to which an organization is directing itself, with the added concept that employee goals will be met in the process (Hersey & Blanchard, 1993, pp. 152–154). An organization without control, or which is running amuck because it is "out of control," cannot be improved. It is adrift. Too many schools are simply clusters of teachers physically connected by classrooms in the same building. We think of one comment by a teacher that, "Curriculum here is what any teacher wants to do."

No organization that is concerned about its performance can leave it up to its members to decide they will or will not become part of the whole; otherwise it forfeits its capability to become effective and mortgages its existence in the future. Schools do not exist to employ teachers. They exist to educate students within a generally accepted social framework. That framework is constantly changing, and the recent flare-ups over OBE (outcomes-based education) have reminded educators that curriculum control cannot be confined solely to the school or to professional discourse alone. Parents can exert enormous pressure on schools to eliminate what they believe to be objectionable (see Manatt, 1994, pp. 226–241).

In the past, control was achieved through bureaucratic or "scientific management techniques" which resulted in rigidity, standardization, routinization, and boredom, especially for students and teachers. While control was necessary, the price to pay for it was high.

Fortunately, today there are alternatives to excessive bureaucratization and routinization. For example, attention to organizational climate and culture can go a long way to reducing the rigidities of the organizational hierarchy. Moving decision making closer to the schools and classrooms is another idea, making the organizational "flatter." The new management literature stresses the centrality of worker involvement, values, and attitudes as well as consumer satisfaction (Vaill, 1989; Senge, 1990).

The basic assumption is that there can be high compatibility between organizational and personal goals or, in the words of Hersey and Blanchard (1993), "The extent that individuals and groups perceive their own goals as being satisfied by the accomplishment of organizational goals is the degree of integration of goals" (p. 152). Organizational performance is enhanced by closing the all-too-common gap between these two sets of goals. Curriculum can serve as a primary means to close that gap. With this in mind it will no longer be the case that organizational performance can only be enhanced as employee deprivation increases. Employee satisfaction and organizational performance are one and the same continuum, not antithetical aims.

Curriculum as a Work Plan

Curriculum is the means to manage the organization—to guide it, shape it, improve it. Curriculum is *the plan* to perform that function. It can assume many forms because there are a variety of *plans.* Curricula is a compilation of sets of directions that serve to guide, shape, and configure what teachers do in classrooms, from simple textbook adoption to complex, interdisciplinary curriculum units and guides.

Part of being able to utilize curriculum *as a means* to improve teaching and subsequently pupil performance is its *manageability.* Plans must therefore be clear, understandable, capable of being implemented with a minimum of extraneous effort, and lend themselves to feedback and subsequent improvement over time.

When teachers begin to use a variety of work plans which exist in schools to make decisions about what to teach, how much to teach of it, the order of teaching, and perhaps the methodology involved, teaching becomes something more than teaching. It becomes *instruction.* Think of instruction as focused and connected teaching, systemized teaching. The function of curriculum is to focus and connect teachers' work. The more the learning outcomes are complex and require continuity and consistency over time, the more instruction is necessary to attain it.

There are several dimensions to instruction. The first is whether or not the focus and connectivity utilizes all that we know about effective learning. For example, effective learning involves developmentally appropriate tasks, solicits learner response and feedback, provides options for different ways of learning, and allows room for students to "construct" their own meaning in the act of knowledge acquisition (English & Hill, 1994, p. 68). An effective curriculum has got to provide "space" for students to engage in such activities. Because teachers represent the critical ingredient in the teaching-learning equation, they must also have room to "construct" what they do within frameworks that provide for opportunities to be creative and responsive to student prompts. This is what makes curriculum development such a challenge. A little bit of curriculum is always "unfinished," in the sense that flexibility must exist within it for *both* teachers and students to engage one another and to find and define themselves in the process of translation from plan to action.

So no curriculum can ever be **done** in the sense that a part of it is always undefined or underdefined.

Curriculum developers are not industrial engineers engaged in elaborate time and motion studies that specify itty-bitty steps and how long it will take to do them. Teaching is a creative activity and some goals cannot be defined ahead of time. However, what can be defined are general expectations, related instructional decisions, and some important processes that are part of the data base. Some work plans can be quite specific. Others must be more general. Uniformity for all curriculum is unwise and standardization is counterproductive. The answer is that it all depends on the type of outcome desired, the assumptions made regarding learning, the nature of the space provided to teachers, and the type of assessment system which is selected or imposed which will be employed to make judgments about effectiveness and efficiency.

The Forms and Manifestations of Curriculum in Schools

There are three forms of curriculum at work in schools. They are the formal, informal, and hidden curricula. The three manifestations of curriculum for each are the written, taught, and tested curricula (English, 1992, p. 9).

The Formal Curriculum

The formal curriculum is that which is officially pronounced, studied, developed and ultimately adopted and implemented. In many states it represents the "sanctioned" curriculum. It is almost always "top down" in development and implementation. This is the curriculum promulgated by state boards of education, accreditation associations, or subject matter recommendations by national associations. This curriculum usually is not developed by democratic means. It is developed by subject matter experts or legally sanctioned government officials. However, in many states it is mainly locally designed and approved.

The Informal Curriculum

The informal curriculum is often the unnoticed curriculum. It exists in the unexplained or implicit values at work in the selection of curriculum content. For example, an attack by religious conservatives that "scientific creationism" be added to a study of evolution in science classrooms is an assault on the assumptions of evolution which they believe contrary to deeply held religious beliefs (Numbers, 1992). The controversy over "outcomes-based education" is over the assumptions which comprise the formal curriculum. It is the value base that engenders the heat that has caused the national OBE thrust to falter (see Chion-Kenny, 1994). The use of tracking plans based on ideas of student variability or "potential" are also based on assumptions about the capacity to learn. Many are obsolete and under review.

Spontaneous pupil groupings based on volunteerism may also be considered part of the "informal curriculum." Often such groupings may be detrimental to the actual operation of the formal curriculum, such as when student gang behavior is antithetical to students doing well in school.

The Hidden Curriculum

The hidden curriculum refers to the way school routines are "lived" by students. This is the curriculum that is truly experienced by all students. The hidden curriculum relates to the implicit cultural values taught without making anyone conscious of them. For example, the teaching of what has been called "monochromatic time," i.e., that students can only do one thing at a time, and even that time itself is important, are peculiar cultural values explicitly taught in lived Westernized school routines (see Hall, 1977). The most pervasive hidden curriculum occurs in the teaching and lived rituals relating to gender identification, i.e., girls are passive and boys are active, and the civic religion (patriotism) (see Bellah, 1970). Schools also enshrine a host of other ritualized activities that are latent but present (see McLaren, 1986).

Exploring the Manifestations of the Three Curricula

There are three manifestations of the formal, informal and hidden curricula. There are the written, taught, and tested manifestations of the formal, informal and hidden curricula. Written documents from state agencies, accreditation associations, national and even international specifications (e.g., the International Baccalaureate Program) comprise the written, manifest and codified work plan. The informal manifestation of the written curriculum might be the tracking plans that present students in different tracks with a more or less rigorous curriculum based on assumptions regarding their "capacity."

For example, a recent study of gifted programs (Sapon-Shevin, 1994) indicated that such programs are not only disruptive of the classroom community but are elitist and racist, particularly in urban school systems, and result in a "better" curriculum being taught to such students through the practice of intense individualization called "compacting" (p. 250).

Tracking plans also present to students in the bottom "tracks" a distinctly inferior, i.e., less rigorous, curriculum as well as having signaled lower expectations for performance (see Oakes, 1992).

Nearly everyone is familiar with testing the formal curriculum. Both standardized and criterion-referenced tests make claims to assessing this curriculum, though the actual match between any local curriculum and a standardized test is usually low (see English, 1992, p. 66). Criterion-referenced tests, or state competency tests as they are sometimes called, claim to assess pupil learning on approved state curricula.

The informal curriculum may be assessed by sociograms, observation, or participant analysis used by trained sociologists, anthropologists, researchers or psychologists where group norms are sketched out as the person doing them "lives with" such groups. Margaret Mead's controversial book on the sexual mores of adolescent girls in Samoa is a famous example (see Howard, 1984, pp. 76–89). School-related descriptions are abundant in sociological research such as Henry's (1963) study of sexual competition between adolescent girls for the attention of boys in school (pp. 182–282) and a more modern study of romance novels most checked out in high school libraries by girls and the messages they receive from them (Christian-Smith, 1987).

Still other examples of the "informal" curriculum are the rules of bureaucracy (Rogers, 1968) and the concepts in educational administration of school climate and culture (Sarason, 1982). School rituals and ceremonies are also representative of informal curriculum (Beck, 1994, pp. 104–5).

The hidden curriculum is not written, but it is evident in blackboard instructions for students; it is taught in lived school routines. It is assessed perhaps best by means of ethnography or photography (see English, 1991, pp. 84–104).

Other Definitions of Curriculum

There are many other ways to define curriculum. Some common ones are:

- a deliberately planned structure (scope and sequence) of learning activities that emphasizes subject matter acquisition, mastery of facts and information, and inquiry skills.

- a deliberately planned structure of knowledge, skills, attitudes, values, and behaviors that emphasizes interpersonal competencies, social problem-solving skills, and equity.
- all the experiences offered to learners under the auspices and direction of the school.

We think these definitions miss the mark for utility.

The Importance of Definition

From our experiences, educators in schools rarely come to terms with a basic question such as, "What is this school's working definition of curriculum?" In the words of one of our students:

> Curriculum is a word you hear inside the walls of educational institutions, but there is no real understanding or purpose to it. It is not perceived as valuable by those in charge or by those who are supposed to use it.

Close scrutiny of the three illustrations of curriculum definitions show that one may emphasize one dimension and perhaps de-emphasize another. In the first instance, the definition would lead the school to focus largely on academic learning (the cognitive domain) (see Bloom, 1956), attained primarily through the formal program.

In the second instance, the definition would lead the school to focus on academic as well as affective learning (Krathwohl, Bloom, & Masia, 1964), attained not only through the formal program but through more explicit attention in that program to issues relating to values, attitudes, and feelings.

In the third instance, the definition would impel the school to focus on cognitive, affective, and psychomotor learning (Harrow, 1972), attained not only through the formal program but through co-curricular programming, i.e., clubs and athletics. What this means is that the school's working definition of curriculum would commit it to skew its attention and allocation of resources to certain dimensions of school life as opposed to others. Managing the curriculum hinges on what *known* curriculum is being offered, including the idea that our understanding of "known" is expanding, i.e., to include the informal and hidden curricula as well.

These alternative views of curriculum are rooted in the vast literature about curriculum development. One scholar has estimated the number of such books to be about 1,200, using 1900 as the publication date (Schubert, 1980, p. 11).

Curriculum Management and Development

Educators commonly refer to curriculum development but rarely refer to curriculum management. Some people use the terms synonymously. The latest review of the ERIC system reveals thirty-eight categories for curriculum with the largest being curriculum development with some 19,000 entries. There is no category for curriculum management even though the concept has been in the general educational literature for a decade (e.g., English, 1978).

As depicted by Figure 1.1, we see curriculum management as the central concept. It is comprised of the major dimensions of design and delivery. Components of management are construction, development, implementation, feedback, evaluation, and modification and institutionalization or abandonment. The intent of the figure is to convey that the components interact in a dynamic/recursive and not linear fashion. Let us examine them in more detail.

Curriculum development is normally concerned with the creation of the formal curriculum. This is the intentional, prescribed curriculum which can be at the teacher/classroom, school unit, or school system level. These processes include the phases of curriculum construction and design which some authors pose as conceptually different.

Zais (1976), for example, presents construction of curriculum as addressing such questions as: What is the nature of the good society? What is the nature of man? What is the good life? What should be the aims of education? What content should students learn? Then design would focus on: (1) aims and objectives for learning; (2) subject-matter content; (3) learning activities; and (4) evaluation (pp. 16–17).

Design should also focus on the nature of the curriculum being developed in terms of its philosophical orientation which should assist in determining whether it will have a subject-centered (content focused), learner-centered (personal development focus), or problem-centered (real living focused) theme.

One of the major problems with these approaches is that by focusing on "what should be," we ignore "what is," assuming that they are on the same continuum and that the future should embrace the present and extend it. The loosely labeled field of "critical pedagogists" has sharply

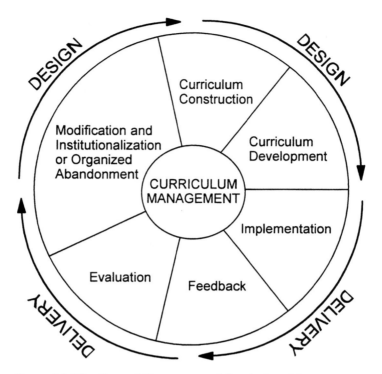

Figure 1.1. The General Components of Curriculum Management.

criticized these practices as ignoring the fact that schools are now a race, class, and gender biased social sorting machine that supports an unjust and elite society (Apple, 1979; Giroux, 1988). Avoiding looking hard at the status quo lets curriculum developers off the hook from any sustained and serious examination of what schools really do. Fundamentally, say the critics, they reproduce social inequity which exists in popular culture (Giroux, 1994).

Curriculum management includes implementation or delivery. That "consists of the process of putting into practice an idea, program, or set of activities and structures new to the people attempting or expected to change" (Fullan, 1991, p. 65). Many curricula are developed but remain on a dusty shelf in the teacher's closet or attic bin. Recently, a workshop participant said, "When I was hired the principal told me to go look in the attic for any old curriculum guides." Another added, "The fourth grade teacher's expectations sort of determine what the third grade teacher does."

We envision curriculum management embracing subactivities such as needs assessment which we have grouped under *design* and *delivery*.

Subsequent chapters will go into greater detail about them. We like the concept of "curriculum thinking" better than the traditional notion of "needs assessment" because it more accurately describes the nature of what is going on at that level. Also, needs assessment in the past has tended to emphasize the "what should be" part of the equation and played down or ignored the problems of schooling in relation to the society in which the school must function (discussed further in Chapter 3). There has been a tendency to overlook the fact that schools connect to and reinforce a society and cannot operate in a vacuum from them. At the same time, one should allow the society, in its continuum of development, to influence what the school should be doing since society is undergoing constant change.

The Dimensions of Curriculum Management

Design Decisions

Step 1: Curriculum Thinking (a.k.a. needs assessment)

1. What should the school be doing to improve our society now? What's wrong with our society now?
2. How is the school helping or limiting achieving the necessary changes in our social fabric?
3. In what ways is our curriculum helping or limiting the necessary changes in our social fabric?
4. Who wins or loses in schools now? Why?
5. How should the curriculum be discarded, modified or replaced to improve pupil success in schools as they now exist?
6. What new information have we acquired about understanding human learning that bears upon curriculum construction? In what ways might it shape our perception of the role of curriculum in the school?
7. How do teaching practices and methods impact the form curriculum might take and how do current organizational practices configure that form? (e.g., non-gradedness, departmentalization, etc.).
8. What impact does or will assessment practices have on defining, evaluating, and changing our concept of pupil learning and how these data are interpreted by learners themselves, parents, professional staff, and other educational agencies to which we are accountable?
9. How do we resolve discrepancies between the many conflicting

demands for curriculum among the viewpoints and information sources we use in creating a work plan?

10. What values are implicit in our work? How do we set curriculum priorities with those values?
11. How will our work be influenced by the expectations of our various publics?
12. What are the most important trends we must acknowledge in our work regarding the future?
13. How should schools be reshaped to be more effective in ameliorating social problems now and in the future?
14. What formats are most conducive to accurate and "user friendly" application?

Step Two: Curriculum Construction

1. The physical creation of work plans which teachers are expected to use in classrooms and which are responsive to questions outlined in Step 1.
2. The piloting of curriculum for modification prior to any large-scale publication of it.

Delivery Decisions

Step One: Publication of Work Plans

1. Supplying each teacher with a copy of the work plan(s).

Step Two: Staff Development

1. Making sure teachers know how to use the work plans.
2. Expressing confidence in teaching staff, developing goodwill and a "can do" spirit.

Step Three: Implementation and Monitoring

1. Implementation of the curriculum on a systematic basis.
2. Monitoring the curriculum as it is implemented to ensure proper implementation and as it is completed to ensure outcomes (results) match those intended.

Step Four: Evaluation and Feedback

1. Determining the effectiveness of delivery and the effectiveness of results with a systematic plan.
2. Acting on information that shows adjustments are necessary to improve implementation and results.

Step Five: Informing Clients and Agencies of Results

1. Provide data on results to students, parents, taxpayers, board.
2. Supply related agencies with data regarding results as required or desired.

Step Six: Connect Design/Delivery Cycle

1. Take reports of implementation and results and apply in subsequent rounds of curriculum thinking (needs assessment).

Considering the Nature of Educational Change and Curriculum as an Important Lever of the Process

"Everything relates to everything else" when it comes to change in organizations. In schools a few of these "things" are budgets, bond issues, new and renovated buildings, school culture and climate, the nature of the student body, the staff, the school board, the community, the quality of supervision—the list is endless and seamless of what impacts education. However, much of the time there is a peripheral impact of these kinds of factors on what Conley has identified, after an extensive review of the restructuring literature, as the central variables of education and restructuring—learner outcomes, curriculum, instruction, and assessment/evaluation. "These dimensions include everything teachers do that relates to the instructional process: What they teach, how they teach it, how it is measured and evaluated" (1993, p. 107). Making change in these areas is the most difficult to achieve compared to change in areas of the supporting variables (governance, teacher leadership, personnel, and working relationships) and enabling variables (learning environment, technology, school-community relationships and time) (pp. 104–112). Fullan states that the central variables are the "hardest core to crack" (1993, p. 49).

Because curriculum management practices *focus on the central variables,* they have the potential to have a considerable impact on them, to alter them in important ways, provided that there is intentionality behind the practices. The practices represent the common, everyday "levers" for change that are present in every organization but are often underutilized (see Larson, 1992a, pp. 109–119). Leverage as a process, says Senge (1990), is when small, focused actions sometimes produce important, lasting improvements (p. 64).

In addition, because they are part of the everyday work milieu, they have *meaning* for educators. "The problem of meaning is central to making sense of educational change" (Fullan, 1991, p. 4). When educators are dealing with curriculum they are dealing with tasks that matter to them, tasks that are rooted in the concrete and immediate experiences in schools. If these tasks can have common or shared meanings, there is a greater possibility of more collective rather than more individualistic change. Glickman (1993) who is involved in a large-scale school improvement project in Georgia, states that, "To be effective, governance must deal with the issues that are within people's power to rectify" (p. 30).

Increasingly, students of school and organizational life are coming to the conclusion that individualistic change can also be an important starting point for larger scale change. Peters and Waterman (1982), in their now classic study of excellent business, devoted a chapter to the importance of the individual to change processes (pp. 55–86). Senge (1990), in his incisive analysis of the "learning organization," does the same (pp. 139–173). Hall and Hord (1987), after a decade of extensive analysis, concluded that, "To change something, someone has to change first" (p. 10). Fullan (1993) put it more dramatically, "I see the individual as an undervalued source of reform" (p. 35).

Clearly then, curriculum management practices must acknowledge the importance of individuals in the process of engaging in curriculum design and delivery. The experiences of the process must create personal meaning that is vital to any successful change effort. Our experiences of the last decade teaching these practices to students in courses, seminars, and workshops have led us to conclude, using the word most commonly uttered by students, that they are *powerful* vehicles of reform. Schools and school systems can only be changed successfully when the individuals in them determine it is time to change them.

Summary

This initial chapter centered on definitional and conceptual distinctions that are important to understand about curriculum management.

Curriculum management is the entire process of the design and delivery of curriculum in schools and other organizations. Nearly all complex organizations have a curriculum, though it may be called different things. Curriculum management includes everything from thinking about the important issues impacting curriculum and how to determine a useful form for it to assume, to matters of implementation, feedback, and evaluation.

The chapter contends that without *control* there can be no focused or cohesive work in schools as organizations because control is central to the assumption that schools can be changed and improved. Control insures responsiveness and accountability. Control is both top down and bottom up. One is not exclusive of the other. Control is also important to ensure stability and constancy of purpose. In organizational life one cannot talk about stability, constancy, and improvement without confronting the issue of control.

It is also not desirable to consider schools without taking into account the nature and type of social system schools are part of, reinforce, and reproduce. For this reason curriculum management can be a radical activity. It can become the basis upon which desirable social change is conceptualized and brought into the school to embrace a different kind of general social response.

For example, students today are much more conservation minded about the environment than students in the authors' generation. That increased "awareness" is at least partially due to a change in emphasis in contemporary school curriculum. As such it represents a *value shift.*

Curriculum management is not a neutral activity. Schools are not neutral places, nor can the curriculum in them be neutral. Our society, government, customs and traditions, laws and mores rest on clusters of values. Every curriculum is embedded in values. The "value free" curriculum does not exist. Given the nature of social diversity in America, the selection of values is one of constant tension.

Finally, the chapter underscores the importance of the individual in the change process. Individuals are the key to change. Ultimately the curriculum is what each teacher decides it is to be in each classroom of each school. That fact is what makes teaching, as work, rather unique from other kinds of work. It is also what makes curriculum management one of the most challenging of all educational activities.

DIALOGUE FOR IMPLEMENTATION

These are the questions most commonly asked of the authors about the ideas in this chapter.

1. The definition of *curriculum* seems quite broad. Is it really everything that exists on paper in schools?

ANSWER: If one defines curriculum as only that which is labeled curriculum, you miss the *primacy* and domination of the textbook in American classrooms. The textbook is the most referenced of all resources for classroom teachers. We say it is the most powerful, but not necessarily *the best* reference. Leaving textbooks out of any curriculum discussion is naive and risky. We concentrate here on the *function* of curriculum *as a work plan.* Lots of school systems have *curriculum,* i.e., work plans, without having curriculum guides.

2. What is the *problem* with all the paper called curriculum in schools?

ANSWER: The major problem is that it is usually unconnected to all the others, developed in isolation, and usually *unaligned* to the regnant assessment tools which are imposed or adopted by the school or school system. No one, including teachers, really knows *which one* will provide the best results on any given type of assessment. The problem is that all the paper, collectively, does not provide an adequate focus for teaching.

3. Why didn't you start this chapter with attention to a *philosophy* of education or something like that? Isn't that where most texts begin?

ANSWER: We think that the word *philosophy* is misapplied in these discussions. What most overall statements really are approach *ideologies,* i.e., statements of values and beliefs, rather than questions about the nature of reality, knowledge, truth, and the like. Those are the province of *philosophy.* Our approach is *organizational* because schools and school systems are forms of human organization. Only universities have the luxury of time to approach organizational questions truly philosophically. Given the governance structure of public and private schools, their existence is much more political than philosophical, at least in the sense those words are commonly used in education.

4. But aren't there values in curriculum? Shouldn't these values be discussed and be made explicit?

ANSWER: Yes and yes. These are discussed in this book but not in the opening chapter. Curriculum design and delivery is a *value-laden* enterprise, i.e., thoroughly embedded in values. There is no "value-free" curriculum of which we know. All facts are attached to somebody's values about them.

5. Where is the controversy over "outcomes-based education" or OBE in all of this?

ANSWER: OBE was an idea long before it had a label, and long before it was attacked by some conservatives as subversive. As *an idea*, the presumption that the results of schooling, i.e., outcomes, should be connected to the activities in schools (a major premise of the concept of accountability) is quite old and nearly unreproachable. What conservatives have objected to are *some of the outcomes* attached to values they question or reject. They have therefore resorted to rejecting the whole idea of "outcomes based" as reprehensible, instead of attacking only those outcomes with which they disagree. Most educators have simply moved around them by relabeling "outcomes" as "standards" and carrying on with their business. This is a demonstration of the fact that even conservatives do not question the premises of educational accountability. They simply differ on the *kinds of things* schools and the teachers and administrators in them should be doing and teaching children.

6. Who determines the "hidden" curriculum? Is anybody in control of it?

ANSWER: The "hidden" curriculum consists of those sociopolitical values that are enmeshed in school activities such as saluting the flag, accepting the authority of teachers and administrators as agents of social, i.e., political control, becoming acclimated to external reward systems (grades, gold stars, awards), and accepting individual competition as the basis of meritorious activity. It is also the "winners and losers" mentality that is the consequence of that decision, behavior regulation by symbolic systems embodied in rules, regulations, dress codes, and accepted ways of "learning" such as being quiet in libraries, hallways and the necessity of forming lines to engage in such activities as traversing halls, bathrooms, cafeterias, showers, playgrounds and the like. The "hidden" curriculum is the "lived" curriculum of schools. Nearly all school authorities are in "control" of it, yet it is difficult to find specific references to it except general provisions of law or local board policies.

7. Doesn't your change in the definition of curriculum also change the idea of it being "developed?"

ANSWER: Yes. If curriculum is simply all of the pieces of collective paper that a classroom teacher might reference in the act of teaching, then development includes adoption of textbooks, legal prescriptions, test specifications, and the like. It also enables us to see the politics of curriculum development in its larger manifestations, and de-emphasizes the naive notion that the developmental process is somehow something other than what it is, a political act of choice and not "engineering" of objective components. Curriculum development is first and foremost a political/cultural activity.

8. Doesn't control imply domination? Isn't management in power to be "in control"? Isn't control antithetical to developing effective curriculum?

ANSWER: Control can be exerted by individuals or groups or combinations of both. If teachers are "in control" of the curriculum, for that influence to be manifested, there will have to be someone who determines if everyone is "in" control. Organizational life requires some conformity. Whether curriculum is generated "bottom up" or "top down" is an option of preference. To ensure effective delivery, someone will have to "execute" the will of the group at the top or the bottom. Control, that is, monitoring of the design, requires political influence and power to carry off. It is a question of "whose will" is being carried out. To equate "control" as synonymous with "top down" is naive. "Bottom-up" management can be as stifling and controlling as "top down," depending upon the form of control it assumes.

ACTIVITIES FOR PERSONAL AND STAFF DEVELOPMENT

We offer some examples of activities as "starters," but encourage readers to develop their own that will fit their situation.

1. Discuss how your previous understandings of curriculum development are different from those presented in this chapter.
2. What do you see as the advantages or disadvantages of seeing curriculum development as a subactivity of curriculum management?
3. Are there any circumstances where curriculum might be considered a "neutral" activity? If so, what are they? If not, why not?
4. What are the common perceptions of teachers in your school or district about the topic of curriculum? How would those perceptions be challenged by the views of the authors in this first chapter?
5. How often is the subject of curriculum discussed in your school? Indicate what forms that the discussion most often takes and the key issues of concern.

6. What are the most common parental and student complaints about your curriculum? Speculate as to the reasons they are common?

7. Describe the ways curriculum is or is not focused and connected in your school or district? How is the issue of control approached? Who is in control of your curriculum?

8. Describe and discuss how the informal and hidden curricula impact and change the formal curriculum? Provide specific examples. Include parental expectations and prohibitions as part of the informal curriculum.

9. Indicate the most controversial aspect of curriculum in your school or school district. Why was it controversial? How was the dispute resolved?

Chapter 2

CURRICULUM MANAGEMENT IN CONTEXT

A curriculum is an internal code that guides the work of the organization. The purpose of a curriculum is not to abandon organizational boundaries but to enable the organization to function within those boundaries more *effectively* and, over time, *efficiently*. "Effectively" means that the organization reaches more of its objectives because it has a curriculum; "efficiently" means that it does so at the least possible cost, i.e., expenditure of resources. A curriculum can accomplish these goals by:

- clarifying organizational boundaries
- defining the nature of the work to be done
- relating the major tasks to be accomplished to one another within the total work process or work flow (coordination)
- defining standards by which work is to be measured or assessed
- defining evaluation procedures by which work results can be compared to work performed
- making changes in the work performed through feedback
- repeating the above steps in order to achieve a higher level of work performance on a consistent basis.

When a new and higher level of organizational performance is attained as a result of the systematic application of these generic steps, then a *breakthrough* occurs (Juran, Gryna, & Bingham, 1951, pp. 2, 15, 16). Such a breakthrough may lead to what some of the current literature is calling, "organizational transformation"—"a set of ideas and actions which take us beyond the nature of our existing institutions and beyond ways of thinking which support them" (Vaill, 1984, p. 33). We must radically change our organizations, says Vaill, because we are immersed in "permanent white water," organizationally and environmentally (1989, pp. 1–32).

There are several characteristics of schools that make it difficult to achieve such a breakthrough, even though schools possess characteristics common to all organizations (e.g., a division of labor, a hierarchy or authority, rules and procedures). Other types of organizations, such as human services agencies, have their special characteristics, too (Hasenfeld, 1992). These characteristics must be considered when applying "rational-istic" approaches, such as curriculum management, in order to increase effectiveness and efficiency.

The Attitude of Educators

Some educators (and the professors who educate them) have attitudes which are antithetical to improving curriculum in schools.

The first is the view that schools in their current form are ineffective or corrupt (Chubb & Moe, 1990; Greer, 1972; Illich, 1970; Lieberman, 1989, 1993; Reimer, 1971). To limit school improvement to improving existing schools is to accept the perpetuation of an imperfect and per-haps unjust organizational form and the society that that form reproduces. This, they contend, is irresponsible and even immoral.

So the argument becomes, "Do schools reflect society or do they assist society to change?" In theory, these two purposes seem incompatible. In practice, however, schools are expected to strive toward both ends (see Chapter 5). The public school curriculum has always included material that reflects these purposes. Consider the current curricular areas that relate to alcoholism, AIDS, teenage pregnancy, birth control, gun safety, recycling, stress management, sexual harassment—the list goes on. Historically, there has always been tension between the school and those advocating for one kind of content or another. Such tensions are exacer-bated in today's "white water" environment.

The boundary which separates what the school does and should/should not be doing in our society has rarely been without ambiguity. It shifts as society evolves, and leads to a periodic reshuffling of curriculum content and priorities (Tanner, 1986). However, there can be little argument that schools in most social orders are, in the main, agents for the status quo rather than change agents.

Currently strategic planning is being promoted as a means to assist schools to deal more effectively with the dilemma of maintaining/changing the status quo. A major component of strategic planning focuses on environmental analysis (e.g., Cook, 1990; Kaufman & Herman, 1990). Such an analysis includes social values and how they must be studied and understood in the development of policy and strategy. The question-ing of the boundaries of responsibility between schools and society would become more commonplace if the "alpha" needs assessment (described in Chapter 3) were applied.

Another attitude which is problematic is that some educators feel uncomfortable about creating a curriculum that guides too closely the work of the teacher. Such perceived prescriptive statements "de-skill" teachers (Apple, 1979). Many individuals are organizational romantics in terms of Drucker's "fallacy of creativity." "Free people from restraint and they will come up with far better, far more advanced, far more productive answers than the experts" (1973, pp. 137–147). Although this idea was popular long before Rousseau, notes Drucker, "there is no evidence to support it. Everything we know . . . the proper structure of work—of any work—is not intuitively obvious" (1973, p. 267). Some of the experiments with alternative schools in the sixties support Drucker's opinion (Popkewitz, Tabachnick, & Wehlage, 1982).

Sound management of curriculum does not preclude a systematic analysis of the boundaries of schooling, and of the nature and values of the society which supports its schools.

There is great variation within the pages of the hundreds of books about curriculum as to what curriculum is or should be.

Authors who are theoretical (Pinar & Grumet, 1976), taxonomic (Eisner & Vallence, 1974), or ideological-political (Apple, 1976) do not appear to understand management or organizational theory. Few, if any, relate the function of curriculum in schools to other similar functions in organizations and examine that function generically. Most of the critics are on the outside looking in. They are concerned with social inequities and the function of schools in society. Many are not concerned with enabling schools to become more effective. They are concerned with changing the society by altering the basic mission of schools, the major means by which society perpetuates itself.

From the perspective of this book, *curriculum is a plan, a set of directions whose chief purpose is to guide the work to be performed in schools.* When teaching relates to the curriculum and is generally guided by it, the result is *instruction.*

As a set of directions for the work of schools, curriculum comes in many forms. The textbook is the most common form. It contains a written set of directions that most often guides teachers in their selection of content, determines the time to be spent on that content, and establishes the sequencing of the content.

If one wants to improve the *operations* of any organization, whether it be one devoted to producing goods or products or one engaged in rendering services, one has to search for what determines how the work is being accomplished. What is it that those engaged in the work use to make decisions about the work? These documents run by many different titles. They may be called job tasks, work rules, work standards or specifications, work guides, practice guides, or standard operating procedures.

In schools, curriculum may be represented by textbooks, programs of study, curriculum guides, syllabi or course guides, plan books, lesson plans, scope and sequence charts, board policies, or state regulations. Any documents that teachers use to make decisions about content or subject matter, about how much time to spend on the content, and the sequence of the content, fulfill the requirement that a curriculum is a set of directions. Content is whatever answers the questions: (1) What am I going to teach today? or (2) What should children learn today? Content can be concepts, facts, skills, values, understandings, or processes as we saw in Chapter 1 when we discussed definitions of curriculum.

To improve curriculum as a guide to work, it is important to know:

(1) if the curriculum being taught is the right "work."
(2) if it is defined in such a way as to be manageable within the conditions faced by the person delivering the work.
(3) if it is connected in substantive ways within the flow of the total work of the organization—it can result in discrete units of work being related to all of the work the organization is doing.
(4) if changed in tangible ways it will result in the student learning more.
(5) if changes in instruction occur as a result of feedback about the effectiveness of the instruction.

Over thirteen years of school, the average student observes close to 13,000 hours of instruction and is taught by dozens of teachers. One's education can be seen, therefore, as simply an unrelated series of "exposures" to whatever teachers decide to do, or schooling can be seen as a coordinated attempt to integrate these "exposures" in order to achieve organizationally determined outcomes.

So curriculum is about structuring schoolwork or any work in organizations. As a guide to work it becomes rather clear that it will be intimately related to the purpose of the organization, the internal authority structure of the organization, and the way the organization divides and subdivides itself (work specialization). This leads us to consider the impact of some other organizational features on curriculum management.

The Nature of Schools and Their Structure

March and Olsen (1979, pp. 10–81) identify special features of schools (and other public organizations) that classify them as "organized anarchies."

In broad terms, organized anarchies lack specific, well-defined, consistent goals; their processes for delivering their service (in this case, instruction) cannot be easily explained, and the participants (in this case, educators and students) vary in their involvement in and commitment to the learning enterprise.

Organized anarchies are rife with ambiguity and uncertainty, characteristics not usually associated with bureaucracy (Miles, 1965; Waller, 1965). Additionally, (1) schools have to accept and attempt to educate all students who come to them; (2) concerns about classroom control are quite high for most teachers; (3) experience is valued much more by educators than is research; (4) the organizational connections between classrooms and schools in the same district are "loosely coupled"; (5) most teachers, despite the trend toward teaming and integrating curricula, work most of the day with children rather than adults, and they work quite independent of colleagues; (6) because most citizens have been through school, observing thousands of hours of instruction from elementary through high school, there is, unlike other professions, little mystique to teaching in the eyes of the public; (7) in the grand scheme of things, the psychic rewards of interacting with learners and seeing them learn are far more important to teachers than are the external rewards of money, prestige, and power; (8) the work of an educator is hectic, filled with detail and an endless stream of decisions, and very present-oriented rather than future-oriented; and (9) the personal instructional styles of teachers are critical to their success; thus any changes that have implications for significantly altering that style may be initially resisted (Larson, 1992a, pp. 27–41).

School structure is also different from other types of organizations. The cellular design of schools evolved over decades, but took on its modern form with the invention of the graded elementary school in Quincy, Massachusetts in 1848 (Cubberly, 1948, p. 756). The graded elementary school was an offshoot of the Lancastrian School of the early

1800s in which a large lecture hall was surrounded by pupil recitation rooms (Tyack, 1974, pp. 44–46).

The principal innovation of the Quincy Graded School was to abandon the lecture hall in favor of full-time instruction in the recitation rooms. Thus we have the genesis of the modern school. Despite attempts to modify this design, the graded school remains not only the dominant form in the U.S. but throughout the world.

Several organizational problems faced educators in the nineteenth century. One of the most troublesome was how to deal with uneven demands of learners. Finding a method of grouping students for instruction within the boundaries of cost was perplexing. The one-room schoolhouse was workable only when the influx of pupils could be controlled. As populations swelled, the whole structure became internally unmanageable, beyond the capability of a teacher to organize.

The Lancastrian School made slight improvements by using older pupils as monitors (hence the name "Monitorial" Schools) to preserve discipline. Yet the noise and confusion was often daunting as teachers dealt with hundreds of students of different ages in large lecture halls. Pupil movement to and from the recitation rooms would present a formidable challenge for a contemporary school faculty; it certainly challenged those half-trained in pupil management techniques of decades ago (Graver, 1954, p. 42).

The graded school was viewed as a significant departure from this depressing dilemma. It resolved several organizational problems.

(1) The grouping of pupils into smaller groups by chronological age (a practice already used in some Monitorial Schools) bolstered the teacher's authority and hence the school became more manageable. The locus of control was reduced.

(2) By shifting from an individual basis for teaching pupils, a common practice in one room schoolhouses, to pupils in groups, a primitive kind of "batching process" emerged. This, in turn, "smoothed out" the demand for teachers and enabled schools to reduce a potentially uneven requirement for staffing to the lowest common denominator (Galbraith, 1977, pp. 224–226). The penalty, however, was that instruction had to be absorbed into the time intervals — the school year of approximately 180 days — selected to process batches of students grouped by age.

(3) Pupils were moved by grades or "batches" after being taught. What changed in the processing was the content of what the teacher taught, but not what the teacher did. Specialization by teachers depended upon the maturity of students and the complexity of the subject matter to be taught. Other than that, a teacher was a teacher was a teacher. Batch processing of this type

required only a minimal level of coordination from teacher to teacher. This gave teachers almost free reign in their classrooms. Teachers came to enjoy a high level of autonomy within this structure.

(4) The absence of schoolwide tests to determine what children had actually learned meant that the existing low levels of coordination between teachers could be maintained. If one teacher strayed from the curriculum or suffered a loss of control, the damage to the entire process was minimal. Early schools, therefore, only had to maintain a very minimal level of internal structure. Coordination and communication costs were negligible. Also, schools then were basically responsible for teaching, not learning. So the emphasis was decidedly on control and order, not achievement. (English 1980, pp. 145–157)

Thus, what sociologist Dan C. Lortie has described as the "cellular structure of the school" (1975) became the mold into which the curriculum was poured and curriculum first appeared in the form of graded school textbooks. However, schoolbooks were not graded until the 1870s, when the concept had become so dominant that the marketplace required recognition of this type of school structure in educational advertising.

Thus, by the late 1800s, the textbook was divided and subdivided, shaped and repackaged to fit the school's organizational pattern. It is difficult to find the word "curriculum" in educational texts of the day prior to 1900. However, the requirement for a curriculum that was central to the work of the teacher was evident, and that curriculum was already being arranged so that it could be taught by single teachers in relatively uncoordinated classrooms.

Other Effects of Structure

As internal structures go, school structure was on the way to being highly decentralized. Today it is called "self-contained" because each teacher is nearly autonomous. According to Bidwell, gaining control over such a structure can take at least three forms:

(1) the bureaucratic rank of the administrator and supervisor as a superior to the teacher who can command the teacher;

(2) the collegial basis of the administration based on group norms as professional educators;

(3) command by assessment of the results or outcomes of the educational/ schooling process. (Bidwell, 1965)

For many years prior to the accountability movement of the 1970s, minimal control—and with it coordination within the school—was a matter of publication, by the office of the superintendent, of a course of study that was to be followed by teachers (Cubberly, 1929, p. 423).

Today, with the advent of statewide minimal competency testing or other alternative assessments, a device for greater control has been implemented which Bidwell noted "is, of course, well adapted to the sequential coordination of instruction, but problematic in regard to universalistic teacher performance and the ultimate uniformity of school-system outcomes" (1965, p. 1014). Support for these comments was presented recently in an *Education Week* story about the Texas Assessment of Academic Skills test which every high school student must pass to graduate. The story described the policy rationale behind the test—a classic example of Wise's concept of "hyperrationalization" that undergirds public policy (Wise, 1979, 1988)—and the realities of the unanticipated impact of the test on students, parents, and teachers (Harp, 1994).

The internal structure of schools is highly compartmentalized and often quite loose despite the need to coordinate the learning of one age grade of pupils with the next. It has been characterized by one organizational theorist as "loosely coupled" which means that the connections between classrooms are "relaxed" so that even at the same grade level or in the same subject, curriculum and instruction have their own identity and physical separateness (Weick, 1976). However, as schools cope with increased external requirements which aim to guarantee that all pupils attain high standards of performance, the necessity for improved control and greater coordination is magnified. At this point, the structure of the school becomes a major obstacle to attaining that goal because it:

- prevents the administration from observing what teachers are really doing on a day-to-day basis without having to be present in all of the classrooms simultaneously—an impossibility in a cell-like structure. The school may work in some ways like an assembly line, but it is not an assembly line in which all of the work may be observed in process simultaneously. Monitoring is limited to observation of one teacher at a time.
- prevents teachers from seeing how what they teach either fits or doesn't fit with what their colleagues are doing in the grade level before or after, so that ongoing and immediate adjustments can take place.
- increases the costs of coordination by moving a task away from direct observation of the entire process to long distance appeal to

follow adopted procedures; these, in turn, drive the system to become further routinized and place more emphasis on specificity contained within written documents such as curriculum, pacing charts, scope and sequence guides, and other such written specifications.

- increases the costs of developing job descriptions because the old descriptions are too global to fit the variety of educational roles in a school. Documents need to be developed which are more precise. These, in turn, require a closer type of supervision and monitoring.

However, moving to a different kind of structure challenges the established authority of the entire school system, not to mention the role and autonomy/authority of administrators and teachers. It also presents a new and different demand for coordination and supervision. Today there is a strong movement across the country to change the traditional hierarchical structure of all organizations from one in which the concentration of power and authority is at the top, to one that is a more "flat," collegial structure, where power and authority are pushed down into the ranks of employees. As Toffler (1990) puts it in *Powershift*, his third volume in his classic trilogy about the future:

> Today in thousands of workplaces, from auto plants to offices, smart companies are experimenting with, or actually exploiting, the new regimen. Its key characteristic is a changed attitude toward both knowledge and power (p. 205). What we see, therefore, is a clear pattern. Workplace power is shifting, not because of fuzzy-minded do-goodism, but because the new system of wealth creation demands it. (p. 207)

In education, the same trend is accelerating. Fullan states that "each and every teacher has the responsibility to help create an organization capable of individual and collective inquiry and continuous renewal, or it will not happen (1993, p. 39). Sergiovanni calls for "substitutes" for traditional leadership whereby new norms, values, and a culture of collegiality need to replace old bureaucratic environments (1992). And integral to this trend is the notion of teacher empowerment (Maeroff, 1988).

Clearly there is enormous pressure on administrators, if they have been leading and managing under the old approaches, to change their styles. In some school systems and communities there is support for making such changes, whereas in others there still are strong norms and values existing that steer practice toward what *has been* rather than what *could be.* The old approaches, in most cases, are no longer appropriate and effective and must change. As we pointed out in Chapter 1, curriculum management practices empower administrators and teachers and thus fit well with the paradigm shifts occurring in modern organizations.

However, because such alterations in power and authority have not happened in many schools, and because even when it is acknowledged that they must happen it takes considerable time to change, some regular means to improve curriculum management might have to be used. Some of these are:

1. upgrade in sophistication the nature, content and use of curriculum guides and any other document that would more precisely define teaching content;
2. utilize more sophisticated techniques in observing and monitoring the work of teachers in their classrooms or work places;
3. utilize more precise assessment/testing instruments which can more adequately identify what things students have not learned and locate more closely where, within the school, such things were not adequately learned or taught;
4. create systems of administration that are responsive to using pupil performance data and teaching performance data in changing the internal work flow (both content and method) within the school;
5. formulate and implement interventions into the work flow of the school so that desired changes result in improved cumulative pupil performance over time.

So while curriculum can be discussed separately and apart from what schools are supposed to do, it makes little sense to do so. Practitioners are left with very pressing demands to make their schools and school districts more responsive and to do so *now.* They have little time nor inclination to pursue curriculum theories which are not immediately perceived as helpful, and particularly those which question the integrity or viability of the entire schooling process of which they find themselves the stewards.

Teacher Autonomy and Authority in School

Teachers are both the means and the major obstacles to attaining a curricular breakthrough. The teacher performs the pivotal role in enabling schools to be more effective. Increased demands for improved pupil achievement require significantly greater coordination of effort among teachers and improved ability to concentrate resources at selected points in the organization where teachers do their work, the classroom.

The self-contained classroom structure of the school is a major impediment to all of these demands. Another is the attitude or orientation to their work that teachers have developed over time. As Lortie has noted, "It is likely that the persistence of separation and low task interdependence among teachers is related to the circumstances affecting the growth of schools and the demographic characteristics of those attracted to teaching" (1975, p. 15). From a historical perspective, there have been several legitimate reasons why schools today are organized as they are and why teachers have the attitudes they have regarding independence.

Teaching as an independent activity attracts people who see themselves remaining pretty much intact apart from the organization to which they belong. Most teachers come to school with a view to work as individuals, a pattern they have observed throughout their K–12 and higher education experiences.

> Unless beginning teachers undergo training experiences which offset their individualistic and traditional experiences, the occupation will be staffed by people who have little concern with building a shared technical culture. (Lortie, 1975, p. 67)

Traditionally, it is teacher individualism that is rewarded in schools and not collaboration. Indeed, until quite recently when many districts adopted approaches to teaching such as the Madeline Hunter "model" (1982), there has not been a kind of technical language through which teachers could even discuss what they were doing in classrooms in specific terms with other teachers.

So there is nothing in the school environment which encourages teachers to work with other teachers except general rudimentary pressures to move students along in a specified curricular area (Sarason, 1982, p. 108). School culture is a mosaic of individualistic, rather than team actions. Therefore, suggestions for change or criticism are often taken personally and individually because there is an absence of a feeling of joint responsibility (Lortie, 1975, p. 81).

Teachers also have mixed feelings about curriculum. First they want good, articulated curriculum (Lortie, 1975, p. 183). but they tend to resist any curriculum that would encroach too much on their own prerogatives to decide what to teach, when to teach it, and how much of it to teach.

The curriculum is good for the other teacher but not necessarily for any specific teacher. This unspoken norm has surfaced in the ambiguity present in most curriculum guides. Such teacher-produced documents first preserve the teacher's individualism against almost all group norms, whether developed in committees or imposed from the top down. Even when teachers develop their "own" curriculum, they may choose not to implement it.

In his penetrating analysis of a failure to implement a highly rational budgetary system in schools, anthropologist Harry Wolcott (1977) took some care to review "recurring themes in teacher talk." He observed that the teacher culture of most schools centered around these ideals:

- autonomy
  Teachers want to preserve their ability to make decisions in their classrooms. They will argue for the "flexibility" required to be responsive to students instead of saying, "I want to do my own thing."
- sanctity
  The duty of teachers is to teach. All else is or should be second or eliminated. Teachers will use this concept to complain about "paperwork" because it "interferes with teaching."
- real experience in the present
  Teachers believe that only those who are currently teaching understand teaching because in a cell-like structure, only day-to-day work would indicate what is really going on there. Teachers will discount a person's ideas because, "They never worked here." If a person once was a teacher who is espousing an idea that they find unwelcome it is because, "They have forgotten what it is like to be in the classroom with the kids I now have." For this reason, only teachers really understand teaching.
- the traditions of teaching
  Teachers present a front which is highly resistant to change. They argue for continuity and stability, yet they will say they never teach the same thing the same way from year to year. For the purpose of curriculum development it presents on the one hand the requirement for a curriculum to codify and identify those traditions, but yet deny them at the same time in the name of flexibility. This apparent paradox is rooted in the need to remain independent from not only administrative control but control imposed from other colleagues.
- teacher isolation and vulnerability
  While teachers shun losing their autonomy they also recognize that this professional isolation makes them individually vulnerable. They will express the view that "nobody listens to me" or that "nobody up there cares what I think." They want to be asked, involved, but are equally fearful of being told what to do. This is a profound dilemma for most

teachers. They want to be left alone but loneliness is not a pleasant state particularly when teachers feel pressures to change.

By now, self-containment has such a long history in schools that it is very hard to separate the physical structure from the mental and emotional mind-sets that have been fostered by it. The people in the structure have become the structure. When schools were built without walls, the walls remained in the minds of teachers until they were physically replaced (Good & Brophy, 1978, pp. 264–273). Like it or not, teachers' sense of self is linked closely to the structure in which they work. They have become one and the same.

As we have seen in the discussion about organizational structure, there is a strong trend in motion today to break down this isolation and to create work environments that are more collaborative and collegial. Teaming is quite common in elementary schools. In the case of the middle school movement, the new organizational structure revolves around teaming rather than individual teachers (Carnegie Council on Adolescent Development, 1989, pp. 38–40). But finding the time to team and to work together more collaboratively—and the need for money to provide that time and training to do so—remain the major impediments to altering traditional patterns of operation (Johnson, 1990, pp. 144–146). As one of our workshop participant's put it, "The only time we plan together is when the shipment of paramecium come in or when we want to know who's using the geiger counter."

Although individualism is important and integral to any profession, carried to an extreme in an organization like a school, it can allow curriculum to be pocket-vetoed at the classroom level. Such a practice means that the *system* loses its capability to be responsive to a changing environment because its individual employees are not. A great challenge today is to create more collaborative work environments while at the same time honoring and supporting the kind of individualism that was discussed in Chapter 1, individualism that leads to *meaning* being attached to the tasks people are experiencing.

The Role of the Principal

Teachers are not the only people in schools who may resist changes relating to their traditional roles. Teachers who become administrators (and almost all school administrators have been classroom teachers) bring with them the same norms for supervision that they had when they were teachers. Principals tend to look at teaching as a solitary activity, so many do not insist (or even think about) linking any written curriculum and subsequent lesson plans to overall cross grade level curricular goals. Therefore, if they monitor instruction at all, they do not monitor the ongoing curriculum but rather focus on teacher performance.

From our graduate courses and in-service workshops we have gathered salient statements. Here are some which illustrate how too many principals (and superintendents as well, because most superintendents were once principals) regard curriculum management.

- "In this school we have a lone ranger code of operation that has been nurtured by administrators over the years and interferes with any cooperative efforts."
- (A principal to a prospective teacher) "You're lucky there's no written curriculum here. You can do your thing."
- "To the best of my knowledge, I have never had an administrator either know or sincerely care about what I was teaching."

Finally, we share this vignette from a recent course. On her way home from the course, one of our students stopped at the market. Rounding a corner she encountered her superintendent.

"My," he said, "you are out late this evening."
"Yes," she said. "I just finished my class at the university."
"What are you taking?"
"Curriculum management."
"Ugh! What a boring subject that must be. I'm sure glad I'm not taking it!"

This kind of administrative behavior reinforces the cellular structure of schools, teacher individualism, and overall resistance to organizational coordination and direction setting. Furthermore, most principals receive little training about how to change these attitudes, and in the conceptual, planning, organizational, and technical skills to deal with improving overall curriculum development, delivery, and management. Larson, in a recent review of the research on the preparation of administrators, found that the subjects of general administration and organization, supervision, law, personnel, and finance still dominate graduate program curricula (1993, pp. 276). Although new studies recommend including major components in curriculum and instruction in future programs (e.g., Hoyle, English, and Steffy, 1990, pp. 83–134; Thomson, 1993, pp. 1–21; 5–30), it will be years before the impact of those components is felt by students and eventually by the schools in which they are employed.

Because of their backgrounds experientially and educationally, many principals do not feel that they have a legitimate right to enforce staff adherence to a curriculum and they may not know how to do it even if they desired to do so. Principals often have the same attitude about "their" schools as teachers do about "their" classrooms; they want the school to be "left alone" by central authorities. They may resist even more strongly than their faculties any move to reduce control over "their" schools. Thus, moves towards centralization raise the ire of not only teachers—all public school educators are grounded in a long tradition of individualism and isolation from colleagues. This tradition is as severe an impediment to effecting large-scale change as it is to the practice of curriculum management with single employees. Listen to this comment by a teacher: "In this school, staff perform their assignments without a written curriculum guide, textbook sequence, departmental organization, grade level coordination, or planned communication among themselves."

These problems stand as significant barriers toward achieving a "breakthrough" in the curricular affairs of a school or school system, a new and higher level of performance as a result of forethought, analysis, and planning. A breakthrough requires problem identification and conceptualization. It requires a sufficient level of detail which is sequenced and related to the real work of the organization. It requires traceable linkages from thought to action. It requires specificity of results.

SOME CONSTRUCTS ABOUT CURRICULUM IN SCHOOLS

At this point in the chapter, it is appropriate to discuss several constructs, common to education, that are relevant to curriculum management. A construct is a representation of a cluster of concepts.

All Subjects Were At One Time Functional

In George Peddiwell's *Saber-Tooth Curriculum,* curricular subjects such as "woolly horse clubbing" and "fish grabbing with the bare hands" were challenged when conditions changed so that Paleolithic tribes were starving when even the most skilled hunters and fishermen failed to obtain food.

The pragmatic observers of Peddiwell's satire then pressed for changes in the curriculum. However, the old subjects, no longer functional, were then defended on the grounds that they possessed "magic" and were good for "mental discipline" (Peddiwell, 1939).

Today, Homer's *Illiad* would be considered a classic but of little direct functional value in modern society. However, in ancient Greek civilization, the reading of Homer was taught by the kitharist or the teacher of music because Homer was read to music. Music in Greek society was tied directly to religious and civic affairs (Pounds, 1968, p. 46). So the future Athenian citizen was being schooled in an important ritual for his societal role. Homer was therefore expected to be put to immediate use in everyday life. His works were functional.

The Greeks also developed some educational theory. Plato described and wrote about education in his *Republic*. Plato envisioned education serving three types of future citizens:

- men of gold—the outstanding intellects
- men of silver—the soldiers and guardians of national security
- men of iron—artisans and workers.

What is important is that Plato saw the need for a basic education for all citizens' success rooted in their accomplishments at the lower basic levels. What students studied did relate to their future role in society. While there was not a formal curriculum as we know it today, education was viewed as a means to social ends.

If one looks to the Romans, one would obviously find that the study of Latin was functional because it was the language of discourse. The Romans viewed the subjects of Greek education as essential, i.e., utilitarian within their own culture. They regarded geometry and arithmetic as quite useful. Geometry was useful for the calculation of estates in surveying and for military usage, especially in laying out encampments. Practical calculations were necessary for navigation, farming, and military applications in forecasting the hours of light and darkness in planning the maneuvers of armies (Bonner, 1977, p. 78).

The field of rhetoric undergirded the practice of oratory in Rome. There were differing points of view about what constituted the best training or rhetoric for grand oration. Cicero practiced daily with exercises called declamations in which he utilized first arguments for and then against. Cicero also stressed that for an orator, philosophy was especially useful. Philosophy permitted the development of "close reasoning" in which a point of law had to be clarified or an interpretation challenged. The study of ethics was also valuable to the orator because no matter what point he was arguing he had to possess the content of morality, knowing the difference between right and wrong conduct.

In these two cultures we generally see curricular subjects stressed because they were useful, and because they were especially valuable to those desiring to acquire applied knowledge or skill. *Utility* was the chief means to determine value.

The Greek-Roman curriculum has become known throughout the Western world as the "classical" curriculum. As it became less and less practical, it was still pursued by the upper classes as an "ideal." When Vittorino da Feltre was invited by the Marquis of Mantua to establish a palace school for the children of the wealthy and powerful in the Renaissance period, his "La Giocosa" or school included the classical subjects from ancient Rome (Pounds, 1968, p. 117).

Later, in the Reformation, the children of the wealthy were required to be prepared for courtly social life. The traditional "classics" did not suit such students particularly well. Therefore, by the mid-seventeenth century certain "knight academies" or *Ritteracademie* were established. The curriculum included instruction in dueling with a sword or pistol and horse-riding skills. Other subjects related to military skills, geography, history, mathematics, and science as well as teaching in the vernacular languages including French (Pounds, p. 156).

As each wave of new schools or subjects is introduced across the ages, a battle ensues as to the value of those areas. Once a curricular area has lost its immediate utility its merits are supported by other arguments. Thus we hear echoes of certain subjects possessing "higher qualities" for preparing the mind, honing the intellect, or instilling cases for emulation of models of courage and character. Witness the current national debate over "cultural literacy" as initiated by Bloom and Hirsch in 1987.

Finally, there is the case for outright status appeal. If something is esoteric, different and expensive, it may be coveted alone by those with the time and money to acquire it. The chief characteristic of any subject vying for a place in the curriculum is still its practical usage in a society. Since societies are always changing, the argument is destined to be rehashed *ad infinitum.*

Curriculum Is a Means to an End

Few curricula, or subjects within a curriculum, are advanced or defended as good unto themselves. Advocates and defenders point out what their area will do or not do for students.

For example, when Philip Phenix argues for six areas to be the guiding force behind the development of a curriculum for general education—symbolics, empirics, esthetics, synnoetics, ethics, and synoptics—he does so on the premise that these areas represent the essential modes of human understanding. As such, these modes of discerning meaning in contemporary life will counteract current social trends which are decidedly negative. In Phenix's view, "the curriculum should be planned so as to counteract destructive skepticism, depersonalization and fragmentation, overabundance, and transcience" (1964, p. 5). The six modes are means to combat these trends.

Mortimer Adler's *Paidedia Proposal* proposes a curriculum which is the same for all students because it is the best *means* to a true democracy. "We are a politically classless society. Our citizenry as a whole is our ruling class. We should, therefore, be an educationally classless society" (1982, p. 5). Because it is an educationally classless society that is the base for a politically classless society, Adler selects the one-track system of school as good for all. His curriculum is the *means* to the desired end.

Perhaps the most vivid example of proposing a different society and dramatically altering the means of attaining that society is B. F. Skinner's *Walden Two.* In this book, Skinner creates a utopia without a ruling class per se and one which "neither sponges nor makes war" (1948, p. 76). Through total behavioral engineering, children are raised in environments in which they are exposed to anger and frustration only as they can learn to positively respond to them. "We build a tolerance for frustration by introducing obstacles gradually as the baby grows strong enough to handle them" (p. 98).

Walden Two is an example of a twenty-four-hour-a-day curriculum in living. It is a totally planned environment. As Frazier, the director of Walden Two, comments:

The English public school of the nineteenth century produced brave men—by setting up almost insurmountable barriers and making the most of the few who came over. But selection isn't education. Its crops of brave men will always be small, and the waste enormous. Like all primitive principles, selection serves in place of education only through a profligate use of material. Multiply extravagantly and select with rigor. (p. 114)

Then Frazier describes the Walden Two curriculum.

> In Walden Two we have a different objective. We make every man a brave man. They all come over the barriers. Some require more preparation than others, but they all come over. The traditional use of adversity is to select the strong. We control adversity to build strength. (p. 114)

Skinner's curriculum is one in which subjects are not taught at all. "We teach only the techniques of learning and thinking" (p. 119). No economic or honorific value is attached to education. There is no curriculum in *Walden Two* because there is no need for one.

So regardless of the proponent, the curriculum, however defined, becomes the means to attain the desired ends. Curriculum is good because it enables us to get something else that we want from it. Whatever that is, however it is described, the *ends* become the basis for defining and shaping the means. In the case of schools, the means is the curriculum.

Of course, schools are not ends in themselves either. Schools are means to social ends. So the means/ends dichotomy goes on and on. It contains a basic paradox: the means by which we might effectively arrive at our desired ends contain elements of ends we do not want, but there appears to be no other way to obtain them.

One of the Major Purposes of Curriculum is Exclusivity

One of the reasons any organization has a curriculum is to limit the focus and energy of the organization. Organizations require a boundary. This boundary separates them from their environment. Organizations have limited resources. Survival requires them to focus their resources on certain activities to the exclusion of others. If an organization cannot focus its energy and resources, it risks going out of business because it will be neither effective nor efficient.

Although public schools traditionally have been seen as "domesticated" organizations—ones that are guaranteed clients and that need not worry about "going out of business" (Carlson, 1964, pp. 266–267)—as we head toward the twenty-first century more and more challenges are emerging to this tradition as witnessed by the rise of charter schools and the increasing experiments where private firms administer school districts.

The nature of curriculum is to bring about internal consistency and enable the organization to muster and focus its resources on essential activities and processes. Sometimes these processes are attached clearly to specific goals or missions and sometimes they are not. Under either circumstance, there must be limits on what the organization does with its resources. This is particularly true in the 1990s where financial resources are so much tighter than they were in the twenty-five years following World War II.

What curriculum does, therefore, is to limit what schools do internally. Curriculum defines and legitimizes some activities and outcomes and declares others out of bounds. Curriculum in schools may include any and all of the following elements:

- a rationale or philosophy undergirding the establishment of the curriculum
- a statement of outcomes or ends, goals, purposes, and objectives
- a description of methods, processes or activities
- time requirements or specifications
- specification of relationships
- schedules
- actual work tasks or job descriptions
- relationships to supplementary materials or equipment required
- evaluation procedures, references to tests
- relationships to larger units of work or work standards
- relationships to external agencies and their requirements or specifications.

These elements all call for more specificity in terms of what curriculum is. When the ends of curriculum are nebulous and global, then it becomes impossible to know if the means are working or not. On what basis would curriculum be evaluated if it was impossible to know what it was supposed to do? The answer is usually what is cheapest, i.e., efficient. How is it known if the curriculum is too large, if there are too many electives? For most school boards the answer is contained not in a curriculum philosophy but within the budget. The questions too often revolve around how much curriculum can be supported by the budget.

Vague curricular ends lead to other values, often contrary to the main thrust of the curriculum, to be substituted for those that cannot be defined. In some cases, the means can become the end as Callahan so masterfully described the "cult of efficiency" movement in American schools in the years up to World War II (1962). If the ends of curriculum are unknown, then curriculum becomes an end in itself. Curriculum becomes the means and ends. In such cases a "good" curriculum is "good" not because it enables a school or any organization to obtain the results desired but because it is "democratic" or "flexible" or "broad." These are terms that describe what the curriculum is and not what it does. In answer to the question, "Is this a good curriculum?", one is forced to say it is by definition good because how would anyone know if it wasn't?

There are people in schools and in higher education who are uncomfortable with too much specificity. Loss of "academic freedom," charges of "routinization" or "dehumanization" or loss of "flexibility" are all reasons given to avoid specificity. Yet these charges can be issued without dealing with specificity in outcomes (Reimer, 1971). Specificity per se is not the problem, because those opposing some schooling practices are usually quite specific about that which they oppose. Rather, when specificity becomes an end in itself rather than as a means to determine if ends have been realized, then routinization may follow.

This is precisely what has happened in schools. Grading practices have brought about a certain mechanization of the learning process. Yet they enabled school systems to be organized. For what ends? (Freire, 1970). Too often the ends have been unstated as efficiency. The lack of specificity in defining the ends of schooling enables those with contrary values about the nature of schooling to continue to undermine measures of effectiveness as legitimate outcomes of curriculum in schools.

The Function of Curriculum Is To Impact Work

In schools, "work" is what people do that relates to curriculum and instruction. It may have little to do with their job descriptions. The purpose of curriculum is to guide and focus the efforts of teachers in classrooms that are loosely connected one to another, and that are not understood clearly by those not being "taught" in them (parents and the general citizenry).

In a highly decentralized work environment, the curriculum becomes one of the only tools, if not the only tool, to logically connect the work of one teacher to the next to provide for the maximum consistency of education for children and youth. The curriculum can become the record of what was taught and the means by which teaching and learning are improved. Curriculum is a kind of work schedule. It defines, enumerates, and orders the teaching process. It links the individual acts of teachers together into a whole. It provides the context for teaching over multiple time periods. It is the work record. It is the means to integrate, coordinate, and relate the actions taken each day in the school.

Too often curriculum provides only a symbolic context for work to occur in schools. In too many schools curriculum does not guide at all. To guide means to help a person determine if her actions are congruent with what the organization had in mind in shaping a job. A guide must proscribe as well as describe. It must be useful as a filter to screen out and allow in. And all of this must be visible within the working environment. Such actions must be visible to supervisors and those responsible for tending to the overall flow of work.

Typically, curriculum guides do not perform this function. Instead, many permit—by design—the almost unlimited application of content, pacing, and stress that any teacher desires. Deliberately defined ambiguity serves to shield teachers from unwanted supervision and hence control over whatever they might want to do in classrooms. In these cases, curriculum does not impact work at all: it keeps administrators and supervisors from intervening in the classroom. The function of curriculum is then to act as a barrier to both administrative/supervisory control and lay interference in the decisions teachers make in classrooms.

For these reasons, teacher-produced curriculum guides (discussed in detail in Chapter 7) are rarely useful as work statements by which the school can become more effective. As quality control tools they are not useful. As records of decisions to be made they are vague. As a means of framing future instructional-curricular changes or interventions they are non-functional. They are neither a record of operations, a clear statement of work, a data base of transactions, nor an inventory of anything that has or might have occurred in schools. Since they rarely have an impact on instruction, even teachers who have developed them do not use them. Instead, they turn to the textbook as the actual work statement to follow. The textbook becomes the "curriculum surrogate" (Fitzgerald, 1979).

Curriculum Must Conform to the
Authority Structure of the Organization

Curriculum properly designed will impact the actual work of any organization. As such it should "fit in" to the way the organization has designed work and how that work is related to the control system of the organization. For work to have direction, it has to be controlled. If this were not so, an organization would not be in control of itself; it would be unable to change direction when it needed to.

As we have seen, some curricular theorists are not only unsympathetic to the idea of better management and hence organizational control over curriculum but are hostile to the concept. They see control as bureaucratic and perverting what they perceive to be the proper ends of education (e.g., Pinar, 1978). Therefore, control is bad and administrators are corruptive agents in charge of our children's future. Critics of the current form of society are loath to provide those in positions of authority with any more power since to do so would only reinforce and perpetuate that form.

Curriculum which is designed to be inherently contradictive of the authority structure has usually been abandoned, modified or completely changed (Tanner & Tanner, 1980, pp. 518–567). Curricularists are often unstudied in organizational theory and in matters relating to the actual administration of a school or district. Many are naive about matters of organizational life outside of higher education. University organization is quite different in both form and process from other types of organizations (Cohen & March, 1974) and does not fit nor work in elementary and secondary school systems. Few curricular academics connect their actual work to any other type of organization as the data base for their criticisms of schooling or ideas for control of schooling.

If one wants to develop a curriculum which is contradictory to the authority structure of school systems, one must first change that control system. Curriculum was not invented first and school formed to fit the curriculum. Rather the form of school was invented first and the curriculum was shaped to fit that form as we have seen earlier in this chapter. This sequence was not mere accident. It was purposive.

Control is essential for the existence of any organization. There is a relationship between what the organization does and what form of control it utilizes. When individual differences in children were suppressed with the implementation of the graded school, the stable form of the bureaucracy was ideally suited to a system of schools. Gradedness remains the most prominent stabilizing force within schools which supports and perpetuates its control system and the division of labor. If and when learners are treated and considered more as individuals and when the current "batch processing" mode is altered, then schools can take steps to de-bureaucratize the control system. This in turn will require a new and different form of curriculum that reinforces a different mode of operational direction.

School systems have generally not been able to institutionalize ungradedness or other organizational forms such as Individually Guided Education (IGE) (Carlson, 1982), the open elementary school, and the non-graded high school. This inability to break the status quo is testimony to the staying power of a nineteenth-century innovation in education. Although there is now a strong movement to create a real middle school that will look quite different from the traditional "junior high"—and with many elementary schools looking quite different in these regards as well—it will take many years to make noticeable modifications in the organizational structure of most schools.

DILEMMAS OF CURRICULUM MANAGEMENT

A dilemma is a situation that requires one to choose between two equally balanced alternatives. According to Aram, "In the complex relationship of individuals and organizations, there are inherent pulls in opposing directions confronting administrators" (1976, p. 3). These dilemmas relate to the persistent issues that grow out of individual and organizational needs. According to Fullan, "those contemplating change are faced with a series of dilemmas" (1991, p. 62). So, too, do educators face dilemmas who wish to manage curriculum more effectively.

From our experiences, we have identified five major dilemmas that relate to the themes of this book. How they are resolved is highly contextual because each organizational situation is different in terms of its history, present conditions and needs, and its future. "Coping with dilemmas is acting, choosing, and creating. The question about dilemmas is not so much how to decide, but rather what values and realities are created by a decision" (Aram, p. 129). Also from our experience, too many educators (and here we refer to administrators and teachers) do not even recognize the presence of these dilemmas and hence simply carry on day to day without confronting new realities.

Dilemma One: centralization versus decentralization

To what degree should the management of curriculum be centralized in the hands of the district central office or office of the principal or curriculum director, and to what degree should it be left in the hands of individual staff? This dilemma is magnified today by the school-based management movement. How can more control be gained over the direction of *the system* while at the same time delegating decision-making responsibilities and accountability to the local school?

Dilemma Two: uniformity versus diversity

To what degree should the management of curriculum strive to create uniformity of behavior among employees responsible for implementing curriculum, and to what degree should individualism be fostered and supported?

Dilemma Three: coordination versus flexibility

To what degree should the management of curriculum control curriculum decision making both laterally and vertically, and to what degree should it allow for individual decision making in these regards?

Dilemma Four: boundaries versus permeability

To what degree should/can a school system preclude the unwanted intrusion of additional curriculum content through a tightly managed curriculum, and to what degree should it allow such intrusions to enter the organization?

Dilemma Five: bounded creativity versus unrestricted creativity

To what extent is creativity among employees stimulated by working within certain organizational boundaries or frameworks, and to what extent is it nourished by an environment that fosters and supports individualism?

Changing conditions dictate constant awareness and response to these kinds of dilemmas. We ought not to follow our natural tendency to think of responses in terms of "either/or" polarities. Rather, we need to recognize that often the "solution" combines elements of both parts of the dilemma. That is especially true in today's complex organizational environments. Fullan, for example, has concluded that to effect real substantive change in schools requires a combination of "top-down and bottom-up" strategies—"the goal being to achieve greater coherence without centralization" (1994, p. 200).

> If administrative behavior were predetermined, certain, and completely predictable, management might be a rather dusty and uninteresting affair; uncertainty and ambiguity create a richness and challenge to administration. While too much certainty may be a threat to sanity, too little is a threat to individual commitment and purpose. Only in the face of choice does purposefulness arise. (Aram, 1976, p. 129)

Educators today, working in the "white water" environments discussed earlier, must operate from "organizational frames" different from the traditional, bureaucratic, "structural" frame that has dominated their thinking, a frame that has stressed predictability and certainty (Bolman & Deal, 1991, pp. 43–116). A frame, according to the authors, is a perspective, a "window to the world" in terms of how we "see" our experiences, understand them, and eventually take action (1991, p. 11). The "human resource," "political," and "symbolic" frames all contain concepts that can be extremely helpful in responding to the dilemmas of curriculum management because they address the conditions of uncertainty and ambiguity that permeate modern-day educational organizations.

SUMMARY

Managing curriculum requires an understanding of the organizational context of schools. Without such an understanding we will not achieve significant breakthroughs that increase school effectiveness through curriculum.

As with all organizations, schools possess certain characteristics that interfere with their ability to become more effective. Historic attitudes relating to the roles of the school in society, the functions of curriculum relative to those roles, the traditional structure of the school, and the roles of administrators and teachers all present formidable obstacles to real change in organizational structure and the type of curriculum existing within it.

At the same time, several constructs about curriculum run parallel to the characteristics: subjects taught should be functional; curriculum is a means to an end; the function of curriculum is to have an impact on work; and curriculum must conform to the authority structure. All of these factors lead to several organizational dilemmas when educators attempt to manage curriculum.

DIALOGUE FOR IMPLEMENTATION

These are the questions most often asked the authors about the content in this chapter:

1. What are the most serious criticisms of the view that curriculum represents the work to be done in schools?

ANSWER: The most serious intellectual criticism is that the work in schools reinforces a view of society that perpetuates our problems. Schools are thus not the solutions to social problems but part of the problem themselves. A Marxist analysis of schools identifies many of the short-comings of the liberal view of society as a collection of individuals with a free will rather than as conditioned people who do not see any social alternatives and believe the current social order is "the best" and "natural." Depending upon the weight one gives to the Marxist analysis and its validity, the whole discussion about structuring work via curriculum may be correct but totally irrelevant in the larger framework of things.

2. But what about more technical disagreements regarding connecting work and curriculum?

ANSWER: Some curricularists are so repelled by the scientific manage-ment movement of Frederick Taylor and others that they find it hard to accept the view that the curriculum should make work any more specific than it does for fear that such specificity inexitably leads to undesirable, unnecessary control, and the exploitation of teachers and students. In our opinion these people are naive, because work will be structured one way or another, if not overtly then covertly. We much prefer the overt approach since it lets everyone know who is doing what to whom.

3. Who do they see will do this exploiting?

ANSWER: Most often, the "exploiters" are not clearly identified by the critics who may label them "capitalist elites" or "corporate power brokers." But often they see them as superintendents, principals, and school board members who want more control over teachers and students than they now have in order to wield their power and authority.

Many feel teachers should simply be left alone to do their "own thing" with as little outside "interference" as possible. Almost always their solutions to school effectiveness lie in "freeing" teachers from organizational constraints, and not adding any more. But as Lortie has pointed out, teachers as a group lack the technical means and the power to improve schools, and, as individuals used to working alone, teachers are disinclined to seek solutions which will change their status.

4. What, then, is the realistic way to change that posture?

ANSWER: Whatever success we've had has been in candidly pointing out to teachers the paradox in their attitude—one that aims to preserve the status quo (with many features they find depressing) while focusing also on proposed alternatives. We can't continue to enhance the cult of personality in classrooms at the expense of a collectivity that can improve schools more collegially. Teachers have to see that they have to alter their course and move towards different solutions that will help solve or alleviate their problems. Teachers can't become more powerful as a body until they act as a body and make an assortment of isolated classrooms into a whole workable organization called a school.

5. What other barriers prevent schools from improving their effectiveness by viewing curriculum as a work statement?

ANSWER: Schools are "loosely coupled"—i.e., they don't behave as a fully integrated organism for reasons explained in the chapter. But we don't believe that the way schools appear to be is the way schools should be. To become more responsive, schools have to become more internally coordinated, which means a closer connection between the teachers performing the work of the organization. The curriculum is the means to connect that work, but it must be tied more closely and logically to the policy directives of boards through the work of the administrative branch of the organization. That means that the actual work of superintendents and their immediate staffs must include tangible means or bridges between board policies/directives and the work going on in schools.

6. Doesn't that mean increased administration control?

ANSWER: Theoretically no, since that control is now undefined and implied throughout all activities. There won't be any more "authority" than before; we haven't added to the power of the administration, but we will have defined and connected more directly what they do to what teachers do.

7. But will that mean that what administrators can monitor will be more specific?

ANSWER: Yes, and in that sense control will be more specific. Some would call it "tight" as opposed to "loose." The connections will also be more visible. Much of what we now call curriculum will be demystified in the process. We think that will be healthy for everyone. It ought to lead towards more manageable teaching. Assuming that the connections to policy are there and the policy or policies are valid, we will have a more effective organization.

8. How is all of this different from the "cult of efficiency" syndrome that cycles through the society and affects schools?

ANSWER: The first thrust of curriculum viewed as work is not to educate children more cheaply. The motivation isn't to cut costs. Rather the motivation is to enable schools to become more effective—to attain more of the agreed-upon objectives for students. It makes no sense to talk about being cheaper if we can't first accomplish what we believe schools should accomplish.

9. What really is the problem with the graded school?

ANSWER: The graded school is like the procrustean bed of Greek mythology. Procrustes was a robber of Attica who tied travelers up to his iron bed. He stretched the short people out to fit the bed and cut the legs off the ones who were too long.

Grades do that to children. Individual differences, strengths and weaknesses become lost within the structure. Such differences don't have to be dealt with since the structure has eliminated them. The graded school is an organizational solution to an organizational problem. It is not a solution to a learning problem. To deal with learning, we have to move around the gradedness of schools. Grades are a hindrance to becoming more effective.

10. Do you see a time when schools won't be graded?

ANSWER: Educators have tried nobly to rid the schools of grades. They have persisted in spite of the arguments against them by some parents and societal critics. But the non-graded movement has never become widespread. The concept of gradedness is intimately connected to the division of labor and power distribution within schools, not to mention the role of the classroom teacher. The graded school is here to stay for a long time, but new structures in elementary schools (such as multi-grade classrooms) are an interesting innovation, and many middle schools have "restructured" themselves into multi-grade teams with integrated curricula.

The high school, for lots of historic and organizational reasons, is the most difficult level to change in these regards. "Block scheduling" is the latest attempt to alter the way curriculum is delivered in high schools, but it is not a "radical" innovation.

ACTIVITIES FOR PERSONAL AND STAFF DEVELOPMENT

We offer some examples of activities as "starters" but encourage readers to develop their own that will fit their situation.

1. Obtain a copy of a statement about the shortcomings of the schools; look for this in materials such as *A Nation at Risk* or *The Paideia Proposal* by Mortimer Adler (1982). Are these statements grounded on shortcomings or deficits of schooling which jeopardize existing social arrangements and social structure, or are they statements which prevent more desirable ones from being formed? What specific deficits are cited? Are the solutions proposed caused by their absence, or are the schools as they currently exist the causative agents of the deficits? Are schools means or ends to social problems?

2. Find a good historical account of some other form of schooling besides the Academy, such as the Dame School or the Lancastrian school. Or find a local example of an innovative school that has been pushed back to be a more traditional school. Trace the causes of the rise and demise of these forms of schooling. What specific social or economic-political factors led to the demise or severe modification of these forms? What forces in these same domains do you see as challenging the present form of schooling? In what ways would educators have to strategize to effect change?

3. Identify some major critics of the present form of public schooling today, critics who represent conservative (e.g., Chester Finn's *We Must Take Charge*) (1991) and liberal views (e.g., Jonathan Kozol's *Savage Inequalities*) (1991). Which of these views would most likely alter the existing social structure and the role of schools? Which view would most likely be receptive to breakthroughs in learning and human growth? Which would be least? Which view would be most acceptable to the general public as represented by results from the latest "Gallup Poll Of the Public's Attitudes Toward the Public Schools"?

4. Trace the experiments in what Drucker calls "the fallacy of

creativity," that range from *Summerhill* by A.S. Neill (1960) to the alternative high schools of the sixties and seventies. What happened to these experiments? Identify specific reasons they may have succeeded or failed. Is Drucker's statement that "the proper structure of work is not intuitively obvious" supported by your review?

5. Obtain a copy of a textbook prior to the 1870s and then one in the 1890s or early 1900s. In what ways do the structure, content, methods and assumptions differ? Which one would teachers find most useful in a school today, assuming they could modify it to some degree? What are the reasons for your choice?

6. Why have such widely heralded curricular innovations as MACOS (Man a Course of Study), BSCS Biology, PSSC Physics, career education, and "the new math" not had the impact they were intended to have? Examine the question from a sociopolitical context, teacher role-teacher training perspective, and impact of the school context on the innovation.

7. Obtain a high school program of studies. Identify the functional source of each offering in the curriculum. Which curricular areas are most difficult to validate functionally? Why? Using a "pure" form of utility—the curricular area has immediate application to social survival—which areas would you eliminate? Would this give you a more useful or valid curriculum? Why or why not?

8. Develop an alternative form of organizational structure at the elementary, middle, or high school level which would recognize major differences between learners, but which would not be a graded or non-graded school. Specify the basis of instruction and grouping, of describing achievement, and the public requirement for accountability. How would the curriculum differ from that which would be found in the typical school today? What would be similar?

9. What organizational factors exist in your school that interfere with more effective curriculum management? Could they be overcome? How? If not, why not?

10. What constructs about curriculum are present in the minds of educators in a school with which you are familiar?

Chapter 3

THE CONCEPT OF QUALITY CONTROL

Few tragedies have rocked the nation more than the January 28, 1986 explosion of the space shuttle *Challenger*. In front of a television audience of millions of people, seven astronauts died, including the first teacher-astronaut, Christa McAuliffe.

This catastrophic event was followed by investigations and recriminations. The once revered NASA name was forever tarnished. The American people and their government were jolted to the core. Quality control had broken down.

What went wrong with such a high-stakes enterprise? While initial theories centered on the fuel tanks, others noticed that the temperature was quite cold and could have caused problems. After an exhaustive investigation in which about forty-five percent of the *Challenger* was recovered from the ocean floor, NASA was able to piece together a scenario that matched the evidence.

We now know that the astronauts probably survived the terrible explosion, but were killed on impact when the space module smashed into the ocean. We know that the O-rings were faulty and that launch in very cold weather was also a factor. In short, a combination of design flaws and operational miscues caused the *Challenger* debacle (Associated Press, 1986).

It was important to know what happened so that steps could be taken to prevent a similar accident from occurring. NASA scientists and administrators had to use all the available feedback to piece together the reasons for the disaster. Unless and until they knew what went wrong, it would be impossible to assure taxpayers and other astronauts that further space adventures would be safe.

Their success was illustrated vividly recently with the docking of the American space shuttle *Atlantis* and the Russian space station *Mir*. For five days the two were "parked" above the earth in graceful, slow-motion maneuvers that were "perfectly executed" (Chandler, 1995, p. 3). Here was quality control for all the world to observe.

Each day, educators confront challenges similar to those faced by the NASA employees. While poor curriculum design and delivery do not have the dramatic effect of a *Challenger* disaster, continued ineffective curriculum and instruction have a serious negative impact on our most precious resource, our children and youth. Dean Corrigan, former dean of education at The University of Vermont and at Texas A & M University, is fond of stating that "education is a matter of life and death." Unfortunately, too many people in our society do not see it that way. A poor education can cause long-term psychological harm or, in Kozol's terms, *Death at an Early Age* (1967).

On a more immediate, practical level, research is also revealing that curriculum and instruction have a considerable impact on student "engagement,"

> ...the student's psychological investment in and effort directed toward learning, understanding, or mastering the knowledge, skills, or crafts that academic work is intended to promote. (Newmann, 1992, p. 12)

Engagement goes beyond general motivation to stimulate active interest, effort, and concentration in the process of learning. Engagement is on a continuum from less to more rather than being present or not present. Today in schools, attaining such a state with students is more challenging than ever due not only to the normal conditions of growth and development with all their distractions from formal learning but also due to the social conditions affecting young people at all levels of education. Hence, curriculum and instruction are pivotal tools for educators as they seek to find ways to promote more engagement and thus learning with the students who are in their charge.

When something happens in a classroom in which a lesson was a dud and failed to attain the teacher's objectives, one cannot tell at the moment whether it was due to a faulty curricular design, poor curricular delivery, a combination of both factors, or other factors. Until the teacher knows, it is impossible to use feedback intelligently to improve performance.

At the operational level, in the midst of the action of a *Challenger* or *Atlantis* and *Mir* launch, it is difficult or impossible to know what went wrong. Certainly that is the case in the "busy kitchen" environment in which teachers (and other educators) work (Huberman, 1983; Larson, 1992a, pp. 36–39). Schools and classrooms are beehives of activity that preclude "in-motion" analysis and deliberation. In the case of the *Challenger*, we can see in retrospect what had to be changed in the design of the rocket, its boosters, and its tanks, and what not to do in the launch or delivery. In the case of schools, we now know enough about curriculum design and delivery that we can *anticipate* probable quality control problems if we fail to attend to certain elements in the system. This is the focus of this chapter.

CURRICULUM DESIGN AND DELIVERY

Curriculum consists of two essential components. The first is its development and the second its delivery or application. *Together they constitute curriculum management* (see Fig. 1.1).

Traditional curriculum development usually includes ideas about how content should be selected and arranged and perhaps how it might be evaluated, but it does not address connections to teaching as feedback, nor monitoring and administration. It would be like trying to determine what went wrong during the *Challenger* disaster by only concentrating on improving the rocket design and ignoring the launch procedures.

What has accelerated the necessity to separate these two functions of curriculum management has been the expansion of statewide testing, in the form of traditional standardized achievement tests or in new forms of authentic assessment. In the latter case, the most notable examples are in Kentucky, where a state mandate requires use of "performance-based" tests (see Steffy, 1993), and in Vermont where the use of "portfolios" is encouraged by the State Department of Education in the fourth, eighth, and tenth grades (Vermont Assessment Program, Summary of Assessment Results, 1992–93).

As administrators, teachers, and supervisors struggle to improve pupil performance on the basis of assessment results, it becomes apparent that many do not know how to use this type of information as feedback. They do not know what to change to do better on subsequent assessment. Some concentrate on instruction by putting into play a specific model such as the Hunter mastery teaching program. This may work if the curriculum design is sound. If it is not, performance problems are not only unsolved but accentuated. Others seem determined to rewrite curriculum, perhaps focusing on more and clearer learning objectives. However, if the curriculum in use was valid but teachers did not know how to use it, they have started with a solution to a design problem when the actual problem was one of delivery. Still others do not really know what to do; often administrators issue "try harder" memos in the hope that that will do the trick. This may work if the problem is motivational and neither design nor delivery in nature.

From our point of view, these kinds of problems persist largely because preservice programs for administrators and teachers do not address these issues. We have discussed this problem relative to administrators in Chapter 2. Goodlad, in his nationwide study of teacher preparation, found a similar situation.

> Data that we gathered in probing into curriculum and instruction strengthen the conclusion that the future teachers in our sample were being prepared primarily for an operational role in the classroom. (1990, p. 251)

By operational role, he means how to perform in the classroom delivering whatever curriculum is school prescribed or teacher designed. There is scarce time or inclination to also examine design/delivery factors within the purview of the teacher and the school.

QUALITY CONTROL AS A CONCEPT

The *Challenger* tragedy was caused by fundamental breakdowns in *quality control.* Many school problems also occur for similar reasons. *We define quality control as the relationship between critical variables that direct and improve human performance, a continuing and evolving process that results in increased organizational effectiveness.* Today "quality" in the form of such trends as TQM (Total Quality Management) is becoming a "household word" in private and public organizations, spurred considerably by the influence of W.E. Deming and associates (see Bonstingl, 1992; Deming, 1986; Walton, 1986, 1990).

However, one can find quality control practiced as far back as the construction of the Egyptian pyramids (Burr, 1976, p. 1). English, in 1978, began writing about "quality" as a concept related to education and central to the management of curriculum.

Three essential elements must be present for quality control to exist within an organization. First is the presence of a work standard—a specification or standard of some sort to which work is directed. The second is some kind of feedback about work which the standard expresses. The last element is the work itself—what is finally delivered to the customer or the client.

J. M. Juran, a contemporary of Deming who has also had a great influence over Japanese management practices, discusses quality control in the private sector as "cost control, expense control, and inventory control" as they relate to quality planning and quality improvement (1988, p. 12). Broadly speaking, he sees quality as "fitness for use," the general concept that quality is ultimately set/defined by the *user or consumer* of the product or services and not their producer. In education, the ultimate consumer is the student.

In education, this means that one of the essential components of quality control is a thorough understanding of the learner and the context in which learning will be assessed. It also connotes an active role for the learner rather than a purely passive one, a role that will promote "engagement."

It is quite different if the learner is considered an animate "product" to be polished and refined on an educational assembly line. "Students in a factory school classroom are generally found working on identical material at a uniform pace" (Grannis, 1972, p. 150). If the learner, and ultimately the success of a school, is going to be assessed on learner achievement in a future state or society (the context), then learners "cannot be done to"; rather, they must be recognized as active participants in the process itself. The same holds true for teachers. Education is the kind of process in which conformance to design must include the fundamental recognition that part of the job will always be unknown and unfinished. A true quality education ends with a question mark and not a statement.

Quality control concepts have been centered around development or production in manufacturing. Quality control in those settings can exert much more absolute hegemony over inputs and processes than can teachers and administrators working in schools, or people working in most other service institutions. Juran's highly technical analysis demonstrates the various options managers have to gain control over production.

Here are two examples of such hegemony. The first is from an engineer who worked for a computer company and the second from an education student who worked in a shoe factory.

Quality control in the scientific world is straightforward. A simple laboratory test requires calibration of an instrument. Calibration is specified by the control parameters designed for the activity, i.e., a scientific test. The test is run using a known mechanism (e.g., an enzymatic assay). The input consists of known and unknown samples. When all the input is tested and the known samples are within the appropriate standard deviations from accepted norms, then the unknown sample is expected to be the correct value. It is relatively easy to prove with reasonable accuracy that the system is in control.

Throughout my high school and college years I worked in a shoe factory in the quality assurance department. My job was to select a random sample of the end product (a pair of shoes), and assess/test the quality based upon predetermined, specified company standards. It was my job to detect defects and to insure that they did not leave the distribution center to tarnish the company name.

These work environments are radically different from those of schools. However, the difference in work environment does not invalidate the essential idea behind quality control. It simply changes the context in which quality control functions. The fundamental concept of quality control is to improve human performance in human institutions, whether it is involved with the production of goods or the rendering of services.

CURRICULUM DESIGN

The first component of curriculum management is *design*. In this section we will discuss the factors of needs assessment, format, specification, assessment, and fit to the organization. Effective management of these elements leads to quality control of curriculum and "fitness for use." Figure 3.1 portrays the components of design and delivery which are the focus of this chapter.

Quality of Needs Assessment

There are many types of needs assessments in schools and service organizations (Kaufman & English, 1979). The word "need" is often misapplied and used incorrectly. Too often a need is really a desire or a want rather than the difference between a future desired state and the actual state. A need in the context of a discussion about curriculum management refers to a specific gap between a future desired condition and the actual existing condition in one or more of five possible organizational states. These states are part of Kaufman's Organizational Elements Model (OEM) (1983, pp. 53–67).

Needs assessment can involve data-gathering activities about any of the five possible organizational states. Data gathering about the actual/required gaps between inputs, processes, products, and outputs come from internal assessments. They are concerned with organizational efforts

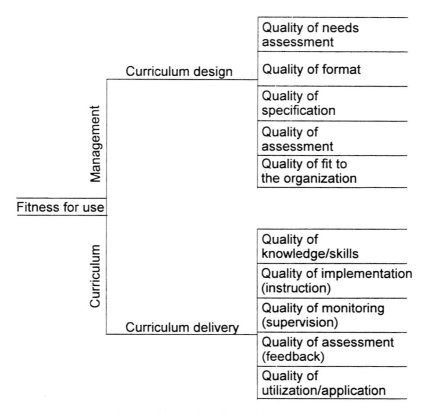

Figure 3.1. Quality Control in Schools.

and organizational results. The last OEM state, outcomes, is external and the results are determined by examining the societal impact of what is happening in schools.

While it is common for the societal impact to be judged largely on the capability of schools to fit the "status quo," there is nothing implicit in the needs assessment procedures that mandates this as an outcome. Kaufman has differentiated between these two types of needs assessments by separating an "alpha" assessment from a "beta" assessment (explained in detail in Kaufman and English, 1979). The "alpha" assessment opens the entire range of values that supports the schools as they exist and the society that sustains them. Both existing social values and those reflected in the schools are open for debate.

However, if this is not the case, then what most schools or other human service agencies do is the more common and less threatening "beta" assessment. This assessment accepts the current social framework

Table 1
KAUFMAN'S ORGANIZATIONAL ELEMENTS MODEL

Kaufman's Organizational State	*Types of Needs (gaps)*
Inputs	• difference between money required and actual money on hand • difference between teachers required and teachers on staff • difference between time required and actual time available • differences between where learners should be and where learners are • difference between what existing objectives or goals are and what they should be
Processes	• difference between existing staffing pattern and required staffing pattern • difference between actual scheduling practices and required practices • difference between actual curriculum design practices and required practices • differences between actual curriculum delivery practices and required practices • differences between on-going teaching methods and required teaching methods • differences between actual managerial practices (MBO, quality circles, etc.) and those required • differences between actual evaluative practices and those required
Products	• differences between courses completed and those which must be completed • differences between grades earned and those required to be earned • differences between actual test scores and required test scores • differences between objectives completed and objectives which must be completed
Outputs	• differences between actual graduates and required number of graduates • differences between those actually certified and those who must be certified • differences between those with job-entry skills and those without who should possess such skills • differences between those who received licenses and those who should have received them
Outcomes	• those who can survive and contribute in society and those who can't compared to those who should

as the "right one." It accepts, with minor exceptions, the purposes of schools as defined by the state regulatory agencies and general societal values. It then goes about determining gaps without questioning the value base upon which they rest or the motives of any group of people in advocating for them as the proper ends of the educational process.

The needs assessment process helps educators select the skills, knowledge, and attitudes they will teach. It is a "value-laden" process which occurs within any given culture; it can never be "value free" or "value less." No curriculum is "objective," neutral. Even a decision to remain neutral about some values is in itself a value. The human condition involves a choice among possible values and conditions. The needs assessment process is a mechanism for choosing among possible values that will be part of a curriculum.

There is no scientific or objective basis upon which to select values. The context in which the selection occurs, a "value system," has been defined as "an interdependent, mutually adjusted, and consistent set of rules" (Smith, Stanley, & Shores, 1950, p. 89). One of the important contributions of some contemporary curriculum critics has been to rebuke the so-called "scientific method" as being anything but scientific and absent of bias (Foster, 1980). Whether a school curriculum in a state-supported school could ever really embrace values contrary to those of the society that supports and controls it is highly dubious. As Thomas F. Green noted:

> The central question is not, "Dare the schools build a new social order?" They probably will not; they probably cannot; and indeed, they probably never could. The significant question is "Dare the social order build a new system of schools?" The answer to that question is problematic, but at least it is the right question. (1969, p. 252)

Perhaps the major contribution of the needs assessment process is that it presents a visible and public process for developing a social consensus about the values to be embraced in a school curriculum. (See Chapter 5 for another approach to needs assessment.)

Quality of Format

The format of a curriculum refers to the shape or structure the curriculum is given prior to the time it is distributed to teachers for implementation (to be discussed further in Chapter 7). Originally, the shape of the curriculum was nothing more than the organization of the textbook. Most early textbooks were simply collections of various passages or concepts into a series of "lessons." These were arranged by difficulty as perceived by the textbook writer. For example, John Pierpont described his organizational plan in an 1837 reader:

> It is hoped that the lessons, in the beginning of the book, are, none of them, so difficult as to dishearten any child, who has mastered the reading exercises that are to be found in his Spelling-book; and that, as the young learner proceeds, if he finds some harder reading, he will, at the same time, find the subject so interesting as to make him disregard the labour of spelling the long words. (p. 3)

This organizational scheme continued to be followed by most textbook writers. An examination of an 1879 version of McGuffey's reader revealed no changes in approach. A 1901 version of this, the most popular textbook in American educational history, revealed no structural changes. What did change were the selections within the reader but not the process of presenting "lessons." Earlier textbooks were also more open about the transmission of cultural values. Noted McGuffey in 1901:

> Lessons inculcating worthy ideas in regard to right thinking and right living form a considerable portion of the contents of this book. (p. 3)

It seems clear that these early curriculum writers were satisfied that "lessons" were all that were necessary to divide a curriculum. A lesson plan is a daily outline of the work of the teacher in the classroom. This was the prime distinction in the developers' minds between curriculum (the selection of content) and the delivery of the curriculum (teaching).

Later curriculum writers would make distinctions between a curriculum resource unit, a teaching unit, and a lesson plan (Hunkins, 1980, p. 342). A curriculum resource unit represented a subdivision of a curriculum. A teaching unit represented the point where the teacher develops a "bridge" from the curriculum—as a stated standard of work—to the actual work in the classroom (the lesson plan).

To educators of this era, "curriculum" was primarily involved in content selection and some content grading (usually by perceived difficulty). Anything beyond this was labeled "instruction." The actual work of the teacher is teaching. It may or may not reference these a priori decisions. The extent to which these a priori decisions serve as guides to teaching constitutes the link between curriculum and teaching.

If a lesson plan does not refer to the prescribed organizational curriculum, it is simply a statement of the independent activities and decisions of the teacher. When teaching refers to the curriculum in its conduct, it is *instruction.* Thus, instruction differs from teaching rather significantly.

Curriculum format is also influenced by how the content is organized. Here too, past practice tends to muddy differences between curriculum, instruction, and teaching. If the curriculum is simply accepted as a collection of "subjects," then the total curriculum format is a collection or collage of these areas portrayed in a variety of combinations.

This fairly rote approach to curriculum development was challenged by John Dewey. He was concerned about the rigidity of schools, their lifelessness, and their sterile pedagogy. He differentiated between logical content organization and content organized from a psychological perspective (Dewey, 1902). The idea was to capture the interests of the learner.

Translations of Dewey's ideas came to be called the activity curriculum or the project method of teaching (Smith, Stanley, & Shores, 1950, p. 417). The activity curriculum was not a curriculum at all in that no predetermined decisions were supposed to be made about what children were to learn. The teacher was supposed to draw from the children their needs and interests and use these as the base for constructing a teaching unit.

This approach to curriculum thinking has been much lampooned and ridiculed (Peddiwell, 1939, pp. 62–73). Often it led to a phony "what do you want to do today children?" in which the teacher asked the question but manipulated the children into the "right" decision. In theory, the activity curriculum was to be defined in large part, if not totally, by the children themselves. The requirement for an a priori defined curriculum was therefore nonexistent. In fairness to Dewey and his disciples, however, much of the criticism of their work came from gross misinterpretations of it, often by people who never read the original writings (Rippa, 1992, p. 181).

As long as there are no precise requirements for specific learning to occur in schools, this type of open-ended approach is as workable as any other. It is possible that children may not learn how to do square root, solve certain algebraic equations or geometric problems, or learn to write legibly and persuasively and it does not really matter. So the curriculum can remain undefined and centered primarily on the spontaneous interests of the students. When it does matter what children learn and when they learn it, the requirement is established for a curriculum as a written plan of work. When negative consequences affect students, teachers, schools or school districts as a result of the lack of learning, the requirement for monitoring the curriculum also becomes more salient.

The quality of the curriculum format is determined by its match to the required outcomes of the school and the educational/political consequences for attaining or not attaining them. If work outcomes are vague, then work specifications can remain vague. As work outcomes become more specific and measurable, so must the curriculum as a statement of work become more specific. The principal criterion—means must be consistent with ends.

If it does not matter whether children learn, or whether any outcome is acceptable as a measure of learning, no curriculum as an a priori designed work statement is necessary. Curriculum is simply whatever happens in the school. It is "all the experiences a child may have in school," whatever they may happen to be. Selecting among them or eliminating some of them is immaterial or violative of some "natural" or "organic" laws of human growth.

What is often missed in these discussions is that school is a *work place*. As such, it is not a "natural" but a contrived setting. In this sense all schools are artificial. To the extent that they capture or build upon what is known about learning as a process, they may become less artificial. Whether schools become more "productive" is in large part not defined by their exemplification of what is known about learning, but how the work is defined and assessed socially and politically. Schools and work in them may be at odds with contemporary notions of how children learn best, but the judgments about schools and what they do may not connect at all to the psychology of learning. Learning theory is but one of the ways the quality of curriculum formatting may be determined.

Quality of Specification

Juran contends that the degree of specificity within the quality control concept of "fitness for use" is determined by the complexity and size of the organization which developed the product or service. The more complex the product and the greater the number of people involved, the less likely that information about fitness can be informally transmitted (1988).

If a vendor in a marketplace has carved some dolls and is selling them, he or she can receive direct feedback about the dolls from potential buyers. But take the case of producing something much more complex—a

VCR unit to show movies. To produce a VCR, hundreds of people may be involved in hundreds of separate operations, so informal feedback is impossible regarding fitness for use. In such cases, notes Juran, specifications substitute for goals. All people involved compare their set of operations to the specifications rather than to the final output.

Applied to school settings, we can see that where one teacher functioned in a one-room schoolhouse and taught all grades, few specifications were required or necessary since the teacher ostensibly *knew* where each child was and made whatever curricular adjustments were required.

As schools grew in size, as teachers were added, as grades provided an internal structure permitting the allocation of resources to be "smoothed" out, and as curricular requirements multiplied, it was no longer possible for a single teacher to be in charge of the child's total education. Teachers saw only a limited portion of a child's program. In most contemporary school systems of a moderate size, a single child may be taught by fifty or sixty teachers over a twelve or thirteen year school career. These instructors may be responsible for sixty to seventy separate curricular areas consisting of hundreds of skills, much information and many processes. In this context, specifications substitute for goals. The major set of specifications is the function of curriculum. Curriculum is a set of specifications which corresponds to the division of labor within schools or any other organization. It defines and regulates the flow or work within the organization.

The problem of deriving a set of specifications that does relate to the desired outputs or outcomes has presented educators with a number of problems. One of the first was that educational outcomes were vague. If the ends of the process of education were not specific, nearly any means would be applicable. How could some means, i.e., teaching, be determined to be more appropriate or effective if the desired outcomes were so broad that they did not indicate which ones were or were not better? In such cases, methods as means to educate evaded empirical testing because there were no standards to determine which were better than others. Thus, to empirically test methods in the content of schooling, the output or outcomes of schooling had to be specified.

From this perspective, we see gradual movement to set up educational systems that permit empirical assessment of methods within schools. Beginning in 1892–1919, educators attempted to establish parameters so that means could be related to ends. First, the Committee of Ten, headed by Charles Eliot of Harvard, recommended standardization of both time and subjects of the secondary school curriculum (Krug, 1964, pp. 18–65). The impact of this late nineteenth century effort led to the removal of many of the "classics" from the curriculum and to the use of the Carnegie unit, a standardized unit of time to measure the schooling process.

Then came a second national committee, headed by math teacher Clarence Kingsley, which addressed the "Seven Cardinal Principles." The Kingsley Report set forth as outcome statements these seven "objectives":

1. health
2. command of fundamental processes
3. vocation
4. worthy home membership
5. citizenship
6. worthy use of leisure
7. ethical character

What was important in this national report was that various courses and subjects then in the secondary school curriculum were to be measured by their contribution to these seven outcomes of secondary schools. Behind this recommendation was the strong conviction that the curriculum as a means should be defined and shaped by the desired ends of the "Seven Cardinal Principles" (Krug, 1964, pp. 336–406). The Kingsley Report accelerated the trend towards the reshaping of the secondary school curriculum. That trend was firmly grounded in the idea that perceived social utility provided the basic criterion upon which to determine what to include and what to exclude from the curriculum.

"The Eight Year Study" (1932–40), sponsored by the Progressive Education Association, sought to determine if secondary school curricula affected students' success in college. The study involved over 300 colleges and thirty selected secondary schools. Comparisons were made between matched pairs of graduates from high schools with "conventional" curricula and those from "non-conventional" curricula.

On criteria strongly affiliated with the "Seven Cardinal Principles" (e.g., intellectual competence, use of leisure time, philosophy of life, social fitness, physical fitness, sensitivity to social problems, practical competence) it was shown that high school students who did well in education at that level did well in college; that there was no pattern of subjects for college admission which was superior to any other pattern; that those students from so-called "experimental" high schools did better than students from the schools with conventional curricula; and, fourth, that students who attained the greatest success in college were those from high schools which most clearly deviated from conventional patterns (Briggs, Leonard, & Justman, 1950, pp. 217–218).

"The Eight-Year Study" was the death knell for the classical high school curriculum that required all students to take Greek, Latin, ancient history, algebra, geometry, and other subjects. It capped a long trek from the curriculum of the academy to the contemporary "shopping mall" curriculum where choice overshadows focus (Powell, Farrar, & Cohen, 1985). More importantly, it continued the practice of viewing the curriculum *as a means to socially desired and approved ends* and further the notion that such means can and ought to be subject to empirical testing against largely social goals (to be discussed in Chapter 5).

One of the offshoots of the "Eight Year Study" was the work of the evaluation team headed by Ralph Tyler of the University of Chicago (Cremin, 1961, p. 255). It was from this far-reaching study that the "Tyler rationale" for curriculum development was created. While Tyler's work in the area of curriculum appeared in 1949 in a course syllabus, he had much earlier argued for precise objectives so that evaluation could occur (1936).

An informal meeting of college examiners attending the American Psychological Association convention in Boston in 1948 furthered that end. It led to the publication in 1956 of the *Taxonomy of Educational Objectives: Handbook I: Cognitive Domain* (Bloom, 1956). The primary motivation for the development of more precise objectives was to create a tool for improved testing. A curriculum could not be empirically examined and assessed by tests unless there was greater precision and uniformity of the objectives from which its underlying rationale emerged. It was no accident, therefore, that the taxonomy accepted and adopted the Tyler rationale to build the relationship between educational objectives and curriculum development. It was also no accident that the illustrative test items contained in the taxonomy were taken from the testing protocols developed by Tyler for "The Eight-Year Study."

As outcomes became more specific, especially as espoused by Robert Mager (1962), they could now not only be assessed but could be related to the curriculum with much more certainty than ever before. It was but a short hop from there to the accountability movement of the sixties and seventies.

The march toward precision in stating educational outcomes has been an example of what Thomas Kuhn has called "the development of a paradigm" (1962, pp. 43–51)—that is, a mindset based on the scientific enterprise. This mind-set consists of rules and regulations, assumptions and constructs which may not all be known at any one time or formally enunciated by all of those working within the paradigm. What one sees from a variety of perspectives, from 1892 to the present, is a progressive movement aiming to consciously relate curriculum to an educational end or outcome. Undergirding this movement is the idea that as the ends become more specific, so must the means. The corollary idea is that curriculum development can also become more scientific.

The quality of specification as a concept of "fitness for use" depends on the framework under which the ends are set forth. Whether means cause the ends may be irrelevant. That they ought to be at least related logically, inductively or intuitively is central to the notion of improving organizations in general, and schools and other service institutions specifically. How such means are verified as being the proper ones may differ depending upon the paradigm at work and the manner in which scientists and educators agree on the process of verification itself.

Few people challenge the idea that what goes on in schools *ought* to have something to do with what learners learn. Thus, the central construct stands: what happens in schools is determined by what learners *should* learn; this is the relationship to be verified.

One of the central issues connected to the quality of specifications is not only the relationship of means to ends—whether curriculum enhances the attainment of certain pupil learnings—but whether curriculum makes the work of the organization more manageable in the process. Too often those who develop curricula are not required to confront one of the facts of life in any organization: work is *time bounded*. As a statement of work, the curriculum must conform to this obvious condition. A workday means that the work force is present only for a fraction of the actual amount of time in any twenty-four-hour period. The time-boundedness of education within schools forces everyone to make decisions about what is to be done with the available time. Two recent reports make this point cogently, *It's About Time* (1993) and *Prisoners of Time* (1994) (time is discussed further in Chapter 9).

When groups of teachers get together to "develop" curriculum, typically there are no organizational specifications to which their efforts must conform. Teachers often have a completely free hand to design their own work—work for which, as we have seen, they are often not prepared based on their preservice education (Goodlad, 1990, 1994). One result is that the definition of the work to be done is stated in ambiguous terms so as not to interfere with teachers' choices in their "own" classrooms.

Curriculum development, therefore, is usually not a process of making work more manageable; rather it often contributes to making the teacher's job less manageable, less realistic, and more frustrating. It is a surrealistic exercise, resulting in a common statement posted behind a teacher's desk, "The harder I work, the behinder I get." These conditions, understandably, lead to the textbook becoming the source of curricula specification.

Quality of Assessment

Until the 1990s, it was common practice in education to design tests *after* the curriculum was designed. Most districts adopted standardized achievement tests without giving a lot of thought about their alignment to the prescribed curriculum, no less to what eventually was taught. Teachers, of course, designed classroom-level tests, usually more aligned to the curriculum.

Today, however, assessment (a broader concept than testing) plays a much larger, *premeditated* role in the design phase of curriculum management. Alternative assessment has exploded onto the educational scene and, in the process, has raised the consciousness of the profession about the need to design *in* assessment practices when designing the curriculum, not afterwards. (Assessment is discussed further in the next section relating to delivery, in Chapter 4, and is the focus of Chapter 9.)

Quality of Fit to the Organization

As organizations, schools must meet certain requirements in order to function. When schools were simple one-room affairs, they had to meet rudimentary requirements. Today, even small elementary schools are complex organizations, reflecting increased federal and state laws and regulations, new programs, many children and youth characterized as disruptive or even dangerous, and often conflicting expectations on the part of segments of their local communities. Schoolwork in the 1990s is challenging and difficult.

Work is different from other types of human activities. Peter Drucker notes: "Work has a result that is outside of the worker. The purpose of play lies in the player; the purpose of work lies with the user of the end product" (Drucker, 1973, p. 169). Here is a connection to the notion of "fitness for use"—the matter of quality being set ultimately by the *user* of the services rather than the *producer.*

Drucker contends that work is impersonal and has its own structure and logic, but working is quite different. Working is transactional. It is a fluid, forceful process. Thus, the work of the teacher is *instruction* to promote learning, but teaching is inextricably bound up with the teacher and who she/he is. While viewing work may be impersonal, dealing with a teacher is always personal. Hence curriculum management *should be* integral to the daily activities of teachers and administrators if it is to have meaning for them.

As schools grew and more teachers were added to staffs, the work of teachers had to be organized and decisions had to be made. Again, Drucker comments:

> Authority is an essential dimension of work. It has little or nothing to do with ownership of the means of production, democracy at the work place, worker representation at the board of directors, or any other way of "structuring" the "system." It is inherent in the fact of organization. (1973, p. 192)

As we have seen in Chapter 2, the box structure of schools has become the dominant way of viewing the work of teachers, work that traditionally has been done apart from colleagues. The structuring of teachers' work has come from documents which provide some sort of guidance about the kinds of decisions they must make. These documents may be vague and directionless in intent, or they may be specific and fairly prescriptive. And there is always the possibility that one can ignore such documents because the system is loosely coupled and supervision is sporadic and often superficial.

As such, curriculum development has been wedded to this semi-autonomous structure in form, content, and ideology. Trends in curriculum practice, which stress the necessity for teams of teachers (working with supervisors) to be involved in curriculum development and management, bump up against these historic patterns. As Fullan puts it:

> We have all seen the debilitating effect of the tradition of individualism in teaching. All successful change processes are characterized by collaboration and close interaction among those central to carrying out the changes. (1991, p. 349)

Currently, in most schools, despite the trend toward collaboration, only state-imposed tests trespass on this terrain and act as countervailing organizational authority in decision making. But, as we pointed out in the last chapter, in the face of this trend individualism must also be honored and sustained.

So extant curriculum practice reflects this authority structure in which teachers are employed. Curriculum making has been an exercise in making *statements about work reflected* rather than about *work to be changed.* There are few curriculum texts which seriously challenge this ideology since most are written by professors who work in a structure with even fewer strictures than those which govern teachers.

Work is not a natural state. It is clearly contrived and defined by its result. Work is a discussion about authority. Work occurs within a social, economic, political and psychological context. It may or may not be of inherent interest to the worker. When workers find their work intrinsically motivating, the outcomes may be of more quality because intrinsic motivators are stronger and more enduring (and less costly) than extrinsic motivators like money, prestige, and power. But, "Individuals are neither motivated *only* (emphasis in the original) by their own internal perceptions, needs, and characteristics nor *only* by external demands, expectations, and environmental conditions, but by an interaction of the two" (Owens, 1995, p. 60).

The industrial revolution brought about the conditions for a study of work. The first person to study work systematically in industrial contexts was Frederick Taylor who presented his basic thoughts on "scientific management" to the American Society of Mechanical Engineers in 1911 (Taylor, 1911). Taylor assumed (and so did many writers of his genre) that inefficiency and waste were rampant in industry and that the solution to this problem was basic, systematic management rather than searching for some esoteric new approach.

These pioneers in the study of organizations and management believed that people came to work to do tasks, but that they usually did not do them in the best way possible. They believed and demonstrated that through work redesign, output and productivity could be enhanced. While they have been subjected to severe criticisms because they ignored the human factors of attitudes, feelings, and values that affect motivation, they broke new ground in trying to understand how the delivery of work in organizations could be improved. But they did not conceive of a concept like "fitness for use" where the definition of quality is ultimately set by the *user* of the services—the student—and not the *producer*—the educator. To scientific managers, "quality" was established by the company.

Work specialization pursued to ultimate detail resulted in worker alienation and lowered productivity. Work can be divided and subdivided until it becomes simply a product or simply a job. Work may be exciting, but most jobs have considerable elements of routine, boring activities.

As we have seen, early school administrators became enamored with the improved efficiencies in factories and industrial settings and saw possibilities of applying similar approaches to attain similar ends in schools (Callahan, 1962). As the public's esteem for American business grew, it was inevitable that citizens would compare schooling and business and wonder how schools could use practices from the private sector to deal with their problems. Since then, American public education has been subjected periodically to similar pressures relating to the country's economic conditions (Toch, 1991, pp. 17–22).

Many administrators in the early part of this century saw connections between ineffective economic practices, the nature of the education profession, and the role of a better managed curriculum. For example, the State Superintendent of Schools in Maine made these prescient comments in 1910.

> A notable waste is occasioned in education by the failure of school authorities to provide courses of study and systematic plans of work. Elsewhere in this report are figures which show that a not inconsiderable number of schools are working without any courses of study whatever. In these schools, it must be assumed, the work goes forward from term to term and from year to year without other plans than are made by the more or less constantly changing teaching force. Haphazard effort of this kind results in the loss of respect of these schools on the parts both of parents and pupils. Teachers who find themselves in schools of this kind must work without accurate knowledge of the results that are expected of them. Under such conditions there can be no continued concentration of effort and waste must result. (Smith, 1910, p. 37)

Here, a year prior to Taylor's "scientific management" paper, we see linkage between work in schools and the requirements for work design, and the reasons they are functionally necessary in educational organizations.

The statement by Smith is strikingly similar to that of one of our students (quoted in Chapter 2) who said that in her school, "Staff perform their assignments without a written curriculum guide, textbook sequence, departmental organization, grade level coordination, or planned communication among themselves." What Smith and the student reflect is the reality that in too many schools, then and now, there was and still is little connection, little "fit," between the work delivered and the design of the work.

Curriculum as work design promotes consistency, allows for more equitable distribution of resources, helps people know the results desired from the work done, and consequently engenders respect from clients and patrons of the schools. A functional course of study or curriculum is as essential then as now for the same reasons. Curriculum follows the organizational structure and its lines of authority. It will be compatible or it will be rejected and replaced by one that is compatible.

CURRICULUM DELIVERY

The second component of curriculum management is *delivery* —putting what is designed into practice. In this section we will examine the factors of skills, implementation, monitoring, assessment, and utilization/application.

Quality of Knowledge/Skills

The person primarily responsible for the delivery of a curriculum in schools is the classroom teacher. There is no such thing as a "teacher proof" curriculum. The best designed curriculum may fall apart in the hands of an unskilled, unprepared, or indifferent teacher. In the previous chapter, we discussed briefly teacher preparation, and in Chapter 4 it is an issue relative to designing and delivering the curriculum.

Complaints about the quality of teachers and their training fill the records of the respective states and city superintendents' reports throughout the time when public education was expanding in the nation. The lack of training was caused by both a simplistic view of what teachers had to do and the lack of government support in allocating funds to improve public education.

In 1839, Henry Barnard of Connecticut organized teachers' institutes. These consisted of brief seminars and workshops for teachers on practical topics. Institutes were later expanded into Normal Schools. Normal Schools were institutions devoted to teaching teachers how to teach. Their curricula were not considered college level. They were not uniquely American, being predated by the founding of the Abbe de la Salle in

Northern France in 1685 (Cubberly, 1948, p. 745). The first Normal School in America (restricted to women) opened in Lexington, Massachusetts in 1839 (Rippa, 1992, p. 232).

The importance of Normal Schools cannot be underestimated. When the Lancaster County Normal School of Pennsylvania began its work in 1855, half of the teachers in the state had no education beyond their neighborhood school. Some were not proficient in the English language. The county superintendent commented that his visits to observe teachers were about as pleasant for them as one from the sheriff, and described his fledgling pedagogues as "young, inexperienced and indifferent men and women whose heart is not in the work, and whose interest is limited by the low salary they receive" (Graver, 1954, p. 188).

Normal Schools expanded into state colleges and finally to state universities that often included a school or college of education.

In the mid-1980s, a group of education deans called "The Holmes Group" met with an agenda to reform teacher education programs. Their goals were strongly reminiscent of the original goals for Normal Schools:

- to make the education of teachers intellectually more solid
- to recognize differences in teachers' knowledge, skill, and commitment, in their education, certification, and work
- to create standards of entry to the profession—examinations and educational requirements—that are professionally relevant and intellectually defensible
- to connect schools of education to real schools
- to make schools better places for teachers to work and to learn (The Holmes Group, 1986, p. 4).

This group of deans initiated a strong reform movement that continues today and has captured the attention of other noted educators, such as John Goodlad who is currently engaged in a major national study of the subject (1990, 1994).

Focusing on "fitness for use" relative to the knowledge base and skills of educators, the delivery of any curriculum must take into account the person with the major responsibility for making sure it is fit for use. Teachers' abilities to bring the curriculum to life depends not only on their background in a pedagogical sense but also upon their knowledge of the content of the curriculum and their desire and willingness to deliver it to learners. Teaching involves a command of subject matter, an ability to inspire the young, and an ability to create an environment in which learner time and interest is maximized within the classroom. According to a recent synthesis of the research related to influences on learning, teacher knowledge and skills in instruction and classroom climate setting were the second most important group of "influences" (next to student aptitude) (Wang, Haertel, & Walberg, 1993–94).

However, despite the abilities of the teacher, writing a curriculum beyond the capabilities of teachers to deliver it would be like trying to build a spaceship in a blacksmith's shop—an exercise in futility, no matter how clear the blueprint. Understanding and doing are two separate spheres of human activity.

If, however, the skill level of the teaching staff is quite low, writing a curriculum at that level does not prepare the "user" (the student) of the curriculum for the challenges they will face in their lives. The education received would not be "fit for their use." For this reason, the skills and knowledge of teachers must be improved and upgraded whether or not they have immediate new curricula before them.

Quality of Implementation

Classroom instruction becomes the focus when considering the implementation of a curriculum. The extent to which teaching adheres to curricular specifications and produces the desired results represents the major consideration for gauging the quality of instruction.

One of the first issues to be confronted in determining the quality of instruction is the matter of how quality is assessed. If instructional quality is to be assessed through utilization of a standardized achievement test of some sort, then it makes a considerable difference whether that test is congruent or aligned with the curriculum. If it is not—or the matter is unknown or not considered—an inappropriate data base may be selected to determine success, one which bears no relationship to the work going on in the classroom. Reporting such outcomes to a school board or community could generate severe negative repercussions for educators in such a system.

Instruction has been defined as teaching which is congruent with the curriculum. That definition must now be expanded to include testing which today is being seen more broadly as assessment. There must be considerable congruence between teaching, the curriculum, and the nature of assessment if we are to achieve instructional effectiveness. "The stubborn problems in assessment reform have to do with a pervasive thoughtlessness about testing and a failure to understand a relationship between testing and learning" (Wiggins, 1993, p. 3). (These relationships will be discussed in greater detail in Chapters 4 and 9.)

Fisher and Berliner et al. examined the quality of instruction in the teaching of reading and math at the second and fifth grades. They used an achievement test battery as the determiner of the quality of instruction. Their findings indicate some of the indices of instructional quality:

- the amount of time that teachers spend in a curriculum area was positively associated with achievement in that area
- the amount of engaged time of the students (attention to the work of the teacher) was positively associated with their achievement
- the amount of time that a student experiences high success is positively associated with learning
- improved substantial interaction between the students and the teacher is associated with higher levels of student engaged time
- feedback to students about their actual answers (academic feedback) was positively associated with student learning
- the structuring of lessons and on-task directions by teachers was positively associated with high student success
- teacher stress on academic goals (which reflects the teacher's value system) was positively associated with student learning
- in classrooms where students took responsibility for their own learning and helped one another, achievement was generally higher. (Fisher et al., 1980, pp. 7–32)

The researchers noted that teachers, for the most part, directly controlled the elements which accounted for improved pupil achievement, and, "If some skills are particularly important for students, it would be reasonable to spend large amounts of time on those skills" (p. 24). (This conclusion is similar to the previously cited synthesis of research by Wang, Haertel, and Walberg, 1993–1994.)

Fisher and Berliner comment that, to be effective in a classroom, a teacher must be a manager of instruction. With groups of thirty students, one-to-one teaching will not occur very often:

[T]he teacher must try to plan generally reasonable activities for the different students in the class and keep everything moving along as well as possible. The teacher cannot consider each student in isolation but must manage instruction for all students simultaneously. (p. 31)

Recent times have seen the development of many systems of instruction, from Benjamin Bloom's mastery learning (1981) to Madeline Hunter's mastery teaching (1982). For purposes of determining the quality of implementation of a curriculum rather than examining instruction qua instruction, these indices connote quality:

- the most appropriate determination of curricular quality is the extent to which teaching reflects and is guided by the curriculum (teaching can be judged apart from whether or not it is referenced to a curriculum);
- the quality of implementation of a curriculum (i.e., instruction) is most appropriately judged by the outcomes in terms of pupil learning that were required or desired to occur;
- for the first two indices to be relevant, measures of learning (outcomes) must be contained within the curriculum and within the measures used for assessment;
- the propriety of means-methods selected by the teacher as well as the structure of interaction between teachers and students is ultimately judged by the measures selected for assessment and how well students perform on them.

What these indices do is link teaching to curriculum and both to assessment. For a curriculum to possess implementation quality it must be used by teachers. It must be referenced in their daily work. It must truly guide by promoting some content and activities and eliminating others. In short, it must *screen in* and *screen out.*

But a curriculum is more than one teacher. Its purpose is to guide all teachers towards common desired outcomes. The genius of curriculum is that across many years and grade levels teaching is consistently directed and purposively shaped to promote required or desired learning. The most fundamental challenge to the implementation of a curriculum is the extent to which it weaves together a coherent *system of instruction* which is directed towards attaining system goals. If a curriculum promotes such a system laterally across grades, it is said to have *continuity* or is *coordinated.* If it does so vertically from one grade to the other, it is said to promote *articulation.* Curriculum management concepts and practices can provide the "common language" for educators in this arena of work to achieve these goals just as the Hunter approach does the same for classroom teaching.

Non-educational organizations have the same problems and use different terms to describe their solutions. The general problem is referred to as one of coordination. First, as Kuhn and Beam describe it, one has to determine the "degree of systemness" required (1982, p. 256). This is the degree to which its components constitute a coordinated pattern, as contrasted to being a simple sum of parts.

Most schools function as a "simple sum of parts" rather than as an integrated, connected pattern of roles and role responsibilities. This is a satisfactory response so long as student learning is not required as a measure of performance or judgment about schools, or as long as student performance is deemed adequate by whatever measures are utilized. When this situation changes, schools are forced to develop tighter connections between their subunits. In short, the external environment requires a greater "degree of systemness" if the system is to adapt and survive.

Now the curriculum becomes a vehicle to establish just what each unit and subunit is to do to attain the required or desired outcomes. This is done "up front" and results in centralization of authority to accomplish that goal. The curriculum becomes a prime agent of control for making the system act like a system. When unity becomes a requirement for effectiveness, the extent to which subunits of an organization can be permitted to deviate from organizational work statements is sharply reduced at all other levels.

Many teachers sense a rather profound change happening when their school is in the process of trying to improve its performance relative to some state test. The dialogue centers on improving coordination, i.e., continuity, and finding time to stress the necessary tested skills or content to ensure mastery rather than creating unique teacher responses that may or may not result in improved performance. Something is lost and something is gained. Lost are autonomous teacher responses to their individual curriculum. Gained is improved performance on approved or mandated measures and a possible increase in public approval and support. If the test is assessing meaningful and important pupil skills or knowledge deemed essential by the school for preparation for citizenship and future employment, the overall result is more desirable. If the test is assessing skills and knowledge deemed essential by the teacher, then the teacher is delivering it more effectively and those results are more desirable.

There are two important points here. The first is that when the external conditions of the school environment are altered to require a higher degree of coordination, articulation, and accountability, curriculum becomes more centralized. It is much more likely to be developed and to be implemented "top down." Despite much resistance from some personnel, a top-down approach does work under some conditions in obtaining better performance on selected measures. In today's turbulent world, "Simultaneous top-down/bottom-up strategies are essential because dynamically complex societies are full of surprises" (Fullan, 1994, p. 201). The second point is that one cannot avoid seriously questioning what the assessment tool is actually evaluating, and whether or not the content of the test is what we really want children to learn in schools. If the answer is negative or incomplete when the loop between testing, curriculum, and teaching is invariably tightened to improve total school and school system response, something of value may be driven—by design or by default—from the curriculum not tested. It may be lost because of a lack of perceived importance or emphasis, or abandoned in the time crunch forced upon a staff when they must narrow instruction to fulfill the requirements of mastery. These consequences ought to be considered prior to implementing changes in curricular practice. What schools are is to a large measure what we expect of them. They cannot avoid being responsive.

Quality of Monitoring

Just as teaching may be thought of as the monitoring of learning, so supervision is the monitoring of teaching. Supervision is performed by school principals and subject area supervisors (discussed also in Chapters 4 and 8).

> No organization can function well if its supervisory force does not function. Supervisors are, so to speak, the ligaments, the tendons and sinews, of an organization. They provide the articulation. Without them, no joint can move. (Drucker, 1980, p. 280)

This is the theory. In reality, the general quality of supervision in schools leaves much to be desired. Some of the prior statements from our students in graduate courses and in workshops about how they are supervised show the shortcomings of supervisory practices in too many educational organizations.

For good measure, here is one more. "In my area of study there is no formal supervision. I am partly monitored by purchase orders!" As Stanley and Popham discovered, "Increasing numbers of educational policymakers recognize that teacher evaluation, as it has been practiced in the United States, is apt to be perfunctory instead of perceptive" (1988, p. ix; see also Castetter, 1986, pp. 318–322).

One of the key problems regarding supervision in schools is the unreasonable spans of control (or coordination) given to those who supervise and the fact that what teachers do is, in most cases, not visible, except in a one-on-one situation. The latter situation differs from many industries where a supervisor can literally "see" several employees at work at the same time. The span of control refers to the number of subordinates a supervisor can effectively supervise on an operational basis. Classical management literature indicates that for high-level executives that number is probably four to eight, and at lower levels eight to fifteen (Filley & House, 1969, p. 282). However, with the onrush to downsize various kinds of businesses that usually eliminates many middle managers, the old concepts of span-of-control have been thrown for a loop.

Most school principals and district-level supervisors have spans of control that are considerably larger than the accepted ranges of supervisory effectiveness (recognizing that one should not equate conditions in the public sector exactly to those in the private). But there is the matter of pure common sense in these regards, since we know all the other demands faced by administrators/supervisors. For example, we know of elementary schools where there is one principal to supervise 30–40 teachers and instructional staff. In extensive studies of teacher evaluation practices, Manatt and his colleagues found that "School organizations seldom face up to the fact that their principals monitor too many employees for effective supervision" (Manatt, 1988, p. 79). In today's economic environment, this situation is getting worse rather than better because school boards choose, as one of their first responses to a budget shortfall, a reduction in the number of administrators.

Because of the unmanageability of the supervisory span, many principals resort to a kind of "management by exception" where they only spend time with "teachers in trouble" or, as a legitimate organizational alternative, skip evaluating all teachers every year (unless one has serious problems) (Manatt, 1988, p. 89). Many systems have resorted to this pattern. This reduces the span to a more manageable number; however, it prevents the principal from being visible and from observing the remainder of the staff. The same is true for many supervisors who often have paper responsibility for scores of teachers in some school systems. This complicates and compromises the supervisor's credibility with teachers who perceive that those who supervise do not really know what they do because they do not spend enough time in their classrooms (Good & Brophy, 1978, p. 29).

Still another problem is the matter of perspective, the *approach* to supervision. In manufacturing, supervision is reduced to a matter of inspection, particularly in American factories. The Japanese take an entirely different view of inspection. Their view is that inspection does no good after a product has been produced. To be effective inspection must occur where the product is being put together—at the source. Whereas Americans think of "defect detection," the Japanese think of "defect prevention" (Schonberger, 1982, p. 35).

"Defect detection" is the view of the supervisor as the "snoopervisor," one who is motivated to "catch" people doing something wrong. "Defect prevention" assumes a posture of an assistant or helper.

Customary observation practices in schools, conducted by either principals or supervisors, examine teaching not as instruction but as an isolated activity. What evidence is there that the designed curriculum is being implemented? Typical plan books do not reveal connections to the curriculum. If they do not, how is the curriculum being monitored? How would any principal or supervisor "know" if teachers were truly implementing the curriculum? It is rare to find a district policy like that of the Essex Junction, Vermont schools that highlights curriculum management and stresses that "All teachers are required to follow the adopted curriculum" (Chittenden Central Supervisory Union, 1993). Even experts in the field, who stress the teachers' knowledge of subject matter when evaluating performance, fail to look at the broader issue of how teacher responsibility for implementing organizational curricula. Scriven, for example, who has developed an excellent framework called "the duties-based" approach never mentions school curricula in his framework (1988, pp. 129–134). However, there are indications that this situation might be changing, albeit very slowly. For example, the new contract just signed by the Boston Teachers Union includes a clause to the effect that, "A new teacher performance evaluation system evaluates the extent to which teachers are cooperating in the implementation of systemwide and school-based educational reform initiatives" (Dowdy, 1994).

While a supervisor usually has subject area expertise—and thus is able to assess well the quality of a teacher's work—a principal is normally a "generalist" and cannot be expert in all areas of the curriculum. Yet the principal has the responsibility for coordination and articulation within the school, while the supervisor has similar responsibilities for the district. When there are two such persons supervising teachers there can be considerable strain between them due to conflicting role expectations, with the result that little more than "perfunctory" rather than "perceptive" supervision is effected.

In addition to helping teachers to improve the delivery of their instruction (so the teaching is wedded to the curriculum), supervisors should obtain *feedback* about the curriculum in order to insure that "the system is acting like a system."

Before concluding this section, we need to point out that traditional practices of supervision, for many of the reasons we have discussed, are being questioned and the overall field is in transition. Emerging as alternatives to "what is" are approaches relying more on peer support and assistance and general collegial interaction, as opposed to centering supervisory expectations in the role of a "supervisor" (see, for example, Stanley and Popham, 1988; Glickman, 1992; Glickman, Gordon, & Ross-Gordon, 1995). Curriculum management practices fit right into this new emphasis because they provide concrete tools to teachers to improve the design and delivery of curriculum; these tools, if joined with peer interaction through collegial processes, can be powerful levers for classroom and school improvement. They can stimulate an organizational climate where self-monitoring becomes the norm and "defect detection" from "the top" becomes a practice of the past.

Quality of Assessment (Feedback)

Feedback is a concept from general systems theory. "Feedback is *evaluative* [emphasis in original] information *about* system action or the results of system action (Immegart & Pilecki, 1973, p. 55). It means that a certain amount of energy from a system is used by the system to improve its relationship to its environment. It is a method for a system to adjust itself externally and internally when there is a gap between what the system is doing and what it ought to be doing within its environment. For this to occur it is assumed that the system has a purpose.

Feedback can be provided to a system at any point where data can be compared to standards. Areas for feedback include inputs, processes, products, outputs or outcomes (using Kaufman's OEM model as the reference).

The most common form of *public* feedback in schools and school systems is achievement testing (but, as we shall see in Chapter 9, many other forms of assessment are used in schools). "An assessment is a comprehensive, multifaceted analysis of performance; it must be judgment-based and personal" (Wiggins, 1993, p. 13). A test, on the other hand, "is an evaluation procedure in which responsiveness to individual test takers and contexts and the role of human judgment are deliberately minimized, if not eliminated" (Wiggins, 1993, p. 15).

It is assumed that the assessment of students provides useful information to educational systems and that, through the use of such information systems, can help bring about improved student performance on subsequent assessments.

For this assumption to be valid the following must be operative in the educational environment:

(1) the test must be related to the goals of the educational system; otherwise, data from the test are relatively meaningless about system performance since they have no reference to what the system is about;
(2) the test must be capable of providing data that can be related to the operations of the educational system internally, or operations cannot be changed with the data;
(3) the educational system must have in place the technology to apply test data, to know what is important and what is not about the data;
(4) the educational system must have a commitment to use and act upon the data on a systematic basis.

From general systems theory, feedback requires *encoding,* the capability of the larger system to break down data regarding performance into meaningful units of information so as to change internal operations.

Historically, encoding has not been present in the use of standardized achievement tests in education. Therefore, standardized test data have been relatively unused by educational systems as a means to improve pupil learning or general system performance. They have been used to classify students. Since they are not a measure of the specific curriculum of any particular school system, they cannot provide information relative to the degree of success to which any local curriculum has been faithfully implemented.

This also means that data provided by the test do not pertain to local standards of performance. At the outset it is impossible for educators to encode it. It may or may not relate to overall system goals and objectives.

These are sometimes unknown to the system itself because often, "The organization operates on the basis of a variety of inconsistent and ill-defined preferences" (Cohen, March, & Olsen, 1979, p. 25).

The whole business is shrouded in mystery when testing content is kept secret and teachers are warned "not to teach to the test." Inasmuch as teaching test content would invariably raise some students' scores, the capability of the test to classify students would be violated by school-based intervention. In turn, this posture rests on the assumption that there is something in the population called "general intelligence," separate and apart from what schools do. However, since schools may include some tasks and content from such tests, they do impact indirectly upon some pupil responses. Thus, we account for the differences in such tests by labeling some "aptitude" and some "achievement" (Popham, 1981, pp. 33–34).

If tests assess content not contained within school curriculum, what are they assessing? Data suggests that they are assessing the environment of the student more than anything else (Jencks et al., 1972, pp. 52–130). Thus the significant correlation between scores on some tests and socio-economic level, i.e., wealth. It is not surprising that such tests do not show much impact from school-related input, since what they are assessing is not connected to what schools do in the first place.

If there is such a factor as "general intelligence," it must nonetheless take on a sociocultural form and be manifested in behavior. Human behavior is acquired, if not from schools then from the environment. If assessment measures are not related to what schools do, they are related to other places where behavior is learned. Human behavior is always context referenced. That context is highly influenced by time, culture, history, and language/thinking patterns. Some contain interactive patterns that are much more conducive to producing the behaviors that tests measure compared to what other tests measure. That such environments are impacted by wealth, status, and race has been well documented (Coleman et al., 1966, pp. 20–23). It seems reasonable to conclude that even under the best conditions, tests will never be able to shed all of the trappings of contextual influence, making the measurement of "pure intelligence" an impossibility. (This topic is examined again in Chapter 7.)

Thus, I.Q. and standardized achievement tests are not well suited as the foci of educational system improvement. The schools cannot be a rung on the ladder to the good life for all the children of all the people, if the measures used as feedback discriminate against some of the children and place them at a decided disadvantage within the very environment committed to eliminating forms of social injustice. To do so places the children of the poor in "double jeopardy." That such practices have been used to do just that has been documented again and again (Terman, 1916, pp. 3–21) in the history of public education (Tyack, 1974, pp. 180–181).

For tests to be used as feedback within educational systems they must be direct measures of what students should be learning in schools, and not indirect measures. They should relate to school instruction and provide information that translates into tasks in the work place—things that teachers do differently in classrooms to improve pupil learning. These characteristics describe effective tests, criterion-referenced tests that are much different in their purpose and assumptions from the typical norm-referenced standardized test (Tuckman, 1985, pp. 109–128). Today, the characteristics also fit what is being called "authentic assessments" or "performance assessments" (Wiggins, 1993). No educator would want a bell-shaped curve after instruction. No educator would accept "failure" as a built-in condition of the educational process.

The quality of assessment is first and foremost a measure of the relationship between what students are taught in schools and what students are tested on and about in schools. Tests are used for purposes of providing useful information about system and individual performance. They can be encoded and the results can help change the direction, content, scope, or emphasis of teaching within schools. Any test that purports to measure pupil performance but does not have such properties simply flunks the most important criterion. Other properties about the quality of tests—such as validity and reliability—are of secondary importance. For quality assessment to occur in schools, tests must directly measure the internal processes of schools and be congruent with the goals and objectives of specific schools and their mission. Work performance and work improvement must be assessed by measures which are congruent with the work being done.

Quality of Utilization/Application

The quality of utilization/application of the feedback data is a function of the presence of previous design/delivery elements. The data have to be the right data (quality of needs assessment), contained within a format that is functional, specific, and fits the organization.

For the curriculum to be utilized, it must match the skills of those implementing it. It requires monitoring, and data derived from the monitoring must be congruent with the work being performed and indicative of the purpose of the system in its environment.

Those who gather feedback must commit themselves to apply the data to adjust any of the previous elements so that, in relationship to one another and to the overall purpose of the system, the system improves over time. All of the elements can be present, but without a commitment to application, the will to change is absent. That will to change depends upon leadership that can transform the feedback into actions that improve operations and total performance throughout the system, at whatever levels the actual work is done.

While the superintendent of schools, the principal, the agency director, or the nurse manager can formally commit the enterprise to improvement, only as this goal is translated into work behavior among all employees is the goal met. For this to happen, the will to improve has to become part of the "working ethos" of an organization—a component of *the total work flow* as discussed in Chapter 9. It must be firmly a part of each person's conscious acts on a day-to-day basis.

This is what Peter Drucker has referred to as "the spirit of performance." It enables an organization of "common men [and women] to do uncommon things" (1973, p. 455).

SUMMARY

Quality control is an old and enduring concept. It refers to a continuous process of organizational self-direction and evolution that increases organizational effectiveness.

In its simplest form, three ingredients must be present: a work standard, work assessment, and activity (the work) directed towards attaining the standard based upon feedback. As the elements become more congruent, work performance is improved.

Within schools quality control of the curriculum breaks down into two domains: those associated with design and those associated with delivery. When the factors within each domain are operational and impact the work done, performance reaches new and higher levels, improved "fitness for use" is stimulated, and a *breakthrough* may be achieved in performance.

There are numerous problems and barriers within schools that prevent significant breakthroughs from occurring. Some are endemic to the nature of the school as an organization, some are technical, and some are attitudinal. All have an effect on curriculum management.

We need to infuse curriculum management processes and practices throughout the organization so that those delivering the service come to rely on them for improving the design and delivery of the work for which they are responsible.

DIALOGUE FOR IMPLEMENTATION

These are the questions most often asked the authors about the content in this chapter.

1. What are the strengths and weaknesses of the needs assessment concept as the first step in curriculum management?

ANSWER: The strengths of the process come from examining the consequences of what schools do with and to children. Wedded to the concept of "fitness of use"—defined by the user—the needs assessment process can help to "open up" work inside of schools so it becomes more congruent with desirable outcomes.

However, few assessments are truly "alpha" assessments. Almost all are defined by special-interest groups—including educators—and reflect the status quo more than anything else. We see this not so much as a "weakness" in the idea but the result of political realities of school governance.

2. What is the dominant way educators think about schools and curriculum today?

ANSWER: The dominant mind-set or paradigm is still "manufacturing" or "the factory." Many citizens and especially policymakers tend to accept the premises of this model as the model for schooling. Witness the current push in some quarters to turn over the administration of schools and systems to private firms.

3. Doesn't the idea of quality control as outlined in this chapter also accept the model of manufacturing as the proper paradigm?

ANSWER: No. Quality control fits non-manufacturing settings as well as manufacturing work places.

Quality control does require the presence of certain elements which are probably going to be found more commonly in manufacturing endeavors. In manufacturing, the "product" is more easily specified and tangible than the "human product" for which schools, colleges, hospitals, and other human services organizations have responsibility. It is also easier to relate work processing to the final work outcome in manufacturing settings; work is also more easily defined and standards more precisely set there as well. But the concept of quality control as "fitness for use" can be applied to most human organizations, irrespective of their function.

4. What is the proper role of testing in the schools?

ANSWER: First, tests should be "frontloaded"—adopted or developed *after* objectives have been created and validated as correct. Then tests reflect the curriculum rather than establish it. In this sequence, it's proper to teach to the test. However, when tests establish the curriculum ("backloading"), it is hard to know if the test content is truly what should be learned or was merely what was "convenient" to test. Thus, the limitations of testing become the same limitations of the curriculum.

If the curriculum is conceived of as work, one first defines the work to be done and then searches for the means of work measurement. If it were the other way around, some work which is necessary to complete might never get done because it was eliminated by the means of extant, cheap, or convenient work measurement at the outset. This is another case of means becoming the ends and replacing them.

Finally, each school district should establish its policy regarding testing and assessment, so it is clear about the proper use of different kinds of tests and newer forms of alternative assessment.

ACTIVITIES FOR PERSONAL AND STAFF DEVELOPMENT

We offer some examples of activities as "starters," but encourage readers to develop their own that will fit their situation.

1. How do people in your situation define and react to quality control? What are the implications of those reactions for how the organization strives to improve itself?
2. How does your organization "measure up" on the design/delivery factors on a 1 (low) to 5 (high) scale? Why the ratings? What are the implications of the ratings for how the organization functions?

3. Given the outcomes in #2, what factors could be changed most quickly and what would be your strategy to do so?

4. Survey a group of teachers through selected informal interviews regarding the utilization of curriculum guides, textbooks, and other related material that are referenced in their day-to-day work. Assess the degree to which this material is used in the classroom.

5. Trace the rise and fall of the "project method of teaching" of the "activity curriculum" in the schools. Examine carefully the major assumptions of this approach and critique each. Indicate in what forms this idea may still be applied in schools today.

6. Find a practical reference on industrial management which sets forth the basic premises of organizing the work place. Trace the arguments, logic and shaping process to the organization of schools in American society since the mid 1850s. Are there actual "blue-prints" as such in which schools were copied from industrial models, or were general arguments and processes followed? In what ways do schools deviate from these models (if they do)? What are some current examples of schools or systems being "run" by private firms, and how is it working?

Chapter 4

ISSUES IN DESIGN AND DELIVERY

There are three basic curricula in schools. They are:
- the written (prescribed) curriculum
- the taught (real) curriculum
- the assessed (learned) curriculum.

These functional curricula comprise the essential elements of generic programmatic quality control in most schools and—with different titles—in other organizations. These curricula and their interrelationships are portrayed in Figure 4.1. They are applicable to the district, school, department or program, or classroom level.

The arrows depict the interactive/dynamic nature of the curricula. When all three are working together towards a definitive purpose, the relationship is called "tight." When the three elements are more or less functioning collectively, the relationship is "relaxed." When there is little conscious connection between them, the relationship is "unconnected" (Figure 4.2). Although they need not always be "tight," totally unrelated curricula are a recipe for school ineffectiveness and harm to students; such schools do not recognize that "education is a matter of life and death." There is no prescription for determining when what set of relationships is best for what situation; such determination requires collegial dialogue and decision making. It can be aided by concepts, processes, and practices of curriculum management as outlined in this chapter and in the rest of the book.

> Curriculum in schools will always be in a state of tension between those requirements that are aimed at ensuring some sort of common content for all and those requirements that demand differences in approach, methods, and materials to attain the common outcomes. (English, 1992, p. 17)

Given the "organized anarchy" and "loosely coupled" nature of schools as organizations, the school's (or district's) work plan must provide for *flexibility* —it can be changed by altering the sequencing and pacing of its delivery without fundamentally altering the basic content of the plan.

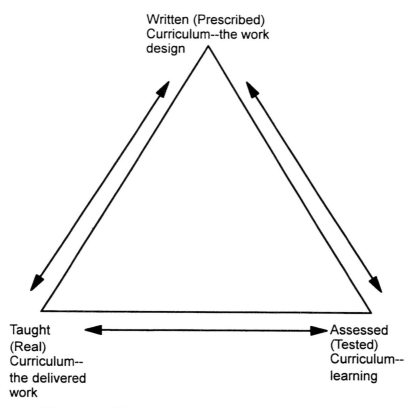

Figure 4.1. Critical Relationships for Curriculum Effectiveness.

Teachers are confronted daily with learner differences that preclude any rigid adherence to a plan that would prevent them from adapting their work to the demands of the situation. School operations cannot be absolutely *standardized* because people are not standardized. Research tells us that effective employees in organizations like schools—which serve a reluctant, often unmotivated clientele—need considerable discretion to act (Katz & Kahn, 1978, p. 159). A work plan must:

> provide for focus and connectivity (coordination and articulation) *without* leading to slavish conformity where every teacher has exactly the same lesson on the same day from the same page in the same textbook. Such a situation would be profoundly unproductive and ineffective. (English, 1992, p. 16)

Achieving this "focus and connectivity" challenges the art and science of curricular design and delivery. There is no single formula that provides "the" method for a work plan. Nor is there a single "fix" for its delivery. The important issue is that the ambiguity of curriculum design

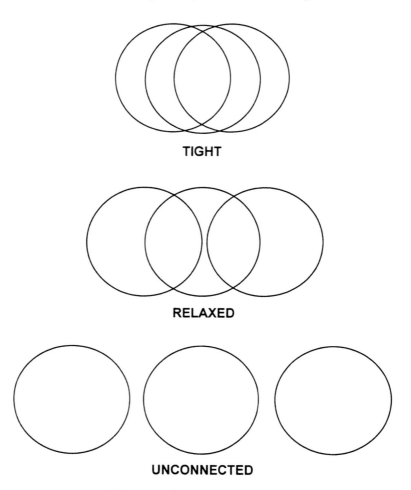

TIGHT

RELAXED

UNCONNECTED

Figure 4.2. Curricular Connections.

and delivery must be confronted deliberately—*with intentionality*—not intentionally ignored. Although individuals can wrestle with and resolve these issues, in most instances it is far more effective to do the problem solving collaboratively as has been stressed in previous chapters.

Some of the student and workshop participant observations that we have cited thus far illustrate clearly that in too many schools the relationships between the three curricula are "unconnected." Attaining knowledge about how to *connect* them will enhance the professionalism of administrators and teachers. Sykes, in his analysis of teaching, contends, "Schools must have means to coordinate and control instruction" (1990, p. 82). Knowledge about how to do this is an important component to fostering the competence and status of educators. As we have argued in

Chapter 1, the three curriculum management curricula are at the heart of teacher work and thus *ought* to have great *meaning* for teachers (and administrators). By assuming responsibility to confront more deliberately the issues imbedded in a tight, relaxed, or unconnected approach to curriculum work, professionalism is *enhanced* rather than diminished.

ENVIRONMENTAL FACTORS AFFECTING QUALITY CONTROL

Important external and internal variables, some different from those outlined in Chapter 3, influence the *interactiveness* of the written, taught, and assessed curricula. Prior to statewide accountability, the relationship in most schools might be characterized as "unconnected." However, when conditions in the environment change and negative consequences relating to "high stakes" testing result (e.g., loss of state aid, public ranking of schools, or state "takeover" of a district), the system attempts to become "tighter" in its management of curriculum. But it ought to manage its curricula more effectively because it has a societal obligation to do so. However, doing so is impeded by the following factors.

The Dominance of Testing/Inspection

Tests and testing exert an enormous pressure on teaching and curriculum development. Current statistics show that some 130 million standardized tests are administered annually in the public schools at an estimated cost of $500 million. That figure is for the *administration* of the tests (Toch & Levine, 1991, p. 64). Madaus and Tan estimate that sales of tests and related services could approach half a billion dollars annually (1993, p. 63). Accurate total figures are elusive. But whatever they are, the fact is that before graduating from high school a typical student will take from ten to twenty standardized achievement tests (Toch & Levine, p. 64). That figure can also be misleading because, as "FairTest" staff (The National Center for Fair and Open Testing) assert, "some batteries include as many as five separate exams" (Neill & Medina, 1989, p. 689).

The compulsion to submit to the pressure to "give" such tests leads to situations such as one described by a workshop participant. He said:

> Every year our district gives the Metropolitan Achievement Tests in grades 1–8. For two weeks in May, each morning is devoted to testing (spread out a bit more to accommodate first graders). We have done this for years. No one ever

sees the results unless they attend the board meeting when they are reported. The teachers hate it.

The reliance on standardized achievement tests in American education (Wiggins, 1993, pp. 1–33, 108–137) has led to a situation where not only districts test but "By 1990, every state had some kind of mandated testing program" (Madaus & Tan, 1993, p. 61). Granted that in recent years states such as Kentucky and Vermont have gone the route of performance assessment rather than achievement testing, but the dominant emphasis is still standardized testing. (The statement is not quite accurate in that in Vermont, as we shall see in Chapter 9, the program is not mandated, but fifty-nine out of sixty districts use it.)

This practice stresses memorization, student ability to recognize sanctioned answers, and a decontextualized and impersonal relationship to the test. Combined with current cries for schools to "teach for understanding," "problem solving," and general modes of inquiry, this practice has created an "Alice in Wonderland world" of incompatible events—"a world in which educators cease to try to make sense of their environment for themselves as professionals or for their students" (Darling-Hammond, 1993, p. 756).

In the past, issues and policies regarding testing were more straightforward. Historically, tests were used to screen, providing the basis for acceptance or rejection into schools and colleges. Later, tests were used to probe into the human personality, reveal tendencies towards vocational preferences, or delve into deeper psychological disorders.

Tests were often used by superintendents to reveal discrepancies in the curriculum, establish a case for greater organizational control of the teacher's work, and to promote many other kinds of reforms (Tyack, 1974, pp. 47–49). The practice of reporting test scores publicly to exert pressures on dissident elements within a school system was criticized as early as 1875 in Portland, Oregon (Tyack, pp. 47–49). Nonetheless, by the early 1900s tests had established themselves as a force to be reckoned with (Callahan, 1962, p. 100).

Tests used by the respective states now serve to define, regulate, and evaluate respective state curricula. Under our federal constitution, states have largely unchallenged power to regulate public education, and in today's environment of "devolution," where more and more power is being delegated to states, that power will increase, not diminish. The general public accepts state regulation and testing. Tests are also one of the cheaper ways to define a curriculum and to monitor it. Without tests, state departments would have to employ considerably more supervisors to perform periodic site visits. Finances alone prohibit adding such staff, but such additions would also run afoul of the "anti-bureaucracy" ethoes that runs in the society. These problems are finessed with statewide testing.

As the rigor of a test is increased to respond to the accountability ethos, more difficult items are included in the content. The more difficult the items, the greater the potential for students to fail. For schools to be responsive to such measures, considerable attention must be given to sequencing the curriculum in such a way as to assure that the cumulative skills and knowledge required to demonstrate a passing score on the test are acquired prior to the test taking. This, in turn, dictates the sequencing of the curriculum and the work of teachers in schools. It is unwise for schools to ignore the political and economic consequences of noncompliance when poor test results lead to general public criticism and often weakened support for schools (see Chapter 9 for further discussion about local policy for use of standardized achievement tests).

Placed in another context, if inspection standards for a product are raised so that more rejections occur and these results are both costly and unacceptable, either (1) work is redefined and gauged more closely to pass such new standards so as to lower the rejection rate, (2) the standards are ultimately changed (lowered), or (3) the enterprise goes out of business. Since it is highly unlikely that public schools will go out of business, the first two options remain the only viable choices, although there is increasing evidence that the very essence of public schooling is being challenged today with the rise of charter schools and the administration of a few districts by private businesses.

Other consequences of tightening the loop are that the purely local control of the curriculum, at least in those areas tested, is lost and that the sequence of teaching is permanently changed to reflect test priorities. One other impact also occurs, and that is the reorganization of time spent on teaching within the school day.

As test standards are raised for minimal passing marks for all students, there will be a great impact on those students who have difficulty learning the curriculum content at the threshold level of the test. True to the tenets of mastery learning (Block, 1971; Guskey, 1985), more time must be spent with these students. This means that less time is available for the remainder of the curriculum that is not tested for the same students.

A certain amount of curriculum content is irretrievably lost. Within a typical school day, where time is not expandable, something may be forced out of the curriculum as a result.

When testing standards are raised beyond a point where a large number of students can easily pass with a minimum of instructional emphasis, then the time within the school day must be reapportioned to meet the new and increased demands. In short, the approach moves from content coverage to content mastery. This may not be an unhealthy result if one views some of the curriculum "forced out" as unnecessary or trivial. The "less is more" philosophy is a cornerstone of high school reform as advocated by Theodore Sizer and his project, "The Coalition of Essential Schools" (Sizer, 1992, p. 207).

What is important to know is that tests which assess what goes on in schools are tools of work measurement. Measures of work not only reflect the work performed, they can also change both the content of the work and the way it is performed within an organization. Schools are not different in this respect. When one changes tests, and when tests are important indicators of what happens in schools, one changes schools.

Today, schools are being changed considerably by the infusion of what is referred to variously as "authentic assessment" or "performance assessment" practices. A little over a decade ago these terms were not even in the popular professional literature (e.g., *Phi Delta Kappan,* May 1981), and as late as 1985 they had not yet entered the popular journals (e.g., *Educational Leadership,* October 1985). Questions such as, "What do we want students to be able to do?"; "How will we know if they can do these things?"; "What can we develop as a means for evaluating their knowledge and abilities in an authentic way?" are becoming powerful tools for educational change (Darling-Hammond, 1993, p. 760). The new testing movement is an example of "osmotic change" —

> . . . change that "happens" or seems to "creep in" to the organization. It is often unclear where it originated or who was responsible for initiating it locally. (Larson, 1992, p. 14)

One outcome of all this testing ferment is that the "assessed" curricula is changing more quickly than the taught curricula and the written curricula is beginning to lag woefully behind both of them in updatedness. This externally driven assessment movement can, in turn, drive a wedge between attempts to attain curricula congruence. It may result in "tight" or "relaxed" curricula becoming more and more "unconnected."

The Impact of Pupil Mobility

Assuming for the moment that a school or school district had the quality of work controlled in the manner described, one of the offsetting factors to improve pupil achievement is not easily controlled—pupil mobility.

Pupil mobility refers to changes in the numbers and sometimes the complexion of the student population within a school year. These changes may occur because of factors such as prolonged illness, pregnancy, employment, enlistment in the armed forces, or physical movement caused by relocation. Mobility means, however, that as pupils drop out, "new" pupils drop in, replacing them as students. Thus, there is a kind of constant "churning" effect within the pupil population.

Many of the nation's urban centers are experiencing this kind of problem. If it is not caused by larger social conditions, then it occurs because of court ordered desegregation practices which also "churn" the pupil population (although recent trends indicate that such practices are less and less relied on by the courts as a means to insure equality of educational opportunity). There are also significant mobility problems in rural states such as Kentucky and Vermont where it is not uncommon to find, over a four-year high school span, close to a fifty percent turnover of students. This migration is usually attributable to families at the poverty line moving in search of cheaper housing or jobs.

If students coming into a system do not have the same skills or level of educational responsiveness as the ones graduating or otherwise "leaving," the system must then compensate by regrouping the students into another class configuration or sometimes, although frowned upon, holding students back.

Coping with swift and sometimes extreme variations in class sizes often presents considerable strain on organizational resources and ingenuity. Despite the valid criticisms of tracking, it remains as a viable option in the face of such managerial problems. As we saw in Chapter 2, the flood of immigrants to this country in the nineteenth century presented schools with immense challenges to educate large numbers of students in the face of limited resources. One solution was the box structured school which is another option when dealing with the challenge of mobility. It is far easier to integrate a new pupil into a self-contained classroom than into a fine-tuned integrated, team-taught curriculum, because such a structure is independent, not interdependent with the rest of the organization.

The structure of schools *internally* does not permit much deviation in accommodating individual differences. As external pressures heighten in the form of test score accountability, the structure will very likely accept less tolerance for deviation from the norm of established practice. Demands on available instructional time have made the pace of schoolwork more hectic and frenetic as schools cope with more and more diversity in their classrooms; with proliferating state mandates and federal legislation—such as the newly enacted "Goals 2000" legislation (U.S. Department of Education, "Goals 2000," May 1994); and with an onslaught of voluntary innovations to accept or reject. As Fullan so aptly puts it:

> The main problem in public education is not resistance to change, but the presence of too many innovations mandated or adopted uncritically and superficially on an *ad hoc* fragmented basis. (1993, p. 23)

For all these reasons, schools now really work for just part of the population. They have difficulty responding effectively to at-risk students, students with handicaps, students with learning and behavioral problems, and other special-needs students because they are structured to educate the group of students who are motivated and ready to learn.

Pupil mobility challenges the production-oriented model to find alternative ways to serve the learner who deviates from the mainstream. Until recently such ways were in the form of Chapter I (now Title I) programs, remedial programs, alternative schools, special education "pull-out" programs, in-house suspension programs and the like. These programs add staff to the regular staff available to process the students. However, today there is a strong trend—partly generated by true concern for the best methods to promote learning and partly for cost-containment reasons—to integrate learners of all kinds into regular classrooms. "Inclusive education" is the common label applied to this broad strategy.

In Vermont, for example, Act 230 of the General Assembly (1990) is a state policy infusing extra resources into schools so that they can educate most children with handicaps in regular classrooms. As a result of the legislation, most of the regular special education system has been dismantled.

Pupil mobility is potentially very disruptive to schools. It presents a serious challenge to continually deal with diversity. While schools have become more diversified, there are definite limits or ranges of tolerance in which they are effective. Even the creation of more heterogeneous classrooms, as a way to reduce the continual segmenting of a pupil population, has run into difficulty in some communities where public pressure demands the retention of more traditional homogeneous grouping practices in reaction to the Outcomes-Based Education approach (Harp, 1993, p. 20). Beyond a certain point of adaptation, schools are unable to respond effectively with their current level of resources. In some cases the problem simply goes away as students drop out, thus freeing the school of any more responsibility to change its internal structure.

Simply changing the nature of the work (curriculum revision or development) will not change what schools do with or to students unless the allocation and application of time is also changed. Curriculum will simply be absorbed into the structure in which time is organized. Changing the schedule will not work either, unless curriculum is also altered and redefined. Finally, if both are changed, one is still left with a support system designed to reinforce the old concepts.

That support system includes the teacher's role within the school, textbooks, grades, tests and their function, administrative authority, and the whole public conception of what constitutes a "good school."

And this system currently views students as more passive rather than active participants in the learning process, although the rise of the alternative assessment movement is a strong indicator that this perspective is changing. This was one overwhelming conclusion from a massive national study of thirty-eight schools and 1000 classrooms at the elementary, middle, and senior high levels conducted by Goodlad (1984, pp. 93–129). These kinds of observations have fueled the present debate about changing this "banking" approach to education where the teacher is the "depositor" of knowledge and the learner is the "depository" (Freire, 1971, p. 58). Countering the banking approach, Sizer and his colleagues in the "The Coalition of Essential Schools" are experimenting with new designs for secondary education where the student assumes much more of a "worker" role (1992).

The more schools focus upon learning, the more necessary it becomes for people in them to examine their own practices. Then educators and community have at least chosen the right starting point for effecting important changes in curriculum and instruction.

The Problem of Complexity

The process of learning is quite complex. There is much that is still relatively unknown about it. The organization of schools appears to have made learning more simple than it really is.

That is the predominant image that the public has resulting from the average of 13,000 hours of observing classroom teaching as cited earlier in research by Lortie (1975). Sykes, in his work on the profession of teaching, arrived at the same conclusion. "Good teaching, then [to the general public], seems to be less a matter of technique, skill, and knowledge than of personality" (1990, p. 80).

In fact, instruction is a complex, not a "simple" activity. Quality control is much more difficult to achieve in an organization where processes are complex. That learners learn in schools is often more a testimony to human ingenuity and flexibility than to the excellence of school design.

For organizations to exist they have to be predictable. Operations have to be routinized. Irregularities have to be flattened out. Without these ingredients there can be no stability and no system. The founders of American schools in the early and mid-nineteenth century were more concerned about rectifying chaotic conditions than with developing an optimum environment for learning. For education to become manageable it had to become stable. *Order* was the primary objective (Tyack, 1974, pp. 39–59).

The more staff there are and the more they use different methodologies to deliver the service, the greater the possibility for breakdowns and errors to occur. While work design must be constructed in a way that optimizes operations by equalizing time constraints, at each step in the process (as with grades in schools), shrinking the processes to very small work operations may result in excessive boredom and inefficiency via routinization. Although a powerful idea in industry, simplification of work takes one only so far in schools before it becomes counterproductive and dysfunctional.

There is an intimate and functional relationship among the processes of schooling as they take shape in scheduling, teaching, curricular, pupil grouping, and supervisory practices. All of these subsets of behaviors are associated with and actually reinforce one another in the school setting. The complexity of schools lies not so much in concentrating upon any one set of operations within them but in seeing them interdependently.

It is the interaction among and between these various operational practices— within the context of features of an organized anarchy and loose coupling—that makes schools complex and often ambiguous as organizations.

Staff Turnover

Staff stability is another crucial ingredient in attaining quality control. Many informal adjustments can be made among staff in schools, adjustments that can lead to modifications in the instructional process. Few, if any, are committed to paper, so there is no *institutional* memory of them. Rather, they are carried about in the heads of the teachers and applied on a day-to-day basis over time. If a staff is stable, has worked together for a reasonable amount of time, and has established a high degree of collegiality, the process of more collaborative instruction can be effective and efficient.

However, in schools with high staff turnover, this process is upset and leads to a reinforcement of the more traditional "individualistic" model of teaching. When a teacher leaves a school, a chunk of the curriculum may go with her or him. To the extent that this set of adjusted behaviors was important in enabling the school to adapt its operations to pupil achievement patterns, the school has lost a good deal of operational effectiveness. "One of the most powerful factors known to take its toll on continuation [of innovations] is staff and administrative turnover" (Fullan, 1991, p. 90).

To offset this problem, schools resort to putting such individual teacher adjustments in writing. The development of curriculum and the implementation of curriculum management practices in such settings assumes an even more serious purpose than mere compliance with rules or regulations.

Staff Expertise

As noted in Chapter 3, the level of staff training, their understanding of instructional processes, their knowledge of content, and their ability to translate this knowledge into effective practices have a critical impact on quality control. In order to make adjustments within schools and among teachers, there has to be a common language and a connectedness among educators that allows them to talk about what is happening in respective classrooms. Based on our work with teachers in courses and in workshops over many years, we have found that they see curriculum management concepts and practices as providing that kind of common language and perspective. They see the concepts and practices as *powerful* (their word) tools for improving curriculum design and delivery.

Without such connections, and even with the presence of work measurement and data, the actual work is not changed; but the presence of a curriculum as a statement of work can be the framework for adjustment. However, the staff has to know how to apply data to alter instruction within that framework. Previously we mentioned that teacher preparation programs (and those for administrators) do not usually help their students learn how to make such adjustments. Although practices are changing, by and large teachers are trained to function apart and in isolation from one another and not as a cohesive work force.

Curricular Utility

If the curriculum provides the mutual framework for work adjustment, its utility is the extent to which it is related to what teachers do in their respective work stations (classrooms), and the extent to which the curriculum provides commonality among those stations through tangible linkages which can be monitored. The curriculum represents the bond which ties together the schooling process over many time periods and many teachers.

Most curriculum guides do not serve this purpose. They lack precision and time references, and they are rarely linked to measurement of work so that data can be used to adjust work. They are open-ended work statements. As such they are usually functionally useless to improve operations within schools since they fail to link the elements of the teaching process into a cohesive whole; rather, they are an idiosyncratic response to outlining the formal curriculum.

Quality and Scope of Monitoring

The traditional supervisory processes in schools (outlined in additional detail in Chapters 3 and 8) do not serve to improve their internal cohesion and management of curriculum. Principals or supervisors typically observe one teacher at a time. Both formal evaluation and ongoing supervision are virtually nonexistent in some schools as exemplified by these "typical" teacher comments.

> In eighteen years of teaching in three schools, no supervisor has ever visited my class, and thus I have never had another adult give me feedback about my work, pro or con.

> None of my administrators has ever asked what it is that I do, nor has anyone asked to see my curriculum notebook—and I've been in this school for ten years.

Also, evaluation may or may not include criteria that examine the relationships of classroom work to curriculum materials. It is unusual to find a teacher evaluation instrument that highlights teacher responsibility to implement district curricula. Here is one such statement:

> The teacher plans instruction consistent with the district approved curriculum for assigned subject(s) and grade(s), demonstration of which include but are not limited to:
> (1) translating district and local school curricular goals into specific instructional sequences. (South Burlington School District, 1994)

Thus, in most situations, evaluation of work at a work station does not examine whether or not the student's work had any connection to work already done or to be done elsewhere in the schooling process.

Teaching, as an act, can be evaluated independently of any specific curricular reference and often is. Lesson plans may or may not contain any reference to the curriculum. In these circumstances teaching may be monitored; but as a means to improve achievement over time, that *connectedness provided by a curriculum* may go unnoticed and unreferenced in the evaluative/monitoring process.

The Potential of Quality Control

Quality control (depicted in Chapter 3) can reinforce current conceptions of school and make them more effective and efficient, or it can also work to reinforce contrary ideas of what schooling may be about. Quality control is the concept that relates the definition of work to what a worker actually does. By noting the discrepancy between what the work should be and what it is, data can be used to reduce the margin of differences over time.

If the mission of schools is about learning and if schools incorporate practices which are not factory facsimiles, then quality control will indicate whether or not the actual work conforms to the various ideas about what work should be in schools. Work measurement would tell one whether or not an ideal was reality. By acting upon the differences, educators could come closer to their new ideal.

That quality control has been applied in the private sector should not discredit it for use in educational and other social service organizations. It is a dynamic concept equally useful in many organizational settings.

To use the concept of quality control in school settings to improve pupil achievement, one must apply it analytically to problems in that work place and then observe whether or not the application results in improved achievement.

To begin the discussion, we have added numbers to Figure 4.3 to contain specific references to its utilization in schools and school systems and have eliminated the interactive arrows in Figure 4.1.

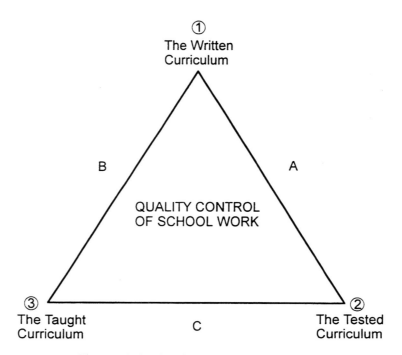

Figure 4.3. Quality Control in School Settings.

Design Problems in Quality Control

As outlined in the previous chapter, many factors go into sound curriculum design. In an operational setting, a generic design problem refers to a breakdown in the linkage between the written curriculum and the assessed curriculum, specifically any situation where the assessed curriculum is not assessing the written curriculum. The design of a curriculum and its subsequent delivery may be "tight," "relaxed," or "unconnected."

In Figure 4.3, the number one represents the written curriculum in whatever form it may be used in school settings (e.g., curriculum guides, textbooks, checklists) and number two the assessed curriculum in whatever form it may be used (e.g., achievement tests, teacher-made tests, performance assessments). The number three represents the curriculum that is actually taught. The letter A represents the linkage between the written and the assessed curricula, the letter B the linkage between the written and the taught curricula, and the letter C the linkage between the taught and the assessed curricula.

When school systems place into the hands of teachers a curriculum that is not linked to the test, it means that the work to be done by teachers is not measured by the instrument that is supposed to indicate if the results of the work have been attained (specific learning outcomes). We have an *incompatibility* between the work to be done and the work measurement instrument.

In this circumstance, the assessed curriculum provides false, misleading, or irrelevant information about the nature of the work performed because it was not measuring that work at all. It was referenced to some other work. This is one of the major problems with using standardized achievement tests to determine either teaching effectiveness or to serve as a barometer of the quality of the written curriculum as a work statement.

To be useful as an instrument of work measurement, the congruence between the work measured and the work to be done must be established so as to know what data should be used to alter the taught curriculum, or what data should be ignored. The process of discovering or determining that relationship is called *curriculum alignment* (to be examined in Chapter 7).

When curriculum alignment is not part of the curriculum development process, the creation of a curriculum may provoke lowered achievement by directing teachers to select content that is not part of the tested content. Children are then tested on what they have not been taught.

Ideally, the curriculum should be defined first, and the tested curriculum adopted or designed second. Testing then follows the curriculum and does not *become* the curriculum. However, in many states and school systems, this is rather hollow advice since tests are designed, adopted, and implemented irrespective of what the local curricula may be. When the tested curriculum is established and applied statewide as a determiner of schooling quality in any form, the tested curriculum quickly becomes the written curriculum. Congruence gets results. The relationship works no matter which end is used as the starting point.

Such a practice of using the tested curriculum content as the written curriculum is called *backloading* — one "loads" the written curriculum from the tested curriculum. The result is congruence and improved test results. If the statewide test is supposed to assess the actual curriculum to be taught, then *frontloading* has occurred — attaining a higher congruence by using test data is part of a legitimate curricular assessment process since the curriculum was defined first.

If the *frontloading* process has been incorporated into the curriculum development process, then "teaching to the test" is good practice and almost impossible to avoid (see Chapter 9). If the written curriculum is totally congruent with the tested curriculum, then when the teacher "teaches" that curriculum he or she is teaching "to the test" simultaneously. Schematically, if A is established first, and then B (congruence of the taught curriculum to the written curriculum), then C automatically happens (congruence of the taught curriculum to the tested curriculum).

Put another way, if the work assessment instrument is designed *after* the work is defined and is totally aligned, then when the work is performed as designed, the work will automatically be congruent with the work assessment instrument. Data produced from the work assessment will be relevant and useful to change the work itself to attain better results. The utility of work data is always defined by its congruence to the work to be done in whatever form that work may be stated. In the case of the classroom teacher, the utility of test data is circumscribed by its relationship to the curriculum to be taught.

Design problems usually occur at the central office level in many school systems, since it is there that textbooks are most often ordered and tests selected. If books and standardized tests are not somewhat correlated in content, then students will be tested on content they have not been taught. However, given that many schools are "loosely coupled" from and perhaps "site managed" relative to their central offices, it is not uncommon for schools to teach a curriculum or portion of it that lacks congruence with a standardized test. As a student put it the other day, "In my school we have perverse congruence."

The importance of textbooks cannot be underestimated. In most school districts, the textbook in most subjects is the curriculum. The textbook is "the curriculum surrogate."

Given this fact, when districts adopt textbooks they are writing their curricula. The textbook is a powerful statement of the work to be completed by the classroom teacher. The importance of ensuring that the textbook is *aligned* with the testing program becomes critical. Not all textbooks are equally well aligned with the various tests available for purchase by school systems.

Textbook alignment with the utilized tests should be the major criterion of textbook selection, if the test is one of great importance to the students and/or the district. Textbooks aligned with tests provide a much better match to work measurement and thereby improve the probability of student achievement. For this reason, the first step of curriculum alignment is most often textbook alignment. A district may not have a written curriculum in all areas, but usually it has textbooks for them. It makes sense to start here.

As an example of this process, the South Burlington, Vermont school district knows that there is an 85 percent correlation between the Ginn basal reading series that it uses and the Metropolitan Achievement Tests given in grades three and five annually. As the former assistant superintendent put it, "In selecting texts and tests the district should first decide what it wants to teach."

Other design problems exist when the curriculum does not rest on a firm and valid needs assessment, when the quality of its format is affected by a lack of critical information, when it is not functional, or when it does not fit the organization's authority pattern or division of labor. Some of these issues will be highlighted in a discussion of delivery problems.

Delivery Problems in Quality Control

Delivery problems are difficulties affiliated with the implementation of the curriculum. The most persistent is that of teacher misuse or non-use of the prepared curricular materials. If school district personnel have taken steps to align the curriculum, thus insuring that there are no design problems, and then that curricula is all but ignored, a breakdown has occurred between the taught curriculum and the written curriculum.

If the curriculum has been aligned, then its "match" to the test is known. If a curriculum with a high match has been designed or selected, not teaching this curriculum reduces the probability students will do well on the test and increases the probability they will be taught something else instead.

So a delivery problem involves both "B" and "C" breakdowns. The solution to the problem of misuse or non-use is classroom monitoring and mapping (Chapter 8 includes material on mapping).

Interaction Between Design/Delivery Problems

Some problems of curriculum delivery may originate with faulty design. For example, if time is not addressed in a curriculum guide and a teacher spends too much time in one area and has to eliminate something which is tested, this is both a design and a delivery problem. Likewise, if the curriculum guide is silent about sequence, teachers may not know what to teach prior to testing and omit important content that would have been aligned with that test. If such data are present in a guide but are ignored by a teacher, then the problem is purely delivery.

After problems are encountered in schools and classrooms with a specific curriculum, educators must ask the questions which lead to identification of the probable causes of the problem(s). Often a set of questions to teachers will reveal the nature of the problem. For example, "Why did you not spend more time with this concept?" may engender the response, "I didn't know how much time to spend on it." If there is no such referent in the guide, the initial problem is design, not delivery. Anytime teachers honestly profess ignorance about what was desired or required in their work definition, the problem is usually faulty design because of poor format or lack of specification.

If teachers say, "I don't use the curriculum guide," then the problem is delivery in nature. Because of the fact that teachers' work in most classrooms is invisible to outsiders and screened off from one another by walls, ongoing work supervision of teachers is a formidable challenge to principals and supervisors.

Trying to use feedback in schools without knowing if one is dealing with a design or delivery problem with curriculum can lead to lowered achievement if one is ignorant about the differences between the two. For example, if poor test scores are the result of the lack of congruence between the taught curriculum and the assessed curriculum, but if teachers were following a written curriculum not well matched to the tested curriculum, improved achievement will not result from enhanced monitoring or "closer supervision" of teachers. Instead, the curriculum must be redesigned via alignment then set back into place. Without alignment, more time on task will not lead to improved test results. With alignment, time-on-task enhancements represent a viable method for better achievement scores.

In too many circumstances, principals and supervisors see most achievement problems as delivery problems, assuming that design problems have been resolved in the developmental stages. When this is not the case and efforts via better monitoring do not lead to enhanced test results, they feel betrayed by the research, or worse, professionally incompetent or impotent.

When work measurement indicates a problem with the work itself, one must proceed in a diagnostic fashion to eliminate the possible reasons. The first potential source for poor work is the statement of the work itself, including its validity, clarity, and alignment with the measures of work performance. When these are resolved to the satisfaction of the investigator, then one looks at worker adherence to the standards, motivation, monitoring, supervisory practices, and the knowledge/skills of the worker.

SUMMARY

There are three basic types of curricula in schools: the written (prescribed), the taught (the real), and the assessed (the learned). They may relate in a tight, relaxed, or unconnected pattern. The degree of their interrelatedness represents quality control. Knowledge about how to achieve quality control through these curricula can enhance the professionalism of administrators and teachers. They are at the heart of effective curriculum management.

However, there are many factors in the external and internal environments of schools that inhibit or even prevent attaining this control. They may lead to breakdowns in curriculum design and delivery. Without an understanding of what these factors are and their impact, one might erroneously fault design for certain problems or delivery, while in reality the breakdown is attributable to other causes.

DIALOGUE FOR IMPLEMENTATION

These are the questions most commonly asked the authors about the content in this chapter:

1. What is the proper relationship between the curriculum and a test?

ANSWER: The relationship is defined by the situation. If the situation is open-ended, then one develops the curriculum first and tests that curriculum second. However, in cases where the test is defined first and cannot be changed or is really the curriculum, then the curriculum simply becomes the test.

2. Is it ever wrong to teach to the test?

ANSWER: If one wants to know whether some students already know something *before* they are taught, then teaching to the test would be misleading. In an instructional setting, it is rarely a problem. If the test data are not to be used as feedback to improve learning, and if the purpose of the test is to discriminate among those tested, then teaching to the test also provides a misleading response. It is always wrong to teach THE test.

3. You seem to be saying that the higher the testing standards for some students, the less of the curriculum they may learn. Is that right?

ANSWER: That's what happens when one can't expand the time to learn. The more time is spent on learning what the test is assessing, the less time there is for other things. It's a myth that some students will ever be able to receive a balanced curriculum in states with very difficult testing standards. Displacement of the curriculum occurs in order to master some items well; the time is spent on them as opposed to something else.

4. Is the tracking of pupils really a viable response for schools?

ANSWER: While we find tracking incompatible with our country's ideals for schools, we recognize that it is one of the few solutions open to schools, given their current organizational structure. For tracking not to be a popular alternative, the fundamental nature of schools will have to be changed so that it is no longer an appropriate response. Simply condemning it as undemocratic doesn't deal with why it has and will continue to be utilized in schools.

5. How difficult is it to change the traditional six, seven, or eight period schedule that still dominates secondary schools?

ANSWER: While no one has written a good history of the national attempts at flexible scheduling in the late sixties or early seventies, those of us who went through that period remember with some clarity the problems schools had in doing away with a rigid, even period schedule. The use of this type of schedule reinforces the custodial functions of the school to "contain" students. The most serious problem we had with flexible scheduling was student unscheduled time for independent study. Unbalancing the school schedule is tinkering with the glue which holds the current model of school in place. It exercises an iron grip over the curriculum and the use of time.

Another major problem was demonstrating that all the time, energy, and money that went into developing more flexible schedules had a real impact on learning. No research, to our knowledge, has been done on this subject either. And, given the multitude of variables that affect learning, it is doubtful that such connections between the schedule and learning could ever be made.

6. What is the preeminent function of school structure as we know it?

ANSWER: The preeminent function is stability. Essentially, the current school structure places a paramount value on efficiency, the use of as little money as possible to attain goals, at the expense of effectiveness, the promotion of learning. Learning is not always predictable. Teaching is much more predictable. Teaching requires order. So schools are first places of teaching and second places of learning.

7. On what grounds would educators object to using quality control in schools?

ANSWER: If one did not see any parallels between what schools do and what occurs in other organizations, then one could object on the grounds that schools are unlike any other kind of organization. Therefore, the use of quality control in manufacturing settings invalidates its use in schools because schools are not like, nor should they be like, factories. The use of quality control would make schools like factories.

We have argued that schools already use quality control and so do many other types of organizations. We've argued, too, that quality control is neutral and that it can be used to reinforce what schools already do, or it can reinforce a contrary or alternative concept. To invalidate quality control as an idea one would have to resort to a completely different paradigm and explain human behavior in very different terms than most people understand it now, particularly in organizational settings.

ACTIVITIES FOR PERSONAL AND STAFF DEVELOPMENT

1. Construct a model board policy that would incorporate the idea of quality control in curriculum. Include text and test adoption practices in it.
2. From a source such as the Education Commission of the States in Denver, or FairTest in Cambridge, Massachusetts, construct a summary of the types of tests now in use in the respective fifty states to assess the curriculum. What are the common areas assessed? What are the areas not assessed? What would account for the patterns?
3. Construct a list of all of the curriculum areas included in your own local curriculum. Perform a simple time log of these areas by asking teachers to indicate what areas they don't teach or spend very little time teaching? What areas receive the greatest impact? The least? What do teachers wish they could spend more time teaching?
4. Develop a list of the pros and cons of tracking. Relate as many as you can to manufacturing concepts such as "line balancing" or the "hidden plant." Are the arguments for or against tracking political, social, educational, mechanical, or structural? Which seem to prevail today?
5. Analyze the types of curricular problems in your school or school system. Which could be called design and which delivery? Are the two interactive? If so, how? How would you attack a problem which was both design and delivery in nature?

Chapter 5

CURRICULUM VALIDATION AND ABANDONMENT

What assures the curriculum developer or policymaker in the area of curriculum that the choices about curriculum content are the most appropriate selections?

The process of determining the selection of curriculum content as work for the teacher *to teach* is referred to as *validation.* It implies a logical set of procedures by which one constructing curriculum *knows* or is *assured* that the "content" included is the "right stuff," even before it is sanctioned or "adopted" by an elected body such as a legislature, assembly or board of education.

The reverse question being asked today is: How to know what curriculum to exclude? It has suddenly become apparent to curriculum personnel that new graduation requirements, new state standards, national standards and even international standards usually mean adding *more* to the curriculum. There is the awareness that there isn't enough time to teach all that might be included in a curriculum (see Hoffman, 1987). How does one "dump" the ancillary and retain and add only the "essential"? That process is called *curriculum abandonment.*

THREE POINTS OF VIEW ABOUT VALIDATION

There are many views about where to initiate a discussion regarding school curriculum. For example, if one asked parents what came to mind when they heard the word "curriculum," they might talk about "subjects" such as math, science, or history. They might also use words like "rigorous" or "interesting for my child" as other ways to discuss curriculum.

Teachers too may discuss curriculum as certain "content" to be taught such as geography or skills to be mastered, i.e., "the times tables." Students may also talk about subjects or content in such statements as "I love spelling, but I can't stand math." Such statements express their sentiments about certain "things" they have experienced in school.

Legislators, critics, newspaper writers, and others may be interested in curriculum as it is reflected in test scores, or rigor, or variety. Rarely, however, are comments directed to the *field of curriculum studies* that is outside of these concerns. There is a body of knowledge about curriculum as a professional subject outside of specific content areas, departments, skills, or questions regarding method of delivery or degree of difficulty in learning or acquiring that content or skills.

Some academics approach the subject of curriculum as an open question regarding the role of schools in reproducing a given social system and consider the curriculum the vehicle which performs that function. Curriculum in this discussion is both something to criticize and something to change, particularly if these writers have criticisms about the kind of society in which we live.

To help clarify the question as to why curriculum discussions are sometimes difficult to undertake and even more difficult to understand, it is necessary to stand back and examine the many perspectives of how one initiates a discussion regarding curriculum. There are at least three axes or perspectives regarding where to begin thinking about curriculum that have been used in the field.

The Societal Perspective: Focusing on Political Justice

Advocates of curriculum change who begin their arguments with specific criticisms regarding modern capitalistic societies, and the characteristics they deem antiquarian, racist, sexist or wealth biased, look at curriculum as the "cloning" mechanism to maintain such an unjust society. Schools are seen as social sorting mechanisms which reproduce rather than reduce inequalities (Katz, 1971; Parenti, 1974; Bowles & Gintis, 1976; Nasaw, 1979; Apple, 1986; McLaren, 1986; Spring, 1988; Giroux, 1994). Curriculum is seen as an elitist tool to sort students by race, sex and class into winners and losers.

Perhaps the most pervasive criticism of curriculum as a professional field of knowledge by those espousing the societal perspective is that unless a discussion of what schools do to reproduce a class, race and sex based society are understood and discussed, practices to "improve" curriculum simply reinforce the way schools work today. Since schools are obviously failing a good portion of the lower classes attending them (see Gonzalez, 1994), to enable them to be more efficient at this task is an absurdity. Such discussions are naive at best and at worst "vulgar" (from a neo-Marxist point of view). The societal perspective is heavily embued with Marxist and neo-Marxist perspectives, which does not invalidate them but simply identifies their intellectual heritage (see Bennett, 1994). Some of the most potent criticism of schools today originate from this intellectual wellspring.

The Learner/Psychological Perspective: Doing What is Developmentally Appropriate

Another view of where to start a discussion about curriculum has to do with one or more of the following perspectives:

1. a philosophical stand on human development or learning;
2. an empirical or quasi-empirical view of human development or learning;
3. a philosophical view of teaching (or the use of a method or approach) and learning or the learner.

The Philosophical Perspective on Learning

A philosophical starting point on human development or learning is represented by the work of Jean Piaget. As Atkinson (1983) has pointed out, Piaget's cognitive development theory is firmly embedded in philosophical theory, and to grasp his ideas regarding human cognition one must come to understand this philosophical focus. In other words, what Piaget assumed about human knowledge colored his experiments and shaped his findings. Piaget called himself a "genetic epistemologist." His theoretical base was rooted in the field of biology and scientific rationalism. Not all of Piaget's claims can be empirically tested, but as Atkinson notes, they can be subjected to scrutiny from the perspective of "coherency and philosophical adequacy" (p. 3).

Central to Piaget's work is the idea of equilibration of cognitive structures. This idea holds that the equilibrium of cognitive systems centers on the concept of order in an open system and includes homeostasis or homeorrhesis, i.e., biological equilibrium or dynamic equilibrium. Cognitive systems engage in interactions with an environment in order to grow and develop *as systems* (Piaget, 1975, p. 4).

Piaget envisioned equilibrium taking three forms: (1) between the subject and object, (2) between schemes and subschemes on the same hierarchical level, and (3) between differentiations and integration into new and superior (hierarchical) totalities (p. 30). At the heart of Piaget's work is the idea that, "no balanced structure can be said to remain in a final state even if it is found to conserve its special characteristics without modifications" (p. 31). So Piaget saw that cognitive or intellectual structure was comprised of wholeness, transformation and self-regulation (Piaget, 1970, p. 5). These capacities are what Piaget defines as *intelligence,* where "its originality resides essentially in the nature of the patterns that it constructs to this effect" (Piaget, 1971, p. 167).

Piaget was convinced that the development of intellectual ability was *social.* The social environment impacted intelligence "through the three media of language (signs), the content of interaction (intellectual values) and rules imposed on thought (collective logical or pre-logical norms)" (Piaget, 1971, p. 156).

What has been difficult with Piagetian notions of intelligence and human growth and development is the translation of them for use in schools and curriculum. Here Piaget offers only the most general kind of advice. He differentiates between traditional schools that put forth predigested knowledge and facts that "must be learned," automatically casting the learner as passive and the teacher as active. Knowledge is visualized as "external" to the child.

Piaget rejects this idea based on his own thinking and limited research. He prefers a kind of place where the successive stages of cognitive equilibrium in dynamic interaction with the environment (which is social) leads the child to *construct* or *reconstruct* the nature of knowledge.

This is the concept of *constructivism.* Piaget rejects the idea that such a concept leads to a "teacher less" school and that all children must learn how to do is "play." The nature of teaching is to "present useful problems to the student" and to "provide counter-examples that compel reflection and reconsideration of over-hasty solutions" (Piaget, 1973, p. 16). A teaching methodology can be derived from this stance because it would mean "speaking to the child in his own language before imposing on him another ready-made and over-abstract one," and "inducing him to rediscover as much as he can rather than simply making him listen and repeat" (Piaget, 1973, p. 19). For Piaget, "knowledge of facts has no value except in relation to the processes of discovery that enable it to be absorbed" (p. 106).

This concept of curriculum is echoed in earlier statements by Dewey when he wrote in 1902 in *The Child and the Curriculum,* "subject-matter never can be got into the child from without. Learning is active. It involves reaching out of the mind. It involves organic assimilation starting from within" (p. 9). In a startling statement which was written long before Piaget did his work, Dewey said, "The only significant method is the method of the mind as it reaches out and assimilates" (p. 9).

The idea of a work plan as an appropriate *curriculum* for a learning place which embodies concepts of Piaget and Dewey is not antithetical to some forms of schooling. It is antithetical to the concept of a curriculum that consists of predigested facts, concepts, skills, knowledges that must be "acquired" by rooms of passive learners. It is also condemnatory of schooling and curriculum which is departmentalized and compartmentalized (Piaget, 1973, p. 31).

The Empirical and Quasi-Empirical Views of Learning

The three best known examples of an empirical view of learning are provided by the work of B. F. Skinner and the operant conditioning model of stimulus and response (see Staddon & Ettinger, 1989), the ideas of J. P. Guilford's structure of the intellect (SOI) model based on factor analytic techniques of Thurstone (Meeker, 1969), and Howard Gardner's (1993) view of multiple intelligences, or MI theory.

These three approaches, particularly Skinner's work, largely dominate the view of learning that guides traditional curriculum development practices in schools. Skinner's work, in which the stimulus is codified knowledge impressed with rewards and punishments on the learner(s), with expected/elicited responses of quizzes and tests leads to a curriculum in which the transmission of that knowledge is viewed as the supreme accomplishment. A curriculum designed from an operant conditioning modality is simply "progressive associations mechanically arranged" by either teaching machines or computers or real teachers. One would then expect to find at more advanced grade levels in schools more complex and sophisticated knowledge being presented. The logic of development is complexity. The idea is that younger learners must be exposed to curricula that is simple and unitary in order to understand basic concepts or acquire initial skills. These are built upon in a "spiral" or staircase manner. The principle of the "spiral curriculum" is the notion that with each grade level older concepts are expanded and used to learn more complex and similar ones.

Guilford's SOI (structure of the intellect model) does not contradict a

Skinnerian view of learning. It simply presents a three-dimensional structure of *operations* made up of five components: divergent production, convergent production, evaluation, memory and cognition; *contents* comprised of figural, symbolic, semantic and behavioral; and *products* which can be classified as units, classes, relations, systems, transformations and implications. The SOI yields 120 distinct types of intellectual abilities.

The curriculum suggestions to be drawn from the SOI fit nicely into conventional ideas regarding scope and sequencing of a curriculum. For example, Meeker (1969) discusses the appropriate curriculum content to reach the figural dimension of cognition in the SOI. The cognition of figural units she defines as "the ability to recognize a figural entity, to 'close' figural information or perceive a complete visual form" (p. 30). She then indicates that this ability can be "profitably explored by the teacher who makes seatwork for her children. Especially useful are ditto masters for hand-drawn work" (p. 31).

Constructivists of the Piagetian bent would denigrate seatwork and such approaches as wasteful of student time. A Piagetian perspective on the carefully sequenced curriculum of the Skinnerians and behaviorism would use Chomsky's work as evidence that the progressivism implicit in the grading of a curriculum by difficulty fails to explain how children learn languages, i.e., children are immersed completely in all of the complexities of language without the benefit of sequential presentations (see Piaget, 1973, p. 7). Shepard (1991) summarizes this insight as follows: "The sequential, facts-before-thinking model of learning is contradicted by a substantial body of evidence from cognitive psychology" (p. 9).

Gardner's (1995) work departs from the idea that intelligence is a one-dimensional general capacity (p. 203), a key assumption of Guilford and Associates, as well as the accompanying notion that this capacity can be adequately assessed in some honest form by a paper-and-pencil test. Gardner's work (1993) expands significantly the types of valued responses students bring to schools, but it does not radically alter schools or traditional concepts about school curricula. A contemporary of Gardner's is Robert Sternberg (1993) who offers a triarchic theory of human intelligence that departs from the idea of a single, general concept of it. The implications are vague for curriculum construction to be based on Sternberg's work.

Quasi-empirical views of learning include such approaches as thinking skills programs or programs involving metacognition as a basis for curriculum construction, learning styles, and studies of hemisphericity of the brain from commissurotomy (Springer & Deutsch, 1981, p. 25)—a practice of split brain surgery leading to viewpoints of teaching on the ideas of a left-brain, right-brain continua.

The so-called thinking skills programs are usually rooted in a desire to include more of the "higher level" thinking processes in curriculum and classroom activities (see Banks, 1991). The use of a hierarchy to discuss "higher" involves the application of Bloom's (1956) famous *Taxonomy of Educational Objectives: Handbook 1: Cognitive Domain.*

The rationale for teaching thinking and informing students about how to think about thinking (metacognition) in schools has been succinctly stated by Beyer (1987) as the improvement of thinking per se as a process, improved subject-matter learning, and enhanced student esteem based on their ability to understand how they think (p. 3) (see also Marzano, 1992).

Metacognition has also involved critical and creative thinking processes. Critical thinking involves the strategy of testing assertions. Creative thinking examines newly generated thoughts and ideas (Marzano et al., 1988, p. 17). Those trying to apply ideas of metacognition to school curricula find that they contradict conventional wisdom (largely Skinnerian practices) regarding curriculum construction. Marzano et al. (1988) note, "As to sequencing, we strongly caution against rigid conceptions and lockstep applications of skill hierarchies and spiraled curriculum . . . little evidence supports objectives that move in a lockstep fashion in Bloom's taxonomy" (p. 131). This is an interesting commentary. While Bloom's taxonomy has been useful in generating ideas regarding "higher level thinking skills," an implicit notion of it that such skills should be stair-stepped into curriculum construction is rejected, partly because even high-level skills depend upon lower-level ones. Thus, the categories in Bloom's taxonomy are not exclusive in thinking about curriculum construction.

The metacognitists insist that high levels of knowledge should be attainable by most students in all subject areas, and that the control of learning should shift from the teacher to the student within their schooling years (Marzano et al., 1988). Beyond these generic principles there is little else very specific about specific curricular content or development from this perspective of learning. Quasi-empirical views of learning which might serve as a base for the development of curriculum pertain to learning styles and to hemisphericity, i.e., left brain, right brain.

There are a variety of viewpoints about learning styles. Keefe (1979) has called them the "characteristic cognitive, affective, and physicological behaviors that serve as relatively stable indicators of how learners perceive, interact with, and respond to the learning environment" (p. 4). Dunn and Greggs (1988) define learning style as "a biologically and developmentally imposed set of characteristics that make the same teaching method wonderful for some and terrible for others" (p. 3). Gregoric (1979) has indicated that styles were hypothetical constructs that help explain the learning and teaching process. They are to be considered as recurring "qualities in behavior that persist" regardless of methods or curriculum content experienced.

The import is unclear for the development of a curriculum which takes into account "learning styles." Most often prescriptions hinge on adjustments in teaching methodologies. Where recommendations are developed, they border on the obvious. For example, if a learning style characteristic of a student was the lack of motivation, persistence or responsibility, one would not place such students into curricular situations in which the student works alone without any help (Dunn & Dunn, 1979, p. 119).

Traces of the idea of *learning style* have dotted the research field as early as 1892 (Keefe, 1987, p. 6), though it was Allport in 1937 that talked about "cognitive style" and Gregorc (1979) and Letteri (1980) that concentrated on school-related applications in more contemporary times. Messick (1976) defined cognitive style as "information processing habits representing the learner's typical mode of perceiving, thinking, problem solving, and remembering."

Despite the revelations regarding cognitive style, implications for curriculum design are far from obvious. Very little has been written about *selecting curriculum content* from a perspective of cognitive style. On the other hand, curriculum delivery is impacted. Style may determine *how to teach* something rather than *what to teach.*

Teaching Approaches as Ways to Determine Curriculum

Preferred teaching approaches are other ways that impact thinking about how to validate a curriculum. What Jones (1987) has called *strategic teaching* is based on a constructivist agenda of enabling students to form meanings based on their experiences. Strategic teaching begins by searching for cues in the backgrounds of the learners (see also Hill, 1992, p. 31).

But even in approaches where curriculum content is to be sampled rather than "covered" (see Durkin, 1993, p. xiii), there is little comment about determining curricular content propriety based on teaching strategies or tactics. Both are considered means (ways) to teach specified ends (curriculum content knowledge).

No matter what approach is selected, all three agree on one thing: there is enough commonality to agree that a curriculum, as a shared content or process, should apply to all learners. Without that assumption, a curriculum is impossible. If learners are so different that they have nothing in common, then curriculum is always confined to one learner and one teacher. A group or class of learners is only feasible if there is something important that is in *common* for all learners.

Curriculum also has to have stability or one cannot be discussed, adopted, refined, field-tested, validated or assessed. Permanency of a sort is a prerequisite condition for a curriculum to exist. Curriculum has tangible properties. It is capable of being defined, designed and delivered. It is not a one-of-a-kind, never-to-be-repeated occurrence. So it has "thingness" properties. While spontaneity can be built into curriculum, it is never the ruler of a curriculum, i.e., dependent upon it to be discussed and adopted.

Real Curriculum Debates and a Curriculum Core

In the realm of public policy debates, curriculum is usually debated around "subjects." For example, when former U.S. Secretary of Education William J. Bennett (1989) discussed curriculum, he proffered a model for a secondary school constructed around his choice of proper subjects. Bennett required literature, both American, British and World, a study of Western Civilization, American History and American democracy. He proposed three years of math around algebra, plane and solid geometry, algebra II and trigonometry, statistics and probability, pre-calculus and calculus. In science he proposed astronomy/geology, biology, chemistry, physics or principles of technology, and two years of a foreign language, two years of physical education and one semester of each of art and music history (p. 15).

Bennett's arguments for a curriculum center around design, not delivery. Similar arguments anchor Adler's (1982) *Paideia Proposal* or Hirsch's (1988) *Cultural Literacy*. Both authors argue for an idea of subjects or topics based on a rationale which is neither psychological nor pedagogical.

Rather, their positions are *political* arguments. Adler believes that the curriculum for the elite in ancient times fits a democracy where everyone occupies the elite. Hirsch bases his premise on a ranking of topics believed to identify mainstream "literacy." Both positions rest on the assumption that culture is static, not dynamic, so static that one could or should create a curriculum which rests upon it. Adler and Hirsch play a kind of cultural politics with curriculum content. Their knowledge occupies a place of "power" by the cultural elites that have chosen to perpetuate a knowledge base that could never be passed off as neutral. Such knowledge privileges those in power and the status quo.

One example of how seemingly innocuous and well-meaning statements conceal hidden assumptions is contained in the mission statement for a large city school district in the U.S. which reads as follows:

> **The mission for the [city schools] is to provide all students with opportunities to learn and reach their optimum potential.**

Who could be against such a well-meaning goal? What is at work here is nothing less than *biological determinism.* It is assumed in this statement that the potential of one human being is set in such a way to become stable and known by some means to another. It also assumes that for every human being there is a "ceiling potential" so that "optimum" can be calculated. What if a person's "optimum potential" is set at birth and becomes a kind of "lid" of development that prevents any further growth from occurring? If all of these assumptions were not true, it would not be possible for a school system developing a curriculum to do what this school system declares it will do: educate all children to their optimum potential. Even the staunchest of defenders of traditional intelligence measures concede that adult calculations of I.Q. are meaningless because one's I.Q. continues to grow after childhood. So even under the most conservative of circumstances, the I.Q. is not a stable target. So how could one really determine if a human being *had developed* to his or her optimal level?

The notion of an "optimum potential" is based on a theory of intelligence that has been both sexist and racist in its historical application in education. The implication of its practice has been to slot some children with "lower optimums" into social garbage heaps based on measurement practices that are insensitive to cultural (and also racial) differences. It condones school practices that excuse poor pupil performance because of alleged pupil/parental genetic deficiencies (see Gould, 1981).

A curriculum core privileges some subjects over others. These are based on value systems which are both explicit and implicit. To argue for a "core" one must assume that whatever ends must be met by the "core" are static over time. Such assumptions have been shown to be false (see Bode, 1930).

Adler eliminates all those curricula which were not part of the classical liberal arts curriculum such as home economics, journalism, drama, athletics, band, and the like. Anything that can be taught anywhere else other than a school he eliminates from school curricula. His premise is tautological, i.e., *true by definition.*

The other approach to defining a curriculum core is *external,* i.e., dependent upon data trends. It is empirical, i.e., testable. This approach begins with the idea of a *needs assessment,* gathering empirical information and sifting it until the major data streams reveal trends. These, in turn, are subject to analyses. From these logical extrapolations are produced statements such as those below.
201

1. The twenty-first century will be known as the Asian century. Therefore, the foreign language to be studied is Chinese rather than French.
2. Other religions and cultures should be studied besides Christianity and Western Civilization since few nations in the Pacific Rim are Christian except the Philippines. Many are Moslem. Students should know something about Islamic beliefs as well as Buddhism.

Adlerians protest that such "data trends" are likely to be fads and not lasting themes. They accept the argument that society is not stable and use it as the base to proffer their solution which is a curriculum "good for the ages."

Empiricists may eschew Adlerianism on its alleged universality. Their argument goes something like this. "You claim that your curriculum is good for the ages and all students. It's clear not all students find that curriculum useful. Furthermore, the classical studies are not practical. They prepare a student for no specific profession nor occupation. How, then, can one substantiate a claim that the Adlerian curriculum core is, in fact, good for all students no matter what their circumstances?"

Adlerians are bound to respond by saying, "Because we know. Our curriculum is time honored and validated. Your empirical data are too narrow and occupation specific. These are but temporary circumstances and no curriculum should be grounded in them."

Resolution of this debate is nearly impossible. An ideological argument not grounded in testable premises is not open to empirical evidence for refutation. So Adler's premises are simply accepted or rejected.

The internally defined *curriculum core* is most likely to be found in higher education proposals to develop a "general education curriculum" in the arts and humanities. The empirical approach to creating a curriculum core rests on constant examination of trend data and the concept of "best practice" anchored in change and discovery. This rationale is most likely to be found in professional schools and the debate centered on "the knowledge base" issue. A professional "knowledge base" is validated by empirical and testable practices. They can be refuted and changed.

Any definition of a curriculum "core" is an arbitrary political act fixing a response to the perennial question, "What knowledge is of most worth"? Knowledge benefits some and disadvantages others (English, 1992, pp. 30–32). It is never neutral. Defining a curriculum core is establishing primacy of some kinds of knowledge as "worth more" than other kinds.

The validation of curriculum involves setting up a series of referents by which curriculum content is selected to be placed into a school or a classroom. The most eclectic process can be envisioned in the form of a curriculum validation matrix shown below.

A Curriculum Validation Matrix

Proposed Curriculum Content	State Law	Possible Curriculum Referents		
		Board Policy	Content Groups	Futurists' Predictions
Foreign language proficiency	Requires one year	Requires two years	French	Chinese

In the example shown above, mastery of a foreign language is part of a recommended curriculum core. State law in this case states that a minimum of one year be spent in a foreign language. Local board policy requires two years. The National Foreign Language Association recommends that the language to be studied be French. Nearly all of the futurists looking to the Pacific Rim as the development economic center in the twenty-first century indicate that the choice of language should be either Chinese or Japanese (see Lehner, 1995, p. A10).

The eclectic process of curriculum consensus involved in *validation* is inherently political. There are no other data displayed except possibly socioeconomic predictions based on status quo projections from present to future. But the process does involve more than self-proclaimed "experts" who pass their opinions off as "objective" such as Hirsch (1988).

Curriculum Abandonment

Getting rid of curriculum reminds curriculum personnel how political curriculum development really is. The interest groups come out in force when something is proposed to be cut from the curriculum pie.

Actually, if one knew by what criteria to "develop" curriculum, the same criteria could be used to assess what was already in place. Curriculum that was already developed and that did not meet the criteria would be abandoned, i.e., discarded.

There are at least two ways to consider abandonment. The first is to engage in *frontloading*, the practice of creating curriculum based on specific criteria or objectives. The second is *backloading*, a process of discarding curriculum that isn't tested (English, 1992, pp. 63–77).

An example of *frontloading* is shown below. In this example, a local board of education adopted eight science goals which should be included as a baseline for all of its secondary courses (grades 7–12). To determine which courses were actually delivering (by design) these baseline objectives, each of the eight was checked against course syllabi objectives for thirteen board-approved science classes. This is a process of matching and involves judgments about whether two objectives stated in different forms are actually similar.

The data show that across the thirteen courses there are 397 course-level objectives. These are referred to as "non-duplicative" because they are counted only once. However, some course objectives may be matched more than once to one or more of the eight board-adopted science goals. These are called "duplicative." There were 545 such matches.

Percentages are computed two ways. First, across all thirteen courses the matching of each of the eight goals has been calculated. This shows that the board-adopted goal that science should demonstrate the "orderly character of matter, energy, non-living and living systems and dynamic nature" comprised 48 percent of all non-duplicative objectives. Board science goal #1 and #8 accounted for a mere 1 percent.

The second "match" is course by course. In descending order, these courses matched the board's adopted science goals in course syllabi objectives.

Table 2
A FRONTLOADING EXAMPLE OF CURRICULUM ABANDONMENT

SCIENCE GOALS	COURSES IN THE 7-12 SCIENCE CURRICULUM													
	Live Science 7	Earth Science 8	Principles Sci. I	Principles Sci. II	Physical Science	General Biology	Microbiology	Botany	Anatomy/Physiology	Animal Development	Chemistry	Adv. Chemistry	Physics	% ALL COURSES
1. Exhibits curiosity, critical thinking about the world.						2					1	3	4	1
2. Scientific inquiry and method of problem solving.	2	3	2	1	1	1	6	1	3	3	3	4	7	7
3. Uses appropriate instruments, terminology, lab skills, modes of data presentation.	8	11	3	10	8	11	12	5	4		11	9	35	23
4. Orderly character of matter, energy, nonliving and living systems and dynamic nature.	15	14	64	33	15	25	20	13	4	10	14	18	14	48
5. Appreciates beauty, fragility, of natural systems.	2	3	1	12	3	14	1	3	5		2			8
6. Science and terminology upon social organization, problems.	1	3	2	8	5	10	1	1		1				6
7. Develops physical well being, mental health of individual.	5			16		8			3					6
8. Knowledge and skills for vocational pursuits.	1	1									1			1
TOTAL NON-DUPLICATIVE OBJECTIVES	27	34	71	38	20	34	26	17	8	12	24	27	59	397
TOTAL OBJECTIVES	34	35	72	80	32	69	42	23	19	13	32	34	60	545
PERCENTAGE OF TOTAL (ND)	7	9	18	10	5	9	6	4	2	3	6	6	15	

Science Course	% of Total
1. Principles of Science 1	18
2. Physics	15
3. Principles of Science 2	10
4. General Biology	9
5. Earth Science	9
6. Life Science	7
7. Microbiology	6
8. Chemistry	6
9. Advanced Chemistry	6
10. Physical Science	5
11. Botany	4
12. Animal Development	3
13. Anatomy/Physiology	2

In this design analysis, assuming that the board determined that its goals were sound, it could move that any course that didn't account for at least 5 percent of its goals in course objectives should be "abandoned." This would see the dropping of the course on Anatomy/Physiology, Animal Development and Botany.

A *backloading* approach to abandonment would see all of the tests displayed with the number of items shown that were tested. Imagine the same data sheet shown earlier accompanied by a legend which showed SAT = Scholastic Aptitude Test, AP = Advanced Placement Test, LCRT = local criterion-referenced test, and SCE = state competency exam entered into the squares. That data would indicate which board-adopted science goals were tested on specific types of assessment *by course*. Such a matrix would be a way to validate the efficacy of the board's goals, as well as re-rank the thirteen courses on how much they separately contributed to preparing students to take different kinds of tests and exams.

Summary

There are several positions which are taken in the development of curriculum. The first indicates that the curriculum should be "developmentally appropriate." This approach is based on some idea of the growth of children. It can be in the form of the genetic determinism of a Piaget, or the idea of cognitive styles, or in the expansion of ideas regarding brain hemisphericity. None of these positions has much to say about the content of curriculum per se. But nearly all have suggestions regarding the delivery of curriculum, i.e., ways to improve instruction.

Other ideas in currency regarding the selection of curriculum content relate to social justice and the elimination of the excesses of a capitalistic society. Other proponents of curriculum content argue from preconceived models of political philosophy regarding the good society or statements concerning desirable cultural attributes and knowledge. Since the selection of curriculum content is a cultural/political act, empirical studies shed little light on the topic. What becomes the curriculum is determined by who is in control of it. In the U.S. the curriculum is the legal creature of state government administered by quasi-state elected boards of education.

Curriculum abandonment is the process of shedding curriculum as newer subjects are added. This too is a supremely political act. One process to be used is that of *frontloading*, determining which areas of the curriculum are most heavily weighted towards delivering a desired set of goals or standards by a process of matching. The opposite tack is *backloading*, a matching process of weighting curriculum content by those areas most frequently tested. If curriculum expansion is determined by a rational process of weighing criteria against internal assets, the same procedures can be employed to abandon unmatched or non-relevant (as determined by matching against criteria) parts (courses, units, chapters, topics, themes).

DIALOGUE FOR IMPLEMENTATION

These are the questions most often asked the authors about the content in this chapter.

1. If the selection of curriculum content is a *political act*, what is the difference between cranks and extremists who demand some changes, and the acts of teachers in developing it according to state guidelines?

ANSWER: Both acts are expressions of political will. Teachers are the recipients of preparation in education and are experienced in classroom protocols and processes. But their action of selection is political. Their decisions are more likely to take into account significant variables related to the learning process. A "crank" is a name we give to a person espousing an unpopular or "extreme" view as assessed against those of the majority.

2. Doesn't viewing the curriculum development process as a political act *degrade* the professionalization of curriculum development?

ANSWER: We use politics in the best sense of the word here, as a process to determine influence in selecting and determining curriculum procedures and content. We don't use it in the sense of pandering to short-term, expedient or venal needs.

3. Is it possible to really consider a politically radical curriculum that is at odds with the existing power structure?

ANSWER: Yes, as long as there is not a severe break all at once with past traditions. School curricula have altered public perceptions about disease, the environment, and racial and sexual attitudes. Schools have enormous leverage to produce social changes, but unless the survival of the society is at stake, they must proceed cautiously and incrementally over significant time periods to prevail and avoid damaging backlashes which would bring change to a halt.

4. What are the major problems with a curriculum core concept?

ANSWER: There is no "objective" way to define a core. The idea of a core is *exclusivity*. The major conceptual problem with a core is the assumption of long-term socio-technical stability. In a dynamic, changing society and world, one decade's core is another's corpus.

5. Why do you say that knowledge isn't neutral?

ANSWER: Because students come from varying social layers and encounter the knowledge contained in a curriculum differently. Some gain and some lose because all layers of society are not equally prepared, nor value some forms of knowledge embodied in schools. Those in positions of power and privilege do the best in schools as a rule.

Secondly what passes for "knowledge" is itself the product of a system of values that is neither objective nor democratic. It all depends on who has it and what they do with it that makes a difference. The knowledge that is contained in a library is somebody's idea of what is important. Books are not random trees in a random forest. They are socio-political constructs of deliberate intent.

6. What's the greatest difficulty with the process of curriculum abandonment?

ANSWER: Developing a sufficiently convincing case for the elimination of content or courses based on logic, demand, importance or cost. While curriculum development is often not seen as a willful and arbitrary political, abandonment is almost always seen in this way.

ACTIVITIES FOR PERSONAL AND STAFF DEVELOPMENT

We offer some examples of activities as "starters," but encourage readers to develop their own to fit their situation.

1. Construct a model of school built around learning and not teaching. Describe the applicability of such concepts as curriculum content and balance, grades and grading, tests and diplomas. Is a school built around principles of learning possible to be systematized and become predictable?

2. Imagine a political party has come to power that has the capability of abolishing schools as we know them. You are asked to develop a strategy that reconceptualizes education in alternative forms. What formal and informal mechanisms would you choose to incorporate in your strategy? Deal with *both* the explicit functions of schooling and the social functions of sorting and certifying children for occupational positions.

3. Develop a position paper which explains why schools have not been able to eradicate poverty and illiteracy in America which does not allow any recognition of inherent or genetic capability, race or sex, demographic or geographic variables. If you believe the schools are successful now, explain why the largest block of those unsuccessful in schools are poor and minority children.

4. Develop a proposal for a curriculum core. Develop a rational procedure which uses historical arguments for including subjects or topics in your core. Do you have subjects which cannot be historically defended or advanced? Explain how you can support their inclusion if they can't be historically defended.

5. Which subjects or courses should be abandoned in your own school? How can you validate your choices? What would be the major barriers to eliminating them? Can the barriers be overcome?

6. Explain the sources for public disagreement over the values embedded in a school's curriculum. Which ones are amenable to change and which ones are less amenable? Develop a general approach to curriculum change which utilizes these public attitudes and values.

Chapter 6

CURRICULUM BALANCE

There is more to learn than time to learn it in schools. Even when educators identify a valid curriculum they must then ask, "Is the **right** content in the curriculum in the **proper proportion?**"

Any question about *how to mix* curriculum ingredients raises the issue of **balance.** Balance is directly related to the question, "What results or outcomes do we want from the curriculum?" Once designers answer this question, they need to diagnose the nature of the learners; determine the best content order; choose the types and proportion of learning tasks; determine instructional methods; consider issues relating to repetition and reinforcement; decide how to maximize time and resources to attain the results; and develop means of assessment (Berliner, 1984). These tasks are often complex and usually quite time consuming, though they appear simple and straightforward in Figure 6.1. Nor do they necessarily fall in the order listed; they can be recursive.

In this chapter we are concerned with the elements from the figure that relate to *content.*

In one set of circumstances, curriculum designers periodically alter the mix of content as feedback from assessments indicates the need for changes. Such modification reflects the "social utilitarian" perspective about what constitutes the "right" curriculum; society, its needs, and its impact on learners is the main referent for curriculum construction.

In this situation, the curriculum is the *means* to stated *ends.* The ends may be clear enough so that the designer can build a logical and empirically validated relationship between the factors depicted in Figure 6.1 and schooling outcomes.

In contrast, the **mix** would be altered infrequently if one approached curriculum from a conservative perspective which is grounded in certain enduring beliefs and values. Around this stable pillar, one develops a curriculum which changes little from year to year. The notion of balance, then, is not seen as critical to all these curriculum developers.

In many respects, then, the question of balance depends not on weigh-

133

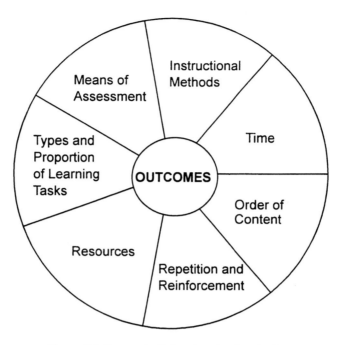

Figure 6.1. Factors in Balancing the Curriculum.

ing or measuring the components included in a curriculum, but on the biases one brings to the curriculum equation in the first place. Educators in public schools face an onslaught of "biases" driven by cultural, economic, political, social, and technological forces; the changing nature of children, youth, and families; pressures from political, religious, and business groups; and increasing expectations from their own professional associations to modify curriculum and instruction. Achieving the right balance challenges and confounds educators (and no less school boards).

An Illustration from History

Long before Tyler (see Chapter 5) advocated for the needs of learners, the needs of society, and the nature of subject matter as the basis for creating a balanced curriculum, educators were using them for that purpose. Here are some examples from the state of Pennsylvania's 1881 *Report of the Superintendent of Public Instruction*.

Before the term "curriculum" was popular in educational literature, educators spoke of "courses of study." J. P. Wickersham (1881), a superintendent of schools, said:

The courses of study in our schools might be greatly improved. The want is most pressing for more attention to moral instruction and culture; we must contrive in some way to establish industrial schools or courses of industrial training . . . . (p. xiii)

In the same document, Superintendent Joseph Gotwals (1881) of Norristown wrote:

In order to create a greater interest in reading, more attention has been given to recitations, declamations, and select readings; by these means pupils are encouraged to read selections other than those found in their regular textbooks. In order to make good readers, a variety of reading matter is necessary. (p. 227)

Superintendent William Kelly (1881) of Jefferson County:

There is a tendency to overcrowd our schools with studies, classes, and recitations, which tends to render them superficial. An attempt to do too much is likely to result in accomplishing too little. Better attempt less and do more; better concentrate our efforts upon fewer branches and master our work more thoroughly. (p. 89)

Here we see a parallel to the "less is more" concept that is one of the nine guiding principles of Sizer's "Coalition of Essential Schools" (Sizer, 1984, pp. 109–119).

Superintendent M.L. McQuown (1881) of Clearfield County:

I have long been convinced of glaring defects existing in the course of instruction. . . . It has been my constant aim, in managing the schools, to see that the instruction given be reduced to something less superficial, and directed more to the development of the powers of the mind. . . . In our higher grade of schools the average pupil manifests but little thinking power. As a general rule, students are not taught to philosophize and draw conclusions that indicate original thought. Not one in a hundred is made an independent discoverer of knowledge. (p. 43)

In this instance, we see a parallel to Bruner's ideas about the *process* of learning (1961) and Gardner's ideas about multiple intelligences (1983, 1991, 1993).

Superintendent John Stephens (1881) of Blair County:

We here urge upon teachers, as we have frequently done in visiting schools, the importance of giving more attention to language lessons and oral instruction. (p. 16)

S.H. Prather (1881), Superintendent of Venango County:

During the past year, writing has received increased attention. In providing copy-books for all the children in the township, the directors of Sugar Creek district have done an act worthy of imitation. The children write a great deal on the slate and soft paper, but need copy-books, that they may learn to write, also with the pen. Writing should be a regular daily exercise. (p. 170)

A.P. Supplee (1881), Superintendent of Hazleton:

> For two years past, quite a number of the high school pupils, together with some of the former graduates, pursued the study of Latin, under the direction of the Superintendent. It is to be regretted that both Latin and English literature are not among the required studies of the high school course. (p. 217)

This brief excursion through Pennsylvania schooling in the 1880s illustrates the recurring nature of issues and forces that affect the balance of curriculum. Schools cannot escape society's web, and educators have always found it difficult not to react according to the push and pull of immediate pressures.

THREE WAYS OF LOOKING AT BALANCE

Balance as an Unmet Social Need

A curriculum may be "out of balance" according to some educators if it does not meet a pressing social need (the social utilitarian school).

Superintendent Wickersham saw a need for improved moral instruction, culture, *and* industrial training—from which one can surmise that the industrial revolution was fast changing Pennsylvania, and that the schools felt the demands of business and industry placed on graduates. Today's educators, politicians, and businesspeople echo Wickersham's theme when they argue that all high school graduates do not need a college education but instead they should prepare for entry right into the world of work.

To further this end, several national reports have been published in the last few years. The most influential of these was *America's Choice: high skills or low wages!*, which emerged from a study conducted by the National Center on Education and the Economy (1990). It proposed the creation of a Certificate of Initial Mastery to be met by all high school graduates (in addition to the diploma); the creation of additional postsecondary school programs for students not pursuing a baccalaureate degree; further investment by business and industry in employee re-education; and the creation of new federal and state boards to organize and oversee the school-to-work transition and training programs.

On the heels of *America's Choice* came the U.S. Department of Labor's, *What Work Requires of Schools: A SCANS Report for America 2000* (1991). It examined how work is changing and what new competencies and levels of proficiency future workers will need in all lines of work. It contains detailed recommendations for curriculum revision in the schools. Such revisions could be effected through the recent "School-to-Work-Opportunities Act" (Council of Chief State School Officers, 1994) which provides grants to states to develop "a comprehensive statewide school-to-work opportunities system." Such a system stresses the integration of school and work-based learning; more integration between academic and vocational curricula; direct experiences in the work place that might link with future careers; and increased emphasis on career awareness, exploration, and counseling.

Consider another connection between current "balance" issues in education and the 1881 Pennsylvania report from Harrisburg County Superintendent, L.O. Foose. His admonition has a decidedly different caste than that of his contemporary, Wickersham.

> The vicious influence of sensational story papers and trashy novels upon the minds and morals of the young, is not unworthy the attention of school authorities. It is not within their province to say what school children shall or shall not read, but much can doubtless be done by calling attention to the matter in a public way, and by turning the moral and religious sentiment of the community against all this vile literature, that is now so cheaply and so widely circulated. Our schools suffer very much from it, the pupils become infatuated with it, and do not only neglect their studies, but often render themselves unfit for study. It absorbs the whole attention, destroys a taste for that which is pure and noble, blinds the judgment, ... (p. 215)

This statement could have come from several of the conservative groups that are currently critical of public schools.

As we approach the twenty-first century, American schools are being challenged to include in the curriculum more and more content relating to the needs of society. In response to drug and alcohol problems, more material on these subjects is either being added voluntarily or mandated by local or state boards. In response to the AIDS epidemic, more explicit sex education units are being added to the curriculum and, in some instances, condom machines are now installed in schools. In response to environmental issues, a fourth "R"—recycling—is either being added voluntarily to the curriculum or mandated by local or state boards. In response to a stressful environment at home and at school, some schools have created "stress management" courses. "Such accommodations make many high schools resemble shopping malls" (Powell, Farrar, & Cohen,

1985, p. 3). These external pressures on schools to meet social needs that schools do not volunteer to meet or that are not mandated for them to do so, exemplify "osmotic change."

Social needs are solved in part—at least according to the social utilitarians who advocate for them—by educating or training children about them. When they consider balancing curriculum, social utilitarians look at society's unmet problems as a starting point. Where this viewpoint prevails, schools find themselves pushed from their roles as conservatories of past knowledge and bastions of cultural preservation into combat centers that attack the problems of the day. De-emphasized are the internal needs of the learner and the selection of a proper body of information and timeless values.

Balance as Adherence to Principles of Learning

Others begin the development of curriculum from the point of view of the learner. They believe that a balanced curriculum incorporates what is known about learning and includes a generic *human curriculum* based on the unique interests and capabilities of each individual.

Based on research about learning over the past three decades, we now know much about the underlying processes of learning. That knowledge enables educators to address individual differences far more effectively than in the past (Marzano, 1992, p. 2). Before 1960, behaviorist-dominated learning theory led to instruction which focused on the acquisition of discrete knowledge and skills. In contrast, cognitive psychology, which today is far more influential, views learning

> as a highly interactive process of constructing personal meaning from the information available in a learning situation and then integrating that information with what we already know to create new knowledge. (Marzano, 1992, p. 5.)

"Constructivism," as discussed in the previous chapter, is the common term for this perspective which also places the learning context at the center of all learning (Glatthorn, 1994, p. 449). This extremely challenging approach to education often requires a complete reorientation to curriculum and instruction (see Brooks & Brooks, 1993).

A constructivist considers first the differences between and among learners as important aspects of balance and then attempts to use theories of learning as organizing principles to structure the curriculum.

Superintendent McQuown alludes to this point of view when he speaks of developing "powers of the mind." McQuown is not so much interested in knowledge per se but in the process of its acquisition. He sees the process—thinking and independent thought—as paramount.

McQuown's viewpoint was moved forward powerfully by John Dewey and came to a head in the Progressive Education Movement which peaked after World War II (Tanner & Tanner, 1975, p. 341). Subsequent writers like Bruner, who espouse critical and creative thinking in a curriculum, represent the continuation of this focal point for assessing balance. From this perspective, a curriculum is "balanced" when it is in harmony with what is known about learning. Superintendent Gotwals is interested in what improves reading to produce good readers. He is less concerned about content than about variety. Variety is preferred because it results in good readers—a more valued outcome than merely exposing children to certain content without aiming to produce "good readers."

Supporting the constructivist movement are Gardner's ideas about "multiple intelligences." Through his research and that of his colleagues at Harvard University, seven types of intelligences have been identified—linguistic, logical-mathematical, spatial, bodily-kinesthetic, musical, interpersonal, and intrapersonal (1983, pp. 73–276). Gardner contends that most people can develop each intelligence to an adequate level of competency and that some people possess higher levels of competence in certain "intelligences." For individual learning to be promoted by schools, therefore, curriculum must attend to "the laws of learning" and not to content per se. Gardner is careful to point out, however, that the intelligences "exist not as physically verifiable entities but only as potentially useful scientific constructs" (1983, p. 70).

Further support for constructivism comes from the work of Marzano and his colleagues at the Mid-Continent Regional Educational Laboratory who have identified five dimensions of learning: attitudes and perceptions, interactive processes, extending and refining knowledge, using knowledge meaningfully, and productive habits of the mind (Marzano, 1992; Marzano, Pickering, & McTighe, 1993). Each of these is integral to a constructivist approach to education.

Balance as Inclusion of Proper Content

Those who de-emphasize social needs and the psychology of learning as beginning points for curriculum development focus instead on a curriculum of "proper knowledge." This represents the conservative educational perspective.

From this perspective, educators may discuss what constitutes the "educated person" over time and then relate these characteristics to subjects or books as the "proper content." Or they may deem some content as more essential and valuable than others, and place it exclusively or in larger proportions in the curriculum than other elements considered of a less valuable or of a transient nature.

When Superintendent Supplee noted that Latin and English literature were not among the required studies for high school, one finds echoes of curriculum classicists such as Mortimer Adler (1982), Arthur Bestor (1956), Robert Hutchins (1953), and E. D. Hirsch, Jr. (1987).

The content-oriented curriculum advocates usually dismiss the social utilitarian point of view as transitory, and the psychological viewpoint as ignoring what students have in common. Instead, they argue that it is what is common among people—not what is different—that should constitute a curriculum. William Bennett, when he was Secretary of Education in the Reagan administration, proposed such curricula in his monographs describing James Madison elementary (1988) and high schools (1987).

Those who advocate for content may employ not only the past as a guide to the selection and proportionate inclusion of subjects in the curriculum. They may also use arguments of *efficiency*. This theme is found in Superintendent Kelly's comments regarding the overcrowded curriculum. The underlying premise is that of *economy*, i.e., scarce resources (time) forces one to decide what to do well or one may do nothing well.

Elements of the efficiency orientation are also found in Superintendent Prather's observations regarding the use of copy-books. For the teaching of writing, copy-books are more efficient than slate or soft paper. Learning is enhanced with their utilization. It is, therefore, "better" and to be preferred.

This emphasis on efficiency in making curricula and instructional decisions led to the previously discussed "cult of efficiency" in public education, an ethos which dominated the schools from around 1910 until the Great Depression in 1929. Callahan concluded that the movement was a "tragedy" because it adopted business practices and values indiscriminately and applied them to the schools with little or no consideration as to their educational values and purposes (1962, p. 244). Although the "cult" peaked in 1929, monetary considerations are very much part of educational decision making today—perhaps more than we think, given the tight economy that shows no signs of abating (Toch, 1991, pp. 17–22).

THE IMPORTANCE OF OUTCOMES
IN DETERMINING BALANCE

The pure content orientation to curriculum balance or the orientation to focus on the principles of learning tend to minimize or ignore the matter of means and ends in curricular design.

The content-orientation advocates argue that it is the acquisition of this content that is the end so the means are the ends. The learner-orientation advocates contend that learning is good in and of itself, that processes are far more important than knowledge acquisition. Furthermore, it is difficult to demonstrate that any specific knowledge has more intrinsic worth than any other.

There are elements of truth in both points of view. However, the moment schooling is embedded in a contextual, time-based framework and specific forces act upon schools, schools tend to become responsive to specific contextual requirements. Laws may compel them to do so. National emergencies cannot go unmet too long. In fact, schools embedded in a society cannot be anything more or less than society permits or demands them to be. As we have seen elsewhere in our discussion of education, the problem of balance is only a problem because society is not static but is in motion.

The argument about specifying curriculum outcomes has recycled over the decades. When Franklin Bobbitt set up a school for women based upon the necessary exit skills of the day, his model was of a "woman's place" of that time (1929, pp. 224–230). Boyd Bode eloquently attempted to dash Bobbitt's approach by pointing out the fluidity of society and the lack of adaptability in Bobbitt's method.

> The genius of democracy expresses itself precisely in this continuous remaking of the social fabric. With regard to curriculum construction it requires, first of all, a type of education that enables the individual, not only to adapt himself to the existing social order, but to take part in its remaking in the interests of a greater freedom. (1930, pp. 19–20)

The argument between Bobbitt and Bode represents a fundamental dilemma regarding curriculum balance. How can a curriculum be constructed to meet social problems if those problems are not static and if the requirements for successful living cannot be captured long enough to place them in a curriculum?

On the other hand, if curriculum content does not immediately relate to social requirements or does not easily transfer to social living, will it not also fall short of the mark? Obsolescence and irrelevancy are possible consequences of both viewpoints.

All three curricular viewpoints acknowledge the existence of outcomes. Where they differ relates to the nature of the outcomes. Precision regarding matters of *balance* demands precision regarding outcomes or results. An approach towards curricular specificity requires equally specific outcomes. On the other hand, if one abandons precision of outcomes because they are either not knowable or unreliable, one moves towards a more global definition of balance.

The quandry about outcomes is reflected presently in what is generically referred to as the "outcome-based education" (OBE) movement. This movement, with roots in the mastery learning work of Bloom (1964) and Block (1971), has been given a considerable nudge in recent years by the work of Spady, widely recognized as the architect of what is formally referred to as OBE.

Spady defines outcomes as "high-quality, culminating demonstrations of significant learning in context" (1994, p. 18). He has conceptualized outcomes into three categories. The first is traditional (discrete content skills which are at the lower end of the cognitive taxonomy). The second is transitional (structured task performances which focus on higher order learnings such as explaining, comparing, and contrasting). The third is transformational (higher-order competencies such as analyzing, determining interrelationships, using complex arrays of data and information, planning complex structures, and communicating with various audiences) (see also Spady, 1995).

As logical and commonsensical as the outcome-based approach is to most educators, a serious reaction in opposition to it has arisen, particularly on the part of some conservative and Christian groups. They object to the "watering down" or elimination of traditional academic content in favor of "new age" affective content that will undermine parental authority and traditional values. They object to no student ever failing and to OBE being a massive experiment in behavior modification and social engineering (Burron, 1994; O'Neil, 1994; Chion-Kenney, 1994). *Value* issues, as we pointed out in previous chapters, are at the root of their objections.

Along with the outcome-based movement, educators are also wrestling with the recent emergence of the **standards** movement. This movement (described in more detail in Chapter 9) was launched by the National Council of Teachers of Mathematics when it published, in 1989, its *Curriculum and Evaluation Standards for School Mathematics.* Then it received a significant political push when the development of "World Class Standards" in English, mathematics, science, history, and geography became a centerpiece of "America 2000" in 1991. Subsequently, these standards, to be developed by states and other groups, sometimes with federal support, were expanded in 1994 by the "Goals 2000" legislation to include other subjects.

Thus as this book is completed in 1995, we are witnessing a significant national debate about educational outcomes or results. The sheer amount of material being produced by states and national professional organizations and commissions is bewildering and potentially boggling for local schools and districts.

> Taken together, the standards documents to date weigh 14 pounds and stand six inches tall, excluding English/language arts and economics. All told, their pages number 2,312. (Diegmueller, 1995, p. 7)

Yet schools and districts must formulate plans to respond to the outcomes and standards movements. The Mid-Continent Regional Laboratory has produced a document for this purpose (Kendall & Marzano, 1995; Marzano & Kendall, 1995).

TIME AND SCHEDULING

In a prescient book, J. Lloyd Trump stated: "How time is used determines the character of institutions and people" (1977, p. 141). Indeed it does, and this is particularly the case where schooling time is limited and where there is more to learn than time to learn it.

Two recent studies focused on the issue of time. They concluded: "As educators are working to change schools to better serve students for the twenty-first century, time constraints are posing the most daunting problems" (National Education Association, 1993, p. 3); and "Learning in America is a prisoner of time" (National Education Commission on Time and Learning, 1994, p. 7). Each report bemoaned the fact that schools generally make their schedules around an allocated "time envelope of 180 six-hour days" (p. 21). And this envelope is in relation to the length of the school year in comparing the United States to other nations. The government report concluded that our students spend a minimum of 1460 hours in core academic subjects during four years of high school, whereas in Japan a secondary student spends about 3170 hours and in Germany 3528 hours (National Commission on Time and Learning, 1994, pp. 23–27).

If one then compares this "allocated" time to "instructional" time — the time a teacher actually has to deliver instruction in the classroom — one discovers that subtracting time for attendance-taking, for passing between classes, for assemblies, and for other non-classroom events, shrinks instructional time to half of the allocated time (American Association of School Administrators, 1982). Thus at the start of a 180-day high school year, a social studies teacher with fifty-minute daily periods theoretically has 9000 minutes or 150 hours to deliver course content. The actual "engaged" time with students, however, could total only seventy-five hours.

The moment of decision concerning time allocation arrives when a school has to translate curriculum into the logistics of the daily schedule. Scheduling requires some precision. If the content of the Great Books determines curriculum balance, how much time should be scheduled for *The Iliad* — a semester or a year? The answer lies partly in a determination of how well one wants students to know *The Iliad* (a consideration of outcomes) and the nature of the learners involved (a consideration of learning).

If one is concerned about developing students' power to think rather than acquiring specific knowledge (outcomes), then how long will it take for them to learn the process? Outcomes determine how one attains balance within a curriculum, and the outcomes are influenced by that balance. They are interactive in this regard.

A schedule assumes some stability within a school. If this were not the case, schooling would be impossible to program because it would consist of non-recurring events. Even a school as non-traditional as A. S. Neill's *Summerhill* had a "timetable" for delivering the curriculum (1960, p. 13). One purpose of the curriculum is to provide the basis for scheduling the work to be done. The logic of the curriculum can define the work flow of the organization.

Work flow requires not only stability but a certain amount of repetition. Continuity grows out of that planned repetition within the work place.

Curriculum can provide the continuity—the plan for recurring events and actions within an organization.

Unfortunately, the traditional schedules of schools—especially high school schedules—now appear to impede rather than facilitate the delivery of curriculum and instruction. For decades these schedules worked quite well as a mechanism for organizing the curriculum, staff, and students so that instruction could occur, instruction patterned somewhat on the "factory" model of schooling discussed in Chapter 2. However, scheduling, especially in secondary schools, has always been a complex activity because it organizes the "fit" between numerous competing variables—numbers of staff and students; the nature of the learners; the competence and motivation of the faculty; the nature of the curriculum (e.g., advanced placement offerings and science labs); sections of courses; the academic difficulty of those sections and student ability to learn; space; and, especially in rural and suburban settings, bus arrival and departure times.

Confronted in the 1990s by new knowledge about learners and learning; by pressures to instruct *all* students for higher order outcomes such as creative thinking, reasoning, problem solving, and decision making; and by subsequent attempts to redesign curriculum into more integrated patterns (see Clark & Agne, 1996), schools have had to find ways to alter their traditional schedules.

Most elementary schools have quite flexible schedules, provided that they are not departmentalized. Most middle schools have implemented block-type schedules (as recommended by the 1989 Carnegie Council on Adolescent Development's *Turning Points*, p. 52) that allow teams of teachers to work with large groups of students within a time frame that can be altered daily to further educational ends.

It is the high school that currently is struggling to "unlock the lockstep" of the typical seven or eight fifty-minute period day (Canady & Rettig, 1993). That pattern emerged in the late 1880s as the separate disciplines found their place in the high school program (Krug, 1964, pp. 5–6, 319–320). It was not seriously challenged until 1959 when J. Lloyd Trump advocated radical changes in the secondary schedule so that, "Both the size of the groups and the length of the classes will vary from day to day" (p. 1). Largely through the influence of Trump, many secondary schools in the 1960s developed "flexible" schedules. "Never before in the history of American education had an idea moved so swiftly from one man's blueprint to such widespread adoption" (Rippa, 1992, p. 283).

But the movement peaked by the early 1970s, and most high schools returned to the standard seven or eight periods per day that structure the delivery of curriculum at schools like Bennett's James Madison High School. But now that high schools face new challenges, they are once again looking at the schedule and how it can be altered to meet better the needs of learners. Just within the last couple of years, new scheduling designs have been proposed that range from the very "doable" yet very different block types that are fairly set from day to day (Canady & Rettig, 1993), to the decidedly radical Copernican Plan (Carroll, 1989, 1993, 1994) which uses variable patterns of time blocks to deliver most of a full year's curriculum in a half year.

How does a school view time and the role of its schedule relative to curriculum balance? Is the schedule seen as an end in itself or a means to an end? Is it in the hands of a single schedule maker who takes pride in fine-tuning it each year so that it runs like clockwork? Or is it in the hands of a schedule maker like the principal who said: "I can manage the curriculum by building the schedule. And the schedule gives the gestalt of the program" (Larson, 1992a, p. 51). Or is it in the hands of a faculty, assisted by the schedule maker, which modifies it each year to further learning goals and which may even entertain an alternative as radical as the Copernican Plan? But regardless of how innovative the schedule is, it will make little difference in what students learn if educators have not grappled with issues of curricular validity and balance.

THE CO-CURRICULUM

A major factor affecting curricula balance in elementary, middle, and high schools is the co-curriculum or extra curriculum. It consists of school-related activities not formally attached to school subjects. Typical activities, depending on the level of schooling, include clubs, student government, dances, plays, musicals, the newspaper and yearbook, intramurals, and varsity athletics. This curriculum has grown over the years in response to student and parent expectations, and the school's response to wider social problems (e.g., counseling programs for students from divorced or "blended" families or whose parents are incarcerated).

Depending on one's definition of curriculum (see Chapter 1), the co-curriculum may or may not be viewed as integrally related to the regular curriculum. To social utilitarians it is an integral extension of the regular program—a *co*-curriculum. But to content-oriented conservatives it is an *extra* curriculum.

The co-curriculum is in itself a unique concept. The authors of *The Shopping Mall High School* refer to it as one of the four main elements of public secondary school programs (Powell, Farrar, & Cohen, 1985, pp. 29–33). Ancient societies such as Greece would have found many of the activities of the co-curriculum an essential component of education. For the Greeks, a balanced educational program included the academic, physical, and aesthetic realms; all were essential to the development of the complete human being.

In European nations today, however, and in most other nations of the world, co-curricular activities are held after school and are not seen as part of the regular school program. They are an *extra* curriculum.

Although financial problems have caused many districts in the United States to cut back on components of the co-curriculum (e.g., dropping football or a club), this curriculum will remain an important part of school programming and thus has to be considered when balancing the overall program.

> The extra curriculum was not created by educators nor can it be abolished by them. The extra curriculum is thus a set of patterns which involve the school, its students, and the community in the larger society. (Steeves & English, 1978, p. 192)

This curriculum requires resources of time, staff, space, and materials and thus has an important impact on the regular program. It can, if properly designed and monitored, support and enhance the formal "content."

CONSIDERATIONS IN DETERMINING BALANCE

Curriculum as work design begins with determining the "right" work to be done or delivered, the **valid** curriculum. It is based on: (1) a set of specifications, i.e., learning outcomes, empirically derived, or logically established; (2) the identification of work tasks and actions that are necessary to accomplish or attain the specifications (e.g., methods of instruction); and (3) the establishment of interrelationships among and between the tasks, the necessary integration of tasks and actions, and the time required to accomplish them.

The work design is *balanced* when the tasks and processes are employed and students achieve the desired outcomes, or attain the necessary levels of performance (learning outcomes) implicit in the original specifications. Actions which detract students from the tasks and processes so that they fail to attain the desired/required outcomes, or realize the specifications, *unbalance* the work design, i.e., the curriculum.

Because schools are dealing with people, whatever is known and pertinent about learning and human growth must also be a factor in work design. While the goal is not to promote growth qua growth but to attain the desired outcomes previously identified, what we know about learning facilitates the design and delivery of the work.

What if the desired outcomes are not achieved or there is general dissatisfaction? What can be changed? If curriculum balance is defined prior to an actual trial in the work place and it does not work or work well, how can the design be altered? The lack of empirical evidence in the work place makes assessment of "balance" a difficult task.

To cope with these challenges in today's rapidly changing world with its constant demands on the curriculum, schools need to create means for periodically assessing or "auditing" balance. Formal written instruments could be used for this purpose as could easily arranged faculty dialogues such as "idea forums" and "research seminars" (Larson, 1992a, pp. 109–130). Given the opportunity and an effective way to interact with one another, most teachers and other concerned members of the school community have the expertise to do—and learn from—such periodic assessments.

SUMMARY

Curriculum balance addresses the basic question, "Are the right things in the curriculum in the *proper proportion?*" It is, perhaps, an even more challenging question than the validity question, "Are we doing the *right* work?" Balance is a neglected subject within the context of broad design and delivery issues.

Balance is the determination of the proper mix among and between the work content, methods, and processes in the work place. Attaining balance depends very much on whether curriculum designers see curriculum as meeting an unmet social need, adhering to the laws of learning, or focusing on proper content.

Depending on one's perspective about curriculum, content, methods, and processes will vary in importance and thus get greater or lesser emphasis in curriculum work.

Curriculum balance is affected considerably by the outcomes or results desired and how these relate to work content and the processes which comprise the work flow. There is quite a bit of controversy in some communities today over educational outcomes, particularly as they relate to what is known as the "outcomes-based education" (OBE) movement.

Available time and schedules also have an important effect on balance. For many years, most elementary schools have worked to make their schedules more flexible, and most of today's middle schools typically use some form of "block" schedule to give teachers more control over time. And just within the last couple of years, many high schools have also implemented some form of block schedule. Major forces driving these changes are new knowledge about learning and "intelligences" and rising expectations for what *all* students should know and be able to do.

Finally, the co-curriculum or the extra curriculum has an effect on balance as well. Whether one sees the activities which comprise this dimension of schooling as *co* or *extra* depends very much on one's philosophy.

DIALOGUE FOR IMPLEMENTATION

These are the questions most often asked the authors about the content in this chapter:

1. Why do you say that social-utilitarians have the greatest problem with curriculum balance?

ANSWER: Because social-utilitarians work from fewer absolutes in determining content. Thus they are much less certain about the "proper" mix of the curriculum. Furthermore, recognizing that social ends are in a fluid state, they are less dogmatic and more flexible in their adherence to preselected and a priori content or specifications than the a priori advocates.

The curriculum classicists already have the answers about content.

Those centered on learning principles may almost be "content free" in their selection, but will insist on adherence to those principles as they see them. Thus social-utilitarians often find it difficult to explain their stances on curricular validity and balance in contrast to the set of core beliefs that guide the more "content" and "principles of learning" advocates.

2. Are any of these starting points for curriculum design and a determination of balance exclusive of the others?

ANSWER: In theory, probably not. We can't imagine even the staunchest classicist desiring to ignore what is known about learning, or what the problems of society may be in shaping a curriculum. But their starting point dominates the others and places them in a subordinate position.

In practice, the classicists often ignore the psychological ordering of curriculum and are reluctant to delete preselected curriculum elements.

3. Why has *balance* been so hard to define and attain in schools?

ANSWER: To understand that one has to understand how schools have evolved and how content came to be defined.

The historical evolution of the curriculum and what are considered "the highest values" were influenced greatly by English society. The academic curriculum represents the Puritan ideal. It was designed to prepare *men* for the ministry. The addition of aesthetic, athletic, and more practical aspects of the curriculum came later.

Given the advent of the technological times we live in, the academic curriculum has come to mean principally science, math, and language knowledge and skills which depend upon reading, writing, and computation. It is hard for other subjects to gain a solid place in the program if they aren't seen as belonging to this "core." For this reason, many people view subjects like art, music, and industrial arts (today often referred to as "Tech-Ed") as less important in the hierarchy of subject matter.

Many of the recent so-called "reforms" of education have all but ignored the social functions of schools, thus overlooking one of the most important activities that occurs there.

4. What forces are at work now in defining curricular balance?

ANSWER: We are in a time of great debate about balance. The pendulum swings between the social need, principles of learning, and content advocates.

We cannot let educational goals become mainly skill acquisition and content attainment as measured by exams and rigidly uniform standards. If we do, we will drive the pupil failure rate up, particularly for those students labeled "at risk." Curricular balance weighted toward skill and content results in more requirements and more time spent on academics and, therefore, less time or no time for everything else.

However, if the goal is to retain as many students as possible and reduce the dropout rate, then the curriculum is "balanced" by including greater curricular diversity for students, and moving away from a single-track curriculum.

Nowhere is this more apparent than in the inner-city magnet schools where curricular diversity is the watchword as opposed to curricular uniformity.

Another force affecting balance is the strong trend toward the inclusion of children and youth with special needs in regular classrooms. As schools respond to these challenges they often have to divert resources from the regular curriculum in order to comply with state and federal laws to serve these learners. In an era of tight resources many educators who we talk with are concerned that the curriculum is being "skewed" toward these learners at the expense of especially the mass of students "in the middle." And some educators are getting concerned that the gifted are no longer being well served.

5. What do you see as the greatest challenges to curriculum balance today?

ANSWER: The development of a monolithic academic curriculum that increasingly alienates more students, the loss of most of the aesthetics in the curriculum, and the divorce of both of these from athletics.

Right now we—in principle at least—have nearly lost track of the diversity in students which our schools serve because we've decided that a "good" curriculum is comprehensive and broad as opposed to narrow and focused.

Another challenge is the "full inclusion" movement spoken about earlier.

6. What are the unique problems of attaining curriculum balance in schools and higher education institutions?

ANSWER: The key to determining "balance" in any organization is the clarity of the organization's purpose. Balance is not an end in itself; it has meaning only as it relates to the mission of the organization.

Most college and university curricula lack clarity, cohesion, and balance. In contrast, schools are more accustomed to and often better at examining outcomes and shaping the means to attain them. School clarity, coherence, and balance are often driven by local and state curricula in various forms as has been discussed throughout this book.

Some of the special problems of colleges in this regard are strong norms of faculty independence and weak norms for faculty supervision leading to inadequate supervision and monitoring of faculty work; the competing and often conflicting goals of teaching, research/scholarship, and service; and lack of knowledge among most administrators about curriculum management and related matters. Even voluntary national curricula guidelines do not break down these norms.

With schools it is the lack of curricular articulation coupled with local, state, and national politics; conflicting expectations on the part of various constituencies as to what "should be" in the curriculum; rising expectations and declining resources; inadequate supervision and monitoring of faculty work; and the lack of knowledge among most administrators about curriculum management and related matters.

ACTIVITIES FOR PERSONAL AND STAFF DEVELOPMENT

We offer some examples of activities as "starters" but encourage readers to develop their own to fit their situation.

1. Obtain a copy of your curricular requirements for high school graduation. How balanced is the curriculum through the lenses of social need, principles of learning, and proper content? Indicate what changes would be required to bring the curriculum in balance depending on the lens used. Do the same activity for any available curriculum guides.

2. Obtain a copy of Thomas P. Rohlen's, *Japan's High Schools* (1983). Compare the Japanese fixed national curriculum and its strengths and weaknesses to the American ideal of diversity and choice. Under what conditions would the Japanese concept of "balance"—as uniformity and orderliness—be superior or not superior to the American?

3. Select a book by Jean Piaget, Robert Gagne, B. F. Skinner, Lawrence Kohlberg, or Howard Gardner and develop a set of instructions that would help determine curriculum balance from their ideas and research. Where are the instructions strong and where do they become more tenuous? What additional study or research is required?

4. From a review of two or three decades of curriculum texts (or educational journals), develop a list of subjects or problems that were once part of the curriculum—in response to a social problem— but were subsequently dropped. What were the causes of the decline in emphasis? Develop a rationale to discern trends from fads in examining any topic for possible inclusion in a curriculum.

5. Develop a working knowledge about "multiple intelligences" and "dimensions of learning." How do they relate to one another? To what extent does your school's curriculum and instructional approaches reflect recognition of the intelligences and the dimensions? How could they be drawn upon more than they are to redesign curricula? How balanced is the curriculum relative to the intelligences and the dimensions?

6. What type of schedule does your school have? How long has it been in place? To what extent does it facilitate or impede your school's curricula and instructional goals? What would be a better schedule? Why? What would be involved in changing it?

Chapter 7

CURRICULUM PLANNING AND ALIGNMENT

S chools are complex organizations. Tinkering around the edges can provide the appearance of change. Committees can be formed. Purposes can be made public. Reports and studies can be written. Pronouncements can be promulgated. The public relations staff can have a field day and the sound bytes on the evening news appear impressive. But teachers in classrooms keep doing the best they can in the same conditions with the same old curriculum. There has been nothing but words. Actual change never happens before, during and after some media blitzes (Wallace, 1995).

Real change comes hard. It involves people. It produces tensions and conflict. It involves the allocation of resources and it is tied to the budget. Since curriculum involves people's attitudes, values and beliefs (LeTendre, 1994), normal conflict regarding scarce resources can be exacerbated enormously.

Deep curriculum change must be planned because there are too many things that can go wrong if it isn't. Planning can't prevent things from going wrong, but it can help anticipate problems and assist personnel to avoid or resolve conflicts when they arise in the course of engaging in curriculum change.

Some Things to Remember About Curriculum Change

Michael Fullan (1993), a recognized, international expert on change in schools, has produced a list of "eight basic lessons" about change. We will review them as they pertain to curricular practices. They form the platform from which we discuss curriculum planning.

1. What Matters Most Can't Be Mandated

The more complex and involved a change, the less a mandate is helpful with implementation (p. 22). Fullan doesn't say that mandates are useless. In fact, he agrees that they are important levers for change.

What he is saying, however, is that mandates alone can't produce new sets of responses from teachers, open vistas for creative ideas, or resolve deep-seated, intricate problems tied to organizational structure (see Carter, 1993, pp. 56–67). On the other hand, *fads can be mandated!* That's why they come and go with ease.

In the case of curriculum, what can be mandated with relative ease are the following:

1. new graduation requirements;
2. new electives (so long as they are not controversial and involve traditional thinking—see Berliner and Biddle, 1995, p. 300);
3. altering existing course objectives or activities to increase or decrease specific emphases;
4. adding onto the curriculum with an activity or a field trip.

None of these activities involve *deep change.* They are "add-ons" and do not disturb the internal operations of the organization. They can be absorbed without changing basic sequencing. While they may cost money, the chances are quite good that the existing program resources for internal support will be reflected rather than altered.

Deep change alters basic organizational relationships. It changes sequencing. It rearranges and reallocates resources. There will be few of such modifications with the traditional "add-ons" to the existing structural approach to curriculum change (see Archbald, 1993).

Newmann and Wehlage (1995) indicate that real restructuring of schools involves changing the intellectual quality of student work, authentic pedagogy, building the capacity of schools, and substantive external support for restructuring processes to work (pp. 3–4).

2. Change Is a Journey, Not a Blueprint

Real change is never linear. It is multifaceted (see Glegg, 1995, pp. 18–24). There is much uncertainty, even chaos at times. Real change is embedded in ambiguity. Sometimes answers are hard to come by and those that surface too quickly are wrong (Stefkovich & Guba, 1995).

Change is a gooey business. Typically, many planning approaches oversimplify reality. The real world is messy, "filled with random noise, gossip, inference, impression" (Mintzberg, 1994, p. 258). Such data are not easily reduced to quantifiable, precise statistics. Managers in these situations are used to making decisions *without hard data.* That they do so with some accuracy is a testimony not to planning but to their intuition and knowledge of the organization. *Deep change* can never be considered precise because of the limitations of information, compressed deadlines, and the dominance of oral forms of communication that are rich in spontaneity. Any kind of planning that doesn't take these conditions into account will be a largely sterile exercise.

3. Problems Are Friends, Not Enemies

Problems are not viewed as detrimental in the change process. Without problems the organization cannot learn and operations cannot be improved. As long as problems are viewed as "things to be fixed" as opposed to "people to blame," the change process can be facilitated.

If change is not a linear and easily programmed set of responses, it stands to reason that there will be many consequences of altering things that simply were not anticipated in the eyes of the planners. So real change, *deep change,* will be a grab bag full of surprises.

4. Vision and Strategic Planning Come Later

Some of the planning literature is full of advice about planning and visioning first, and then moving into a change modality second. Fullan (1993) cautions that this advice is erroneous. He insists that a *vision* comes after *action* and not before. Second, the "sharing" of a vision involves a dynamic interaction of people who develop a common understanding of what they are trying to accomplish. In all cases, action *precedes* the development of a vision. So it is necessary to get in there and "muck around" awhile before a purposive vision can be developed.

Robert Eaton, Chrysler's new chairman, says this about vision. "Internally, we don't use the word vision. I believe in quantifiable short-term results—things we can all relate to—as opposed to some esoteric thing no one can quantify" (Lavin, 1993, p. A1). When Lou Gerstner took over the failing corporate giant International Business Machines he quipped, "The last thing IBM needs right now is a vision" (Fuchsberg, 1994, p. B4).

5. Equal Power Between Individual and Collective Work

"Productive educational change is . . . a process of overcoming isolation while not succumbing to groupthink," warns Fullan (1993, p. 33). Business has been a victim of fads, more so than in education. The trendy words often found in business, such as "re-engineering," "benchmarking," "broadbanding," "outsourcing," and "dynamic competitive simulation" or "wargaming," have generally produced disappointing or negative results. Harvard economics professor James Medoff notes, "The success rate of any of these approaches is pretty low ... [there is] no empirical evidence that any of these things increase productivity" (Bleakley, 1993, p. A1).

Benchmarking, a practice of examining how one's competitors do things better, meant trips to observe their operations. However, in the case of the Pacific Gas & Electric Company, the observers were "just industrial tourists," until they were given specific tips on what to look for (Bleakley, 1993, p. A1). Another problem with benchmarking, according to a Japanese businessman, is: "Doing the same things as your competitors is the risk. If they fail, you fail" (Williams & Kanabayashi, 1994, A1).

When Johnson & Johnson tried *broadbanding,* the idea of collapsing multiple salary grades into a few to encourage job movement, a third of the work force (3000) complained that clear job paths had been eliminated. The "experiment" was abolished (Bleakley, 1993, p. A1).

Similarly, when *re-engineering* was tried at American Express it meant the elimination of layers of middle-management jobs. With the ensuing hiatus went opportunities for promotion from those who had counted on them for advancement. The company had to make changes to maintain productivity (Bleakley, 1993, p. A1). Such management "quick fixes" improved effectiveness between ten to twenty percent, but many employees were fed up, remarking, "Stop with the fads. No more posters, seminars and training classes" (Bleakley, 1993, p. A1). Even in Japan, a country that invented worker empowerment with the notion that good ideas would percolate up to the boardroom, the result was stagnation and duplication. At one point, Nissan had "300 different ashtrays in its cars" (Schlesinger, Williams & Forman, 1993, p. A-4). Many Japanese companies have adopted the American viewpoint of "top-down" decision making to extricate themselves from an unproductive, unprofitable economic quagmire.

Outsourcing is the practice of *subcontracting* the development of a part, product or service. In theory, this allows the main company to concentrate upon its "core competencies" and also reduce internal costs of production. In 1996, American companies will spend about $100 billion on outsourcing, reducing their labor costs by ten to fifteen percent ("The Outing of Outsourcing," 1995, p. 57). The downside of outsourcing is that if the main company reduces costs to a maximum point, the outsourcer can't turn a profit. Then the main company may have to take the product or service back into the fold because they can do it cheaper. It should be clear that *outsourcing* is a way to reduce labor costs.

Dynamic competitive simulation or *wargaming* is the latest corporate boardroom practice of trying to anticipate the moves of a competitor in the marketplace. It is different from the practice of game theory which is of a more tactical nature. In business, tactical decisions pertain to pricing. Wargaming in business involves breaking the corporate boardroom into teams and providing them with market and product information. The teams then establish objectives and build capacities. By taking "turns" they implement their decisions. After three turns an impartial panel of "adjudicators" determine the most likely outcomes (Treat, 1995, p. A12). Some of these concepts have filtered into education in recent times and lie behind the notion of privatizing schools.

The idea of allowing for-profit companies to "take over" failing schools was attractive for awhile. But claims by the private sector that they could run failing schools cheaper and better proved unworkable. The Minneapolis-based Education Alternatives Inc. was brought up short in Hartford, Connecticut when the school board rejected the idea that to pay for new computers they should lay off 300 teachers. The board had already agreed to freeze teacher salaries to save $6 million before it rejected EAI's budgetary trade-off scheme of teachers for hardware (Judson, 1995, p. A13).

6. Neither Centralization Nor Decentralization Works

Fullan (1993) sees the debate over centralization and decentralization as unproductive. "Center and local units need each other," he advises. "You can't get anywhere by swinging from one dominance to another" (p. 38). Two attempts to downsize and de-bureaucratize state departments of education in Kentucky (Steffy, 1992) and Virginia (Troutman, 1994) indicated that both efforts underestimated the complexity of the undertaking and despite the reform rhetoric of getting rid of "incompetents" embedded in the bureaucratic woodwork, "89% of former employees were rehired at similar levels" (Troutman, 1994, p. 318). As Steffy (1992) observed, "The more correct title for what happened . . . in the Kentucky Department of Education was simply *re-organization*" (p. 30).

Let us consider another example. In one urban school system, a board-adopted school busing plan was put into effect to desegregate the system along racial lines. Quotas were installed which were to be followed by nearly every school. The premise of the busing plan (centrally adopted from a court order) was to *equalize* the *opportunity to learn.* That assumption rested on the notion that the curriculum at each school for similar levels was *comparable.* However, due to the impact of unbridled site-based management, each school was free to form its own curriculum emphasis. Vast differences between schools flourished. A study revealed that programs were not *comparable;* they were radically different.

The *opportunity to learn* concept is centered around equalizing the "playing field" for all students. It became a victim of the unequal embrace of differences. Students at one high school had no access to courses readily available to students at other high schools. For example, AP Calculus was offered at only one of six high schools. If students did not attend that high school, they had no access to AP Calculus. In this scenario, a central solution to solve one problem in the schools (busing) was ineffective because of unregulated program diversity at the schools (decentralization). Successful change is neither centralized or decentralized. It is both.

7. Connection to a Wider Environment is Critical

Educational systems are not social islands. What goes on in them can be supported or annexed by external groups and forces. Newmann and Wehlage (1995) indicated four types of external support that were central to successful change. They were standard setting, staff development, deregulation, and parental support (p. 41).

One of the key forces driving change in the Kentucky reform was the establishment of state learning standards based on the involvement of 900 Kentuckians from business, the communities and educational leaders (Pankratz, 1992, p. 144). The input from these groups, which included fifty classroom teachers, led to adoption by the statewide Council on School Performance Standards. What was driving educational reform in Kentucky were mandates externally set and imposed on all school systems.

While parental support is critical to change, it clearly has limitations. Emerging research indicates that the involvement of parents creates suspicions among teachers of parental motivations. In one study in Western Australia, teachers were threatened that the involvement of parents displaced teacher influence in curriculum decision making (see O'Donoghue & O'Brien, 1995, p. 412). In England, parental involvement hinged on the necessity for teachers to learn to trust parents by being more open to constructive criticism from them (Wikeley & Hughes, 1995, p. 308). Empowering parents in the guise of their roles on school councils has led to the removal of school principals who have been judged to be ineffective (Hess, 1992, p. 278).

8. Every Person Is a Change Agent

It has been easy to characterize educational change as mass movements involving impersonal forces that need to "restructure" schools. The idea is that of "systemic" or "third wave" reform (Murphy, 1992, p. 9).

Steffy and English (1996) aver that the concept of "systemic" change derives from linguistic structuralism and, as such, marginalizes the contribution of individuals in the change process. As such, change viewed as impersonal mass movements cannot really be empirically tested. Such movements become self-fulfilling prophecies only with implementation.

Larson (1992a) has indicated that individual teachers pursue change mainly for "psychic rewards" and that these are largely idiosyncratic, classroom to classroom (pp. 57–59). In a study of the variables which accounted for successful implementation of the primary school concept in Kentucky, Settle (1995) found that the one critical factor was the leadership of the individual school principal (p. 180).

Now that we have examined the conditions of change, let us look at the planning process for curriculum change.

The Planning Process for Curriculum Change

Planning models that assume reality is static, change is linear, and humans predictable are ineffective. Very few such models take into account future trends, so they are essentially extensions of the status quo arbitrarily placed into some future moment (see Bailey, 1991). Planning can be envisioned to occur at three levels: strategic, tactical, and operational (Kaufman, Herman & Watters, 1996).

Curriculum planning is necessary for three reasons: (1) to conceptualize and operationalize the nature of curriculum; (2) to think through the major steps in the process within the context for development; and (3) to construct procedures to create the necessary political consensus to support the curriculum products once they are developed.

The Nature of Curriculum

The "stuff" which becomes the curriculum can be thought of as processes, facts, activities, experiences, data, or knowledge. What the teacher ultimately decides to do in a classroom is en toto *the curriculum.* Curriculum has properties, and it comes to be seen as being stable enough to debate, adopt, and publish in some form. In this way one can speak of the "history curriculum" or the "third-grade curriculum."

Such "stuff" is never neutral or objective. Curriculum content is subjectively determined within a structure of implicit and explicit values (English, 1992, pp. 23–34). In fact, the traditional construction of curriculum is largely a tautological process, i.e., those desired ends also become the means of their delivery and the criteria to determine effectiveness.

As we have seen in Chapter 5, one thinks about curriculum within a values structure that serves as a screen for what is ultimately included in a curriculum. What is "in" a curriculum does not stand independently. It was selected to reinforce, support, and exemplify the values screen which led to its creation. In turn, the "results" of this selection will be matched to the values inherent in its construction. Such curriculum is tautological, "good" or "true" by definition.

In the construction of curriculum it is recommended that as many values which are implicit in the selection of the "stuff" which goes into a curriculum be made explicit. In this way, at least the developers/creators can come to understand their own biases.

Let us take a controversial decision to distribute condoms in schools. One value screen for inclusion rests on the premise that students will most likely engage in sex and so they ought to be protected from disease, notably AIDS. The lethal nature of AIDS has come to override other values which rest on notions of privacy and the values taught in the church or in the home.

Another value screen against the distribution of condoms indicates that this places the institution in an implicit posture of "approving" sexual activities among students. Such a posture violates the alleged "neutrality" of schools on sensitive value issues or assumes a stance that is unacceptable to school patrons. Since no one can hide from the terrible tragedy of AIDS, the way to deal with "the problem" is to develop abstinence campaigns until marriage. Neither approach is neutral. The distribution of condoms or any discussion of birth control are decided by a priori decisions implicit in the values which led to the selection or rejection of curriculum content.

Making values explicit is risky. Part of the problem with the OBE movement (outcomes-based education) is that many implicit values in schools were made public, ushering into the public spotlight assumptions of which many parents had been unaware. One response has been the development of "stealth politics" in which Christian fundamentalists counterattack by running for school boards on hidden agendas (see Manatt, 1995, p. 34–35).

Americans do not agree on the values that should be included in a public school curriculum. For example, in 1994, when a member of the House Education and Labor Committee suggested that a national conference be held to promote the teaching of such values as honesty, responsibility and caring, Richard Armey, a conservative Texas Republican, glowered, "The fact is that these people don't know my children and the fact is they don't love my children. And the fact is they don't care about my children and the further fact is they accept no responsibility for the outcome . . . and they ought to, by God, leave my kids alone." The amendment to teach values was defeated, 23–6 (Sharpe, 1994, p. A20).

Conservative newspaper columnist Cal Thomas (1995) regularly dispenses folk wisdom about what is wrong with the public schools. Claiming that poor national history test scores are the result of the enemies of education and real history creating an Orwellian "memory hole," Thomas decries trends of secularism and the loss of American heroes being dumped in favor of politically correct fourteenth-century African kings in school curricula (p. 13A).

When a national poll was conducted by Gallup of 1306 adults about the values which should be taught in the public schools, 97 percent responded that honesty should be taught. Ninety percent indicated they thought that "the golden rule" should also be in the curriculum. Only 87 percent believed that people should be accepted who hold different religious beliefs, 56 percent indicated that they would accept the right of women to choose abortion, and 51 percent believed that homosexuals and bisexuals should be accepted (Sharpe, 1994, p. A20).

In a study of why Canada's and the United States' test scores were average to low compared to children from other countries on the International Assessment of Educational Progress (IAEP), Gaffield (1994) suggested that the traditions of family in both nations placed its value above academic skills acquisition and may be responsible for lower test performance as a consequence (p. 51, 60).

The Major Steps in the Process

The major steps in the *ideal* process of planning follow the explication of the values framework within which curriculum is to be developed or written. Leaving aside for the moment whether it should be created in committees or by elite groups, there are steps in the process that are important to consider. The most crucial is called needs assessment (English & Kaufman, 1975) which was discussed in Chapter 3.

Step 1: Establish Goals. Goals represent non-time bound aspirations for any level of a school system or business. There can be system goals, school or business goals, department or division goals or classroom goals. Goals may represent idealized learning results, hoped-for organizational conditions, or the installation of new processes or procedures.

A goal can be and usually is a desired result, process, or condition which currently does not exist or is not attainable. As such, goals are usually not measurable in conventional terms.

In curricular affairs, goals normally are abstract statements which are supposed to guide the developers of curriculum in specifying objectives or in delineating curriculum content. While the development of goals is helpful as a beginning point to lay out the boundaries of curriculum development, their lack of specificity means that concrete linkages to organizational behaviors and practices are absent. Furthermore, if goals are stated in terms of subject-matter content mastery, they do not assist in the process of selecting content at all. Rather, they bypass the selection process altogether and move straight to content specification.

For example, if a goal is for a student to attain mastery of "essential mathematical operations," then math as a field or subject area is accepted as a curriculum program. Goals ought to question the validity of any a priori curricular categories used in schools. However, this cannot be the case when they are stated as attainments to be achieved within content areas at the outset.

In this case, the *forcing function* of examining any array of curricular categories has been lost. The existing curricular categories are simply accepted. Goals ought to be stated outside of specific curricular content. They should be *contentless* in the abstract. Then in the process of translating them into organizational activities they may assume a content form.

Fundamentalists and those in the liberal arts tradition (see Adler, 1982) will object to this process of goal development since they assume that some subject matter has been *proven* to be more worthy of curriculum inclusion than others.

Step 2: Developing Objectives. For idealized conditions, processes or results can only have an impact on an organization if they become tactical and operational. In this case, nebulous goal statements have to be made more definitive or they cannot be accurately translated into things people do. In short, abstract visions cannot become work unless they are changed into work statements and work measurement.

Objectives are tangible, realizable and measurable aspects of work. Objectives provide both focus and economy within an organization's resources. Here is an example of the translation process.

The Translation Process of Goals to Objectives to Assessment Procedures*

Goal: The student will observe, design, and/or conduct an investigation demonstrating the concept of change over time.

Objective: The student will observe, design and/or conduct an investigation where a change in the state of matter is observed over a period of time and will manipulate and draw conclusions about the variable responsible for the change observed.

Assessment Procedures: Given the results of an investigation the student will demonstrate and conclude that the manipulation of heat energy results in a change in the state of matter from solid to liquid and liquid to gas.

No organization can be responsible or accountable unless and until its work processes can be connected to larger aims which rest on a political consensus. In many cases school operations are not connected to larger political purposes. They operate independently from them. The process of moving from goal to objective to measurement is part of the business of establishing internal organizational connectivity. It is fundamental to operational accountability.

Step 3: Locate Objectives in Curricular Content. Once objectives are defined and validated via a consensual procedure, they should be placed within curricular content areas. Think of such objectives as results of the instructional processes to be employed. The curriculum is grouped by subject matter, sometimes separately, sometimes in relationship to other content areas.

The different types of curricular groups are a subject content curriculum, an interdisciplinary curriculum, a core curriculum or a thematic or activity curriculum. Sometimes the type of curriculum employed has been determined prior to the location of curricular objectives.

The *subject content* curriculum is the "traditional" subject or discipline-centered curriculum. In this model, the subjects are dominant and

---

*NOTE: The above science goals/objectives taken from science protocols developed by the Texas Education Agency in Austin, Texas are in the public domain.

separate. The delineations of math, science, social studies, physical education, and foreign language are regnant.

The *interdisciplinary curriculum* combines aspects of team teaching, flexible scheduling, and blocks of instructional time where combinations of subjects are possible in fluid situations (Jenkins, 1992, pp. 101–104).

A *core curriculum* has traditionally implied two or more subjects taught or fused together, the most common being language arts and social studies (McNeil, 1996, p. 188).

The *thematic curriculum* is one where themes are selected such as "the global community," or "health and the environment," and these themes constitute ways of cutting across curriculum subjects. They are conceptual "hooks" which integrate learning within many subject content areas.

An *activity curriculum* may be thought of as "writing across the curriculum," where the function of writing and its improvement is applied to every subject field a student may encounter in his or her day (see Earley, 1992, pp. 91–99).

Step 4: Sequence the Objectives. Objectives must be located within a curriculum. Most often such objectives are contained within *curriculum units* (Jones, Grizzel & Grinstead, 1939). Curriculum units are simply "chunks" of content or processes around which and into which objectives can be placed or clustered. Freeland (1991) indicates that such units are comprised of eight parts beginning with an overview and followed by concepts, generalizations and facts, understandings, attitudes and skills, motivational activities, developmental activities, evaluation techniques, bibliography and other sources (p. 27). Within these units are subunits, chapters or even individual lessons. Needs assessment is simply a kind of gap or discrepancy analysis (Kaufman, 1988, p. 15). Prior to undertaking the actual assessment, objectives must be placed or located in some form in the curriculum.

Step 5: The Discrepancy Analysis. Desired objectives pertaining to expected student results must be evaluated to determine if they are being met. This involves a search for the extant data which existing assessment or tests produce in the school or school system. Such results can be "matched" against the objectives to determine differences. The discrepancies or "gaps" become the future "needs" which must be met by the school, program or school district, depending upon the level or area of analysis which has been undertaken.

In many cases, there may not be an appropriate evaluative tool available, and so the "gap" may not be documented with anything but anecdotal data or other qualitative data. Such data can be very legitimate.

Step 6: Harvest the Needs. All of the gap data (needs) can be displayed by showing them *within* the type of curriculum format selected. Needs with an interdisciplinary curriculum may be somewhat different than those within a traditional curriculum structure.

Gap data can be illustrated by area, school level, or district exit data (twelfth grade). In the end, it must be prioritized and costed out. Once again, the implicit and explicit value screen used by administrators and boards of education become important decision-making points in determining which "gaps" are to be harvested first, second, or third.

Needs assessments, like the process described, assume that curriculum development is a logical, data-driven approach to determining priorities. But we have seen that both on the front end and the back, deciding how gaps are defined, and then determining which ones are most important, are highly subjective, political decisions (see Giroux & McLaren, 1992, pp. 99–110).

(For a *highly* useable book on curriculum development, see Carr and Harris, 1993.)

Curriculum Alignment

After a determination of the propriety of the curriculum content, the next most important aspect of *curriculum design* is *curriculum alignment*. Alignment refers to two dimensions in the curriculum development process: (1) the relationship between what is specified in the *curriculum content* and the *assessment tools* (design alignment), and (2) the relationship between what is *taught* and what is *specified* and *tested* (delivery alignment) (see also Chapter 4).

The concept of curriculum alignment is not new in the field of curriculum. Near the turn of the nineteenth century Joseph Mayer Rice began a series of pioneering studies that represented an attack on American education for its mindlessness and rigidity. Rice's views later became centered on the need for goal clarity and measurement which would indicate whether such results had been attained (Kliebard, 1982).

It took some time for educators to see the requirements between the work to be performed (curriculum or courses of study), work measurement (testing), and work performance (teaching) as integral to one another.

The testing movement grew separate and apart from the early curriculum movement, though paths often crossed. Early advocates of testing were more concerned with using tests to classify children prior to, or during instruction, than as a means to assess instruction directly (Terman, 1916). Some early school superintendents who used tests to show poor pupil performance were more concerned with improved structural efficiencies and enhanced control than with curricular change (Tyack, 1974).

The expansion of statewide competency testing and the publication of school and school system scores have not only brought about increased pressure on local officials and teachers to improve pupil performance as measured but has reduced local control of the curriculum (see Tyree, 1993).

As state testing content becomes more complex and difficult for students to demonstrate mastery, the requirement for a more interconnected curriculum across grade levels and within schools soon becomes apparent. Since tests are assessing cumulative skills and knowledge, changing the school environment becomes a matter of looking for those tools that direct the work of teachers over many years. Chief among these is an approach which provides the student with an activity, realistic task, problem or simulation that relates to a standard being measured called *authentic assessment* (Steffy, 1995, p. 6).

The congruence of the curriculum to the test, then, is of paramount importance, or what some researchers have come to call "curriculum coverage," i.e., the extent to which curriculum taught is also that which is tested (Baker, 1993, p. 18). This is sometimes referred to as *content* alignment. It is this factor which Ian Westbury (1992) believes helps explain why achievement in Japanese schools is consistently higher than in the U.S. and enhances Japanese OTL (opportunity to learn). Says Westbury:

> But the analysis I have offered here suggests that the difference between Japanese and U.S. achievement can be seen as a consequence of different curricula.... when U.S. teachers teach a curriculum which parallels that of Japan, U.S. achievement is similar to that of Japan. (p. 23)

What is at work behind OTL is an older idea called *the transfer of training*. Originally, the idea of *transfer of training* was dominated by the metaphor that the brain was a muscle which if exercised through systematic drills would become strong and effectual in the world. The school was the place for such exercise. Curriculum consisted of much memorization and rote work as a result. Difficult subjects like Latin and Greek were supposed to produce razor sharp mental faculties because of their inherent rigor.

The work of E. L. Thorndike (1924) put an end to such notions when he showed that physics and Greek did not produce better reasoning than the content of physical education or drama in schools. In place of the mental faculties view of the transfer from the schooling environment to the real world, Thorndike proffered the *identical elements* idea of transfer. He postulated that elements in the school were successfully transferred to the real world to the extent that those same elements in the schools were *present* in the real world.

What this means is that if a specific task is required of a person in the real world of work, the extent to which that task is included in the school and taught there will be more successfully transferred than if not so included in the curriculum (the idea of "curriculum coverage" in Westbury's article previously cited). Not only must it be included in the curriculum of the school, it must be taught *as encountered* in the real world. This view of transfer is the underlying principle behind *curriculum alignment.*

Tests designed to make judgments or inferences about the quantity or quality of school life must have some element of "real world" credibility. If they did not, why should the schools care about them? Why should parents or legislators care about them either? It is assumed that tests assess something important about either the world or attributes or abilities that will make a difference in the real world. For this reason tests are situations of "real world surrogates" in one form or another. As one type of situation they can be transferred to another situation in a school and *taught.* The principle of curriculum alignment rests upon an accurate assessment of the test as a reality surrogate.

If the test is assessing the ability to generalize from one situation to the next, then generalizability as a process is best taught in the identical situation existing in the school. If it is the "wholeness" of the situation that is desired to be learned and the capability of understanding *relationships* within a variety of situations, then the schooling environment should include these elements within it to maximize transfer. If knowledge of a gestalt is required, then gestalt recognition and utilization should be included in the curriculum. This assurance, that *how* the content taught facilitates and reinforces *learning*, is called "context" alignment.

The principle of alignment is anchored in contemporary notions of accountability. If a teacher or a principal is being held accountable for pupil learning as well as the students themselves, they must have access to learn that which is tested. Access or opportunity to learn is the fulcrum for control to exist. Legal requirements for job protection or rewards and sanctions require *due process*. That idea rests on adequate notice of intended actions and the capability of behaving responsibly in a situation.

If students are tested on knowledge or processes they have not been taught, then such tests cannot be adequate measures to determine teacher effectiveness nor student responsibility. Non-aligned tests measure SES (socioeconomic status or poverty levels). Simply put, poor students do worse than rich students when tests are not reflective of the taught curriculum in schools (see Battistich, Solomon, Kim, Watson & Schaps, 1995, p. 644). SES is a consistent variable which predicts pupil perform-ance on non-aligned tests. In one study conducted by Robinson and Brandon (1994), 89 percent of the variance of the NAEP math scores in 1992 were explained by four variables which had nothing to do with the quality of education students were receiving in their schools. They were: (1) number of parents living at home, (2) parents' education, (3) commu-nity type, and (4) the state poverty rate (p. 7). Tests which are reflective measures of poverty result in the idea that there are no poor schools, only schools that serve the poor. How can schools be accountable for pupil performance on tests which do not reflect their curriculum and which *do align* with wealth and related measures of wealth which are beyond the control of the school and its agents?

It makes no sense for poor performing schools to engage in rational planning activities to improve pupil performance when the tests they give do not align with the curriculum they teach their students. No amount of involvement, empowerment, or being "outcomes-driven" will show improvement without alignment as the critical linking variable (Hendery, 1992, p. 9).

Understanding Alignment

Alignment consists of several dimensions. We shall discuss four here shown in the diagram on the following page.

DIMENSIONS OF CURRICULUM ALIGNMENT

	Design	*Delivery*
Content	Establish in the construction of curriculum.	Taught as specified.
Context	Match formats in the construction of curriculum.	Teach formats as exemplars.

Content refers to the substance of the curriculum to be developed. It may be facts, processes, skills, or broad ranges of expected results. *Context* refers to the format in which the packaging of curriculum is matched. Sometimes it is referred to as "format" alignment. It is most often used to reference the match from the curriculum to a textbook or a test. *Design* refers to how to put together the curriculum in themes—interdisciplinary or multidisciplinary or traditional disciplines. *Delivery* relates to the implementation of the curriculum. This aspect involves the teacher as an active participant in the process.

An Example of Alignment

The textbook is perhaps the single most influential (not necessarily the best) resource for classroom teachers. Textbook/test alignment is therefore the easiest and most pervasive place to begin looking at alignment.

Here is an example of textbook/test alignment:

OBJECTIVE: To engage in problem solving.

TEST ITEM AND FORMAT: Eleven people tried out for the class play in the morning. Twenty-eight people tried out in the afternoon. Which pair of numbers would you add to estimate the total number of people who tried out for the play?

1. 10, 30	3. 10, 20
2. 10, 25	4. 15, 20

TEXTBOOK ITEM AND FORMAT: On Mary's twelfth birthday, her grandfather gave her $10. He gave Mary $20 on her thirteenth birthday and $40 on her fourteenth birthday. Following this pattern, Mary's grandfather plans on giving Mary $70 on her fifteenth birthday, but Mary expects $80 on that day. Mary's sister says that both amounts may be correct. Who is right—Mary's grandfather, Mary, or Mary's sister? Explain your reasoning.

COMPARISON OF THE TEST/TEXTBOOK: The difference in format is substantive here. The test format is multiple-choice versus essay, scoring is based on the correct answer versus rubric scoring, and basic skills versus higher order thinking (Ferguson, 1994, p. 2).

This is an example of low alignment. High alignment would demonstrate a much better match between content/context than the example. The higher the content/context match, the easier the transfer. It is important to maximize transfer that the alignment match both the content and format of test/curriculum or test/textbook.

One can attain *design alignment* by developing curriculum first and then developing the test, a process called *frontloading. Backloading* is the opposite. One begins by working "back" from the test to the curriculum. Examples of backloading occur in advanced placement courses and in commercial tutorial courses to improve scholastic aptitude test (SAT) scores. When the test and the curriculum are considered synonymous, "teaching to tested objectives is synonymous with good instruction" (Shepard, 1991, p. 7).

On the other hand, when the purpose of the test is diagnostic or to measure some psychological trait, no such assumption can be made about test/curriculum parallelism. In this case, the teacher would not "teach to the test" because such tools would have no function as accountability measures.

The widespread use of standardized tests as accountability tools represents a serious misuse of their function. As Archibald and Newmann (1988) note:

> It is impossible for many students to experience relative success on standardized tests. To achieve a normal curve, the developers deliberately choose certain items to ensure that at least half the students will always score below average. This process produces rankings that are influenced very little...by school learning. (p. 54)

Standardized tests replicate the normal curve by: (1) keeping the test a secret and (2) ensuring a low alignment to any locally developed curriculum. Both of these practices ensure that school learning as an important variable one is reduced to randomness (chance). Standardized test makers are more interested in what the results look like (the bell curve) than they are in ensuring that the test itself is a good measure of any specific curriculum. In the case of low alignment, SES dominates how students come to be ranked on nearly all standardized tests. Since SES, I.Q. and race are related in America, and incorrectly considered to be singular measures of a stable generic inheritance, such tests are historically racist in their application (see Singham, 1995, pp. 271–278). The recent furor over *The Bell Curve* by Herrnstein and Murray (1994) perpetuates the fallacies of early test makers in the U.S. It never received positive feedback from a critical, well-educated audience. *The Bell Curve* pandered to popular misconceptions and prejudices. (Standardized tests will be discussed further in Chapter 9.)

Curriculum alignment remains one of the least understood and most potent forces for improving pupil achievement on all kinds of assessments in schools except those which insist on secrecy rooted in assumptions of false scarcity (randomness) misapplied as reliable measures of in-school learning.

Finally, in concluding this discussion of alignment, it is important to refer readers back to Chapter 4 and our discussion of the concepts of "tight," "relaxed," and "unconnected" curricula in terms of design and delivery issues. There we pointed out that the connections need not always be "tight," but that "unconnected" curricula are not justifiable. The same holds for alignment. Educators must decide what kind of alignment is required by what situation through processes of collegial dialogue.

Summary

Curriculum change is neither a simple nor linear process. Society is not stable but dynamic and changing. Any curriculum posited on social stability will ultimately become outdated. School systems and most organizations are multifaceted and interactive. Planning can assist curriculum leaders in trying to anticipate the many reactions and interactions which will occur in any process of change. Yet any planning process or model will never be able to anticipate each and every reaction to change. Change cannot be controlled, but it can be guided.

Consensus about what should be placed within a curriculum is necessarily a political process. There are no "true facts" which can stand alone. Americans have historically been in disagreement about the virtues and values to be embraced in their schools. Many of the values and beliefs about what should be in school curricula remain implicit and hidden. They are exposed during times of conflict and controversy.

The development of curriculum generally follows a process of developing *goals*, making them more specific through the translation into objectives, and tracking them into the existing curriculum structure. These are then assessed and gaps or needs explicated. These "needs" form the basis for curriculum change and the development of smaller action agendas to improve curriculum.

Curriculum alignment is primarily concerned with improving the OTL (opportunity to learn) by ensuring that curriculum tested has been taught. There are assumptions from some test makers that run contrary to both alignment and accountability when the purpose of tests is to identify traits or abilities among students (see Halayna, Nolen, & Haas, 1991).

The widespread use of standardized tests to determine accountability has been a misuse of what they allegedly demonstrate because large portions of the test content are not part of any local or state curriculum. They cannot be used to determine "quality education" because what they are assessing is not known to local educators. Since they cannot control the test content, local educators cannot be accountable for test score improvement. In such cases, the socioeconomic status of the students is the variable which explains the largest percentage of the variance.

DIALOGUE FOR IMPLEMENTATION

These are the questions most commonly asked of the authors about the ideas in this chapter.

1. You seem to be downplaying the idea of planning. Is planning a worthwhile activity?

ANSWER: Planning is essential to improve upon luck in the change process. But planning should not be allowed to become something which one does by itself and is good "by itself." Planning should be viewed as a temporary truce with reality rather than a way to "control" reality. All plans should be considered as containing large chunks of ambiguity. Planning should be a dynamic and continual activity as opposed to a one-time, monumental effort.

2. How can "problems be friends" if school administrators insist on the idea that a "good school" runs like a "smooth ship"?

ANSWER: The notions are antithetical. Even "good schools" have problems. A school without problems is in serious trouble because it means that administrators, teachers, and other staff are sitting on them instead of solving them.

3. The concept of *action* first and *vision* second runs contrary to the idea of thinking about the future instead of the status quo. If one followed Fullan's advice, wouldn't there be no change?

ANSWER: All future actions are reflections of the present anyway. Grounding the future in current actions ensures that when the "vision" is developed it is not esoteric and unattainable.

4. You indicate that curriculum development is inherently a *tautological process*. Is there any way to develop curriculum that doesn't fall into this trap?

ANSWER: Probably not. As long as schooling is seen as a way of reproducing a culture, the function of schooling will be subverted to perpetuating the status quo. The implicit and explicit "value screen" by which curricular goals and objectives are selected will not stray very far from sociopolitical notions of acceptability. In the U.S. and Canada, public school boards and committees reinforce that status quo.

5. Isn't the most controversial aspect of *curriculum alignment* the idea of "teaching to the test"?

ANSWER: Particularly on the concept of *backloading*, the notion of working from the test to the curriculum, "teaching to the test" is usually raised. There is nothing wrong with "teaching to the test" as long as the test is a valid measure of the curriculum to be learned. It is when the function of the test is *to diagnose and classify* that "teaching to the test" becomes problematic. Secrecy protects the content of diagnostic tests from potential *misclassification*. However, when the test is misused as a measure of accountability for *in-school learning*, "teaching to the test" becomes subversive as a measure of school learning, the determination of appropriate curricula, and test integrity.

ACTIVITIES FOR PERSONAL AND STAFF DEVELOPMENT

We offer some examples of activities as "starters," but encourage readers to develop their own that will fit their situation.

1. What are the key assumptions of the *needs assessment* process and in what ways are they faulty? Examine closely the notions of

rational system functioning and social stability in responding to this query.

2. Curriculum alignment has a bias towards specific notions of learning. Among the various theories such as gestalt, organismic, field theories, or behavioristic theories, identify which one most strongly supports alignment.

3. Explain what standardized tests really assess if they are not aligned to any local or state curriculum. What is actually being compared? How would you respond to parents who claim that they "need" to know test scores from such instruments to "know" how well their children are doing compared to children elsewhere?

4. Do a survey of curriculum changes or controversies in your school or school system for the last five years. What kinds of changes were proposed and what kind of changes were implemented? Were any of these activities related to *deep change?*

5. Provide at least one example of curriculum development being tautological in your school or school system. Can you think of any example that *wasn't* tautological?

6. Examine past curriculum development practices in your school or school system. To what extent were such activities *anchored* by a needs assessment? If yes, were such activities complete as described in this chapter? If not, why do you think they were not used?

7. Develop a narrative or theory which describes how curriculum development typically reinforces the socioeconomic status quo. What sociopolitical changes would have to occur to change this? How likely is it that such changes will or would occur in the future?

Chapter 8

CURRICULUM GUIDES, MAPPING, AND
TOTAL QUALITY EDUCATION

One could hardly find an activity in which more fruitless money has been spent in education than employing teachers to write curriculum guides. Instead of being viewed as the creation of *a functional work plan*, guides have been seen as the authorization to engage in philosophical speculation, endless theorizing, or as short-term summer work products. Rarely is the development of curriculum guides attached to a long-range plan for curriculum development, or even as a short-term investment to improve curriculum alignment. Teachers are almost always never trained to write curriculum, nor are they required to demonstrate if they understand the cutting edge issues in the areas they volunteer to work on or are selected to develop.

It isn't that teachers don't want to develop something of which they can be proud and to which other teachers refer in their daily work. It is, rather, that curriculum guides are a subject about which there is very little clarity regarding their function in schools and classrooms and about which there is a lot of strong political opinion regarding teacher "ownership" and whether they should be "bottom-up" or "top-down" documents. No one seems to remember that most textbooks are not written by teachers but are adopted hierarchically. Despite that fact, once purchased most teachers are either directed or guided by what is between the covers. And confidential interviews with teachers often reveal that even when they are "involved" in developing curriculum, they hardly reference it in their classroom decisions. So what's all the talk about ownership, and "bottom-up" empowerment, and being creative in the classroom?

What Is a Curriculum Guide?

Start by asking yourself, "What is a curriculum guide?" Is it *the* curriculum? Or is it *a* curriculum? Is it supposed to direct classroom

176

teaching? If so, how? Or is it supposed to guide the selection of textbook topics? Or is to supplement the textbook? Or is it supposed to be the textbook? Is a curriculum guide just a cookbook? Is it a repository of techniques? Should it be monitored, or is it just a set of benign suggestions teachers are free to use or discard as they see fit?

Part of the problem with curriculum guides is that various audiences see their function differently. Boards may see guides as prescriptions. Supervisors may envision them as yardsticks of accountability. Teachers may see them as well, *guides*. (See "Assessment of Work Design" section in Chapter 9 for more information about guides.)

When teachers develop guides they aren't inclined to write tight prescriptions for themselves that could become the means for critical evaluations from their superiors. So teachers will write loose, vague, and flexible specifications. Administrators want guides that are more specific, tighter, more prescriptive and should be followed once developed.

The board may be thinking of a public relations document that can be distributed to parents and may object to educational jargon being part of the guide content.

The *function* of curriculum in any organization is to create continuity *within* that organization and to wed together the actual work performed with desired results. An analysis of the obtained results should reveal if they are in harmony with the purposes for which the organization exists. The key resource involved with curriculum development is how to use *classroom learning time*. Herbert Walberg (1993) puts it this way: "The body of research literature suggests that large increases in productive learning time (other things being equal) can be expected to result in correspondingly large learning effects (p. 1).

The Battle Over Classroom Control

Like all other professionals, teachers want to protect the autonomy they enjoy in scheduling, defining, and performing their work. One reason teachers prefer "loose" and "vague" documents is to preserve such autonomy in dealing with children. For some time teachers have been able to ward off tighter control. However, these conditions are changing with mandatory state assessment programs that place accountability at the school or even classroom levels. High-risk tests establish accountability much closer to the classroom than ever before. As sanctions and rewards come to be distributed, there is great pressure for teachers to "pay" attention to what is tested, often overruling their own sense of priorities and sensibilities.

We view this trend with some alarm, particularly given the overwhelming political nature of decisions regarding what is tested in the schools. There are no "facts" which stand free from a system of belief. Neutrality is a myth. Someone's interests are being advanced and other interests are marginalized in selecting curriculum to teach in the schools. Because teachers stand at the center of the delivery system in schooling, they cannot be removed from the scene, but their personal sense of priorities can be eroded and blunted by high-stakes testing systems (Tanner, 1992, pp. 9–10). Often the only thing truly balancing a curriculum is the *common sense* of the *classroom teacher*. While it can sometimes be wrong, rarely is it wrong for very long. And for much of the time teachers have a sense of what is important of all the things they could teach. The genius of curriculum development is to "capture" that innate sense of importance from teachers in the translation from purpose and aims to curriculum content and classroom activities. (See Chapter 2 for the discussion about schools as organizations.)

The Challenge of Total Quality Management

W. Edwards Deming's work (1986, 1993) has become well known globally. We discussed it earlier in Chapter 3. He was considered the master architect of a revitalized Japanese economy after World War II had left that country devastated. But his work in education has been sadly misconstrued. In fact, Deming did not speak about education directly until very late in his life (1993, pp. 148–157). While he was laudatory of Japanese management, he was equally critical of Japanese schooling practices.

From his observations about organizations that supposedly epitomized the essence of his managerial outlook, he derived fourteen aphorisms. They are shown in Table 3 with practices in education that support or negate them. Deming had little patience with managerial practices which assumed individuals possessed control over their work lives, but in reality had very little. He was a true organizational radical in that he challenged conventional wisdom regarding productivity. Deming focused on the entire range of organizational criteria that impinged upon productivity, and these were almost always controlled by top management. He was vigorously opposed to systems of counting and rewarding people revolving around variables over which they had no or only marginal control such as MBO (management by objectives). He tirelessly pointed out that such schemes rooted in quotas and slogans created *suboptimization* within an organization, i.e., the situation where a subunit is successful at the expenses of the whole organization. He was against merit pay plans or job target setting by numerical standards or any scheme which robbed people of "pride of workmanship" (p. 24).

Table 3

DEMING'S FOURTEEN POINTS COMPARED TO EDUCATIONAL PRACTICES IN THE SCHOOLS

	Deming TQM Points	*School Practices For*	*School Practices Against*
1.	Create constancy of purpose.	strategic planning	no planning
2.	Adopt a new philosophy.	strategic planning	annual budgeting
3.	Cease dependence on inspection to achieve quality.	authentic assessment	standardized testing for accountability
4.	Cease awarding business on cost.	concept of equity	job to low bidder
5.	Improve constantly.	annual planning	fads, one-shot change efforts
6.	Institute on-the-job training.	constant staff development	unplanned staff development
7.	Institute leadership.	reward leaders, risk-takers	reward rule followers
8.	Drive out fear.	open communication	chain-of-command
9.	Break down barriers.	curriculum chunking	departmentalization
10.	Eliminate slogans.	create group synergy	individual work targets
11.	Eliminate quotas/MBO.	create group synergy	focus on individual teachers
12.	Remove barriers.	pride in work done	merit pay
13.	Initiate self-improvement.	focus on growth	focus on failure
14.	Initiate transformation.	everybody involved	top management only

He saw many pay plans that focused on individual workers as creating an atmosphere of fear where change was impeded and adversarial relations developed which impeded organizational creativity and responsiveness.

Deming's principles challenge many conventional ideas of schooling in the U.S., Japan, and the world. He was opposed to creating artificial "winners and losers" and thus to standardized achievement testing (English & Hill, 1994, p. 4). He was opposed to all forms of competition with the exception of games in schools. He was opposed to conventional systems of grading, saying, "There is no scarcity of good pupils. There is no scarcity of good people. There is no reason why everyone in a class should not be in the top grade" (1993, p. 151). Another practice which produces false scarcities is that of ability grouping or tracking.

Deming saw departmentalization as inherently a poor way to create organizational *synergy*. Departmentalization created barriers. Barriers led to internal rivalries and competition which in turn produced suboptimization. Deming was against *inspection* as an effective antidote to quality in any organization. Nearly all of the statewide testing movement is aimed at *inspecting quality* as opposed to *building it in via curriculum development.*

The schooling practices that support Deming's ideas of *quality* were those that encouraged people to work together, across departments and divisions, that focused on growth, rewarded risk-taking and creativity, and open communication (see Bradley, 1993). He believed everyone's responsibility was to transform the organization, not just the workers, nor simply management.

Curriculum chunking "is a swath of curriculum that includes many concepts, ideas, values, skills, knowledge, and attitudes. It is a large interconnected fabric of interdisciplinary experiences and activities" (English & Hill, 1994, p. 72).

If one uses the "chunking" idea, one is rejecting "behaviors" as desirable "ends" of curriculum. A "chunk" of curriculum is worthwhile to learn in itself. It requires no other justification, and it is not a means to an end. It is like Deming's concept of the intrinsic idea of learning. The joy of learning is *in learning*. All humans can and have done it. No external rewards are necessary to "make" humans learn.

Deming's ideas were not particularly novel. Applied on a grand scale in war-weary Japan, they appeared to have worked a "miracle" there. Deming's ideas are rooted in classical management literature, notably McGregor's (1960), *The Human Side of Enterprise*.

Yet Deming was no saint and his vision of the future was limited (English, 1994, p. 212). He never challenged the role of hierarchy or the existence of bureaucracy. He never poked a question at managerial authority except to say it was misused. This "blind side" to his work often led overzealous companies to engage in "top-down meddling" (Gordon, 1994, A12).

Two Ways of Thinking About Curriculum Guides

With Deming's work as contextual background, there are two major approaches to creating curriculum guides. The first is the *behavioral* and the second is the *constructivist*. (See Chapter 5 for additional discussion of these learning theories.)

The *behavioral approach* envisions curriculum guides as specific templates which link teaching to learning by building detailed linkages between them. Teachers *follow* guides to attain desired and required pupil learning. Guides are *work specifications*. They are as detailed as need be, given the complexity of the learning desired and the presence of high-stakes testing to assess it.

In the *behavioral approach* the main emphasis for the teacher is "how" to successfully conduct lessons to *transmit* the curriculum in such a way that prespecified outcomes are attained. The idea of "coverage" fits this model. There is nothing inherently "wrong" with this concept. We might even say it is the dominant one in theory, though not necessarily in practice in most schools. The *behaviorist approach* is the one people tend to talk about. Behaviorists start thinking about developing guides by creating goals and moving towards objectives through *needs assessments*.

The *constructivist approach* abandons the means/ends dichotomy and sees curriculum in chunks, containing endless possibilities, with considerable room for both teachers and students to select and engage in learning that is meaningful to them. Constructivists do not envision all learning as capable or desirable of being prespecified. Personal meaning cannot be prespecified and must be "open."

Let us discuss how these two approaches differ through a common set of steps by which curriculum guides *could* be developed.

Step 1: Defining the Purpose of Curriculum Guides

Both approaches would envision curriculum as a set of documents *for teachers* primarily, though constructivists would see students as more active partners with teachers than behaviorists. Behaviorists see curriculum as more of a shaping tool than constructivists. Behaviorists like detail. Constructivists see detail as providing models but not prespecified channels to be followed.

Step 2: Defining the Content of Curriculum Guides

For behaviorists, curriculum content is primarily the delineation of facts and knowledge with attention on some occasions to processes. Behaviorists see curriculum content as *paths* to take to attain prespecified *results*. Behaviorists have linked ends definition to be part of means specification in the form of the *behavioral objective* (Mager, 1962). A *behavioral objective* has measurement of the learning outcome "built in" to its form. For example, "At the end of the unit on the Civil War, the student will be able to list three probable causes which led to it." Now "the unit" may contain many things, but *it must* contain and teach the "three probable causes" which led to it. Furthermore, this result takes precedent over anything else that might be learned. Nearly all other learning has been pushed aside, or *marginalized.*

The *constructivist* would reject such delineations as arbitrary and superficial. The constructivist would be content with allowing students to examine the American Civil War with many themes in mind and with many different connections. The learner "engages" in the content, but prespecified learning that is deemed fit for all children no matter what the context or circumstance would be quite rare. If one takes into account individual learning rates of students based on their unique development, the result will be different outcomes.

Individualized instruction therefore has two meanings. In the behaviorist model, individualized instruction refers to tactics the teacher employs to "reach" all students. It refers to such things as using different tacks for engagement, motivation and follow-through. It *does not mean* that learners select or reject content which must be learned. It refers to the designation of *variable means* to attain *prespecified universal* ends.

With the constructivists, individualized instruction means that there is "room" for the selection of content and activities which would lead to varying outcomes. Constructivists consider *variable means* as *ends themselves.* The "means" are the "ends" in the constructivist model of curriculum.

Step 3: Selecting the Format of Curriculum Guides

Behaviorists are anchored to ideas of *efficiency.* They see time lost as a problem. They want to cut immediately to the problem, engage in solving it, and attain the results. They want to reduce *waste.*

Constructivists see learning as inherently serendipitous. Since learning is enjoyable and pleasurable, time engaged in the process is neither wasted, nor can it be *efficient*.

These two viewpoints produce very different ideas of curriculum formats. *Behaviorists* want "lean and mean," "user-friendly" curriculum guides which contain all relevant information and nothing more, and which lead to optimization of results with minimal effort.

Constructivists want basically very loose statements or even "blank pages" where they can write the curriculum as they go, or as learners "discover" it. Behaviorists see constructivists as wasteful, fuzzy-minded romantics. Constructivists see behaviorists as preoccupied with trivia and detail which drive out the enjoyment in learning inherent to all humans, leading to boredom or rebellion in schools. Behaviorists talk about *mastery*. Constructivists talk about *engagement* and *intensity*.

Step 4: Specifying Alignments to Tests

Behaviorists are concerned about alignment (matches) to tests because tests are tools to determine quality and accountability. Constructivists see current testing as corruptive of the process of learning and teaching. Testing drives out serendipity. It creates schooling sterility, particularly if there are rewards and consequences which follow test score publication.

Constructivists decry the hollow emphasis on tests much the way Deming protested against the concept of *inspection*. Constructivists see tests as diagnostic, not as devices to frighten teachers into teaching content in which they do not believe. Constructivists see the child as "in control" of the curriculum and learning, and not the state (see Dewey, 1902). Behaviorists see children as *means* to the state's ends. Constructivists see children as *ends themselves*. The idea of *alignment* to a constructivist is not to match the test to the curriculum but to match the child to the curriculum and perhaps later to a test.

Step 5: Field Testing Curriculum Guides

Since behaviorists see curriculum as providing *directions* to teachers on at least *what to teach*, guides should be field tested to ascertain if they do so expeditiously, i.e., unambiguously and efficiently. Since constructivists see curriculum guides as much more open-ended, ambiguity is built in and there is not a need to "field test" guides. In the constructivist approach, field testing occurs everyday.

Step 6: Adoption of Curriculum Guides

In the behaviorist model, curriculum should be field tested, improved, and finally adopted as specific work statements aligned with extant tests. Constructivists would be hard pressed to have curriculum adopted except as the most general kind of policy statement.

It should be clear that the *concept of accountability* is superbly fitted to the *behaviorist mind-set.* Behaviorists are oriented to quantify and measure. To them constructivists appear to be hopeless idealists who can't cope with modern demands for precise means/ends relationships and the quest for the *one right method.* Behaviorists see constructivists as "anti-accountability," or "irresponsible" quacks, misfits in the age of school reform.

Constructivists view behaviorists as "efficiency experts" a la Frederick Taylor's scientific management. They view behaviorism applied as a kind of pseudo-science, a form of civil religion of short-term, shallow thinking about the purposes of education and schooling. Constructivists see accountability as a corruptive influence on what makes human learning enjoyable and powerful. Constructivists see adoption of curriculum guides as an unnecessary political act interfering with teaching and learning in schools. Table 4 outlines some major differences between behaviorism and constructivism.

Issues in Developing Guides

What Should Guides Look Like?

The format of a guide is its physical shape and internal layout. Too little thought is given to format with the result that substantive content may rarely be used because guides are as thick as a telephone directory and tip the scales in weightiness. And they can cost a bundle to produce. A student told us recently about developing guides in his district, one comprised of 250 teachers. Over a five-year period about $150,000 was spent (primarily for consultants and substitute teacher pay) to produce catalog size, three-ring binder guides. Now most sit on shelves and are only dusted off when the board asks about them or there may be a periodic internal need to refer to them.

Guides should be "user" friendly. They should fit the work situation and enable the faculty to focus on the essentials for purposes of making

Table 4
MAJOR DIFFERENCES BETWEEN BEHAVIORISM AND CONSTRUCTIVISM AT A GLANCE

Variable	Behaviorism	Constructivism
Advocate	B. F. Skinner	Jean Piaget
Epistemology	environmental determinism	genetic determinism
View of Learning	external stimulus/response	internal development
Curriculum content	externally set, specific	internally defined, general
Sequence strategy	logical, simple to complex	psychologically determined
Focus	learned similarities, lock-step	learner differences, maturational
Classroom activities	pre-defined and set by teacher or system	self-selected by learners
Preferred assessment strategies	criterion referenced tests or norm referenced tests	authentic assessment, projects, exhibitions

necessary curricular improvements. Functional guides focus and connect the work of teachers. They are well-organized, easy to read, and easy to update.

Debates sometimes rage regarding format, particularly whether the traditional three-ring binders are the way to go versus thin, stapled "flight guide" size guides. Recently, some districts have developed guides that are more tabular in form with components listed briefly in columns and rows. Such a format allows components to be interfaced explicitly. Our recommendation is that format should be discussed by *the staff* of the local school or district in terms of practicality criteria. Such a decision should never be made by supervisors.

What Should Be the Components of a Guide?

Lively debates are usually held about what should be in a curriculum guide. The discussion itself can be a rich staff development activity. At a minimum we feel that guides should:

- define what is to be taught
- describe the means of assessment to be used

- provide linkages to instructional materials, especially textbooks if they are a dominant mode of curriculum delivery.
- provide cues for the teacher for delivery
- indicate *ranges* of time to be spent on objectives or clusters of objectives

The presence of *behavioral objectives* may be a requirement for the behaviorist. On the other hand, many functional curriculum guides from the constructivist perspective do not include them. It is important that a clear charge is given for what the teacher is to do, even if the outcomes of teaching activities are not defined precisely.

We feel strongly that time needs to be a component because schools today have an "overcrowded" curriculum—the day (as we saw in Chapter 6) has not been extended for decades, yet more and more content is expected to be taught. Without the parameter of time (*a constant*), the designed curriculum has a proclivity to become larger than the time available to deliver it. In essence, one can design a plane that is too heavy to fly. No pilot (teacher) would want to be held accountable for achieving lift-off. And this is particularly the case today, where schools and other organizations are often subjected to severe political and economic pressures and expectations, pressures and expectations that are often unfair and unrealistic (see Berliner & Biddle, 1995).

Lastly, guides should be tailored to the local situation. The amount of detail and degree of flexibility in guides depends greatly on factors such as the degree of accountability expected locally to deliver the prescribed curriculum, staff expertise, experience, and turnover, and range and diversity of students served (see English, 1992, pp. 44–46 for further discussion).

The Role of Technology*

Computers and accompanying software hold considerable potential for the development of guides. The problems of updating could be solved if guides were on disks. As teachers edit their guides they could share their ideas with colleagues via local networks. As district committees work on altering guides, the information could be shared among all relevant staff groups.

---

*We are indebted to Doctor Jurg Jenzer, Principal of the Putney Central School, Putney, VT, for these technology suggestions.

Shortcuts to Guide Content

There is no need to begin a process of developing guides from "ground zero." It is eminently sensible to borrow guides from wherever one can in initiating the process. Other local districts, districts such as ones in Aurora and Denver, Colorado, sell them; departments of education such as the Wisconsin Department of Public Instruction (which sells them, too), the national ASCD *Curriculum Handbook,* and the Kraus *Curriculum Resource Handbooks* (hard copy) and *Curriculum Development Library* (microfiche) are also rich sources of content.

Curriculum Mapping

Mapping was created as a technique to chart the *taught curriculum* as opposed to analyzing the *written curriculum* (English, 1980). It is grounded in teachers' sense of time, the present rather than the future (Lortie, 1975). By comparing the discrepancies between the taught and specified (written) curriculum, adjustments could be made to bring about better alignment. Mapping in this application is *behaviorist.*

Under any circumstance, mapping occurs *after teaching,* not before. It can be utilized in the constructivist model for curriculum development to reveal patterns teachers took in making sense of the curriculum. The patterns discerned become the *taught curriculum.* The only difference between the two approaches is that the *behaviorist* would compare the patterns to prespecified ones and results. The constructivist would see the patterns as definitive of what was meant by a specific group of children and teachers as they *defined* the curriculum (see English & Steffy, 1983). Let us take an example of a curriculum map and note the two differences in interpretation.

The map shown in Table 5 regarding three tenth-grade U.S. history teachers shows time spent by half-periods (.5) on a hypothetical 180-day school year. To read a line of the map take the curricular topic, "The Age of Big Business," as an example. Mrs. Cox spent five instructional periods on it. Mr. Pope taught the topic for two periods and Mr. Smith used five periods. Between the three U.S. teachers, they spent twelve instructional periods on the topic for an average time spent (ATS) of four periods per teacher. The range between the three teachers (the difference between the highest and lowest amounts) was 3.0.

Between the three teachers the topics which received the greatest amount of time (on the average, or ATS) were:

1. World War II
2. The Civil War
3. World War I

However, here are the topics given most attention *by teacher.*

Cox	Pope	Smith
1. World War II	1. The Civil War	1. World War II
2. The Sixties	2. Transportation	2. World War I
3. The New Century	3. War with Mexico	3. Vietnam

Variations between teacher can usually be explained by the interests of the teachers and students on the topic to be studied and/or the availability or suitability of relevant materials (films, textbooks, etc.) to assist teaching.

If one were to examine the map by the topics of the greatest *differences* between teachers (established by the range), then they would be:

1. Reconstruction
2. Transportation
3. War with Mexico

A behaviorist would examine the map and focus on these questions:

1. Was the time spent on the most important topics as established by the curriculum framework, policy, or law?
2. Was the least time similarly construed?
3. Were deviances or variations between teachers important discontinuities?
4. What were the *causes* of the differences? Were differences caused by attempts to individualize instruction or by lack of teacher interest or competence?
5. Mr. Pope failed to teach 17 percent of the curriculum. What were the reasons for this?
6. Several topics show very wide variance between teachers. How can such variances be reduced to improve focus between teachers?
7. What do end-of-course exams show about pupil learning? Are there areas where learning is not occurring as specified?

A constructivist would ask these questions:

1. What important patterns among the three teachers show commonalities and differences?

Table 5
UNITED STATES HISTORY
TENTH GRADE CURRICULUM MAP
ACTUAL TIME SPENT FROM TEACHER RECORDS
(TIME BY .5 INSTRUCTIONAL PERIODS)

| Topic | History Department Teachers | | | | | |
	Cox	Pope	Smith	Total	ATS	Range
Age of Discovery	2.0	1.0	2.0	5.0	1.66	1.0
Colonization	3.0	1.0	4.0	8.0	2.66	3.0
English Colonies	5.0	2.0	3.0	10.0	3.33	3.0
American Revolution	5.0	15.0	4.0	24.0	8.10	11.0
Confederation	2.0	.5	.5	3.0	1.00	1.5
Constitution	10.0	2.0	11.0	23.0	7.66	9.0
New Government	1.0	.5	2.0	3.5	1.16	1.5
Washington/Adams	3.0	5.0	4.0	12.0	4.00	2.0
Jefferson	2.0	0.0	2.0	4.00	1.33	2.0
War of 1812	4.0	11.5	3.0	18.50	6.16	8.5
Industrial Revolution	10.5	10.0	5.0	25.50	8.50	5.5
Westward Movement	10.0	14.0	8.0	32.00	10.66	6.0
Missouri Compromise	.5	1.0	1.5	3.00	1.00	1.0
Transportation	4.0	20.0	3.0	27.00	9.00	17.0
Jacksonian Democracy	1.0	1.0	2.0	4.00	.75	1.0
War with Mexico	2.0	15.0	1.0	18.00	6.00	14.0
Territorial Slavery	1.0	4.0	1.0	6.00	2.00	3.0
Kansas Struggle	3.0	0.0	4.0	7.00	2.33	4.0
Social Progress	5.0	0.0	5.0	10.00	3.33	5.0
The Civil War	10.0	25.0	5.0	40.00	13.33	20.0
Reconstruction	5.0	2.0	4.0	11.00	3.66	3.0
The New West/South	2.0	10.0	4.0	16.00	5.33	8.0
Age of Big Business	5.0	2.0	5.0	12.00	4.00	3.0
Political Reforms	4.0	0.0	2.0	6.00	2.00	4.0
War with Spain	3.0	0.0	2.0	5.00	1.66	3.0
The New Century	11.5	1.0	10.0	22.50	7.50	10.5
World War I	8.0	10.0	15.0	33.00	11.00	7.0
Harding/Coolidge	4.0	0.0	3.0	7.00	2.33	4.0
The Depression	5.0	2.0	5.0	12.00	4.00	3.0
Spanish Civil War	3.0	2.0	3.0	8.00	2.66	1.0
World War II	18.0	5.5	19.0	42.50	14.16	13.5
The U.N.	5.0	1.0	10.0	16.00	5.33	9.0
Korean War	5.0	5.0	5.0	15.00	5.00	0.0
The Sixties	12.5	10.0	10.0	32.50	10.83	2.5
Vietnam	5.0	1.0	12.5	18.50	6.16	11.5
TOTALS	180.0	180.0	180.0			
Percentage of Curriculum Taught	100%	83%	100%			
% Time Used	100%	100%	100%			

2. In what ways do the differences reflect student engagement or lack of engagement with the curriculum?

For example, only nineteen of thirty-five topics show a variance of more than three full periods. This means that only 54 percent of the topics revealed significant variance in time spent. This is much too much *conformity* to argue that significant pupil engagement has occurred among the three teachers. Small bands of differences negate pupil interest. Teachers were not paying enough attention to finding ways to connect to the interest levels of their students.

It ought to be clear that *behaviorists* see differences as problems, while *constructivists* see conformity as the problem. Any conformity over too many topics can only mean that teachers are ignoring the profound differences which are assumed to exist in their classroom between students.

Behaviorists see variance as aberrance. While they do not want to see strict conformity, they view significant differences as too idiosyncratic and envision the curriculum as a way of "tightening" or "focusing" the behaviors of teachers towards more specific targets (goals or objectives).

The Benefits of Mapping

As a tool, curriculum mapping can be seen as a process for determining finding out how much conformance/variance exists within the actual curriculum being taught. The interpretation of the mapping data will vary according to the persuasion of the observer.

The mapping technique described in this chapter could be classed as a "Type II" map in that it addresses the dimensions of *content* and *time*. One can do a "Type I" map that just addresses content—what is included or excluded from a curriculum. The particular curriculum can be a year or semester course at the secondary level, or subjects taught across grades at the elementary level. Although not very sophisticated, we have found that Type I maps can be "powerful" learning tools for teachers. "Simply" becoming aware of what the patterns are among colleagues in terms of what is or is not taught can lead to important (and sometimes conflictual) discussions. But adding the dimension of "time" always leads to even more rich and evocative dialogue.

The third dimension of mapping is that of *sequence.** Such mapping becomes complicated and must be carried out for longer periods of time than need be the case with Type I or II approaches. But there can be high payoff through Type III mapping because the issue of *ordination* is central to many curricula.

Mapping can also address the issues of slack, overage, substitution, and repetition. *Slack* is when most of the prescribed curriculum was delivered and the teacher has time to teach other material. *Overage* is when 100 percent of the allotted time was used but not all of the curriculum was delivered. *Substitution* is when a teacher eliminates some content and replaces it with content not in the prescribed curriculum. *Repetition* is when content is repeated either knowingly or unknowingly.

As is the case with curriculum guides, today it is possible to utilize technology for mapping. Software is available or could be written that would enable a school or district to engage in the mapping process through computers. Mapping data can also be portrayed graphically via bar charts and histograms.

The context for mapping is critical for its successful use. If teachers work in a harsh and punitive environment, they will very likely see mapping as an accountability tool to give administrators more leverage over what they do in their classrooms. In such an environment, proposing mapping through technology would no doubt boomerang. Conjured up would be visions of "big brother or sister" snooping in the work place. Thus, mapping data more likely would be of questionable validity because they might be manipulated out of fear. Mapping data are not to be used for evaluative purposes.

But in a positive professional environment, mapping can be a developmental tool to improve curriculum, to manage it more effectively. It can also be a stimulating staff development tool. Teachers will recognize that to be more accountable to the public for delivering the approved curriculum, it will be to everyone's advantage to close the curricular gaps that ought not to be there. Teachers will recognize that mapping can create a more collegial base for curriculum development and problem solving because it is rooted in data and not opinion. Teachers will recognize that an overloaded curriculum is an unmanageable curricu-

---

*Anyone interested in learning more about the finer distinctions between these three approaches to mapping should consult English, F. W. (1987), Chapter 7.

lum and that the curriculum needs to be designed so that it can be delivered.

Curriculum mapping is not a way to fine-tune a curriculum. Rather, it is a procedure to reveal gross trends in content, time, and sequence that may not be evident from classroom observations or even from examination of plan books and lesson plans. A penchant for over precision in the process strains credibility of outcomes and enhances the natural flaws in the process. Weinstein's approach to mapping is, in our opinion, an example of over precision (1986). So caution is in order when considering use of technology. Finally, mapping should be used *only* when it appears that alignment is not resulting in desired data. Mapping too frequently can subtract from its value.

Summary

The construction of curriculum guides is a necessary activity to provide a teacher with **directions** or a **framework** in which to function in a classroom. School curricula definition is a shared responsibility between largely state-local governing bodies, but teachers are expected to know how to translate the definitions into meaningful classroom interactions with students.

Curriculum guides represent attempts to both translate and localize state curricular frameworks and intentions embodied in law and regulation. Depending upon the context of the translation process, guides may not be functional responses. For example, if the context is overwhelmingly *behavioral* with a high-risk state test at work, loosely created documents may lead to wide divergence which impede improved assessment results. On the other hand, if the state assessment system is based on authentic assessment strategies, too much conformity in teaching may impede pupil growth in problem solving and originality.

Total quality management, or *quality* as it is known, is a perspective made famous by W. Edwards Deming. It is not a science but an *ideology*. Resting on a series of assumptions, TQM aims to improve quality, however defined, and productivity, by not focusing on costs but on working conditions within an organization. These conditions are premised on ideas about how to treat people, what management must do to create working teams, and how to engage workers in continual improvement processes.

Deming's beliefs about education are radical; they would change many of the operational practices in schools all over the world. Deming was opposed to competitive practices, grading, schemes which created false scarcities and external rewards that destroyed the innate sense of the joy of learning. For the most part, his ideas have remained in business and the non-educational side of organizations.

Curriculum mapping is the practice of learning what the *taught curriculum* is by tracking it as it has been taught by teachers. Mapping can become an important data base to learn what the existing patterns of topics or processes are that have been taught. The interpretation of mapping data depends upon whether one sees variance as healthy or unhealthy in educational organizations.

DIALOGUE FOR IMPLEMENTATION

These are the questions most commonly asked of the authors about the ideas in this chapter.

1. Why has it been so difficult to develop quality curriculum guides for schools? Is it the fault of teachers who write most of them?

ANSWER: We believe that muddy purposes are the problem, not teachers. We hold administrators and supervisors responsible for the lack of clarity. If one is not sure what curriculum is to do, then most any product will be acceptable.

2. Wouldn't constructivists prefer an open-ended model for curriculum development?

ANSWER: For the uninitiated it might look the same, but it isn't. An open-ended guide developed to fit a clear picture of what the teacher and students are to do is different than a muddle where any response might be adequate.

ANSWER: Yes. Teachers will write more specific guides or plans when they become convinced that ambiguity is not purposeful or functional. Our experience has been that teachers will trade ambiguity for genuine improvement most of the time as long as they retain a semblance of control over other aspects of their work.

5. What's really revolutionary about *total quality management*?

ANSWER: If something is wrong in an organization it isn't the worker's fault but managers, because they control the conditions of the work itself. Poor quality or poor workmanship is management's province. It can't blame labor. If American products are second rate it's because America's management is second rate or has a second-rate mentality. In Deming's eyes, if schools were not right, one would never blame the teachers. One would start with legislatures, school boards and superintendents. They have the power.

6. What exactly is wrong with *behavioral objectives?*

ANSWER: Behavioral objectives emanated from evaluators, not curriculum developers. They have been overused in most curricular documents since they don't impact work as powerfully as let's say the textbook has done. Behavioral objectives are part of work measurement; in and of themselves they don't lead to improved work design.

7. What are the most common mistakes administrators make when approaching mapping?

ANSWER: Administrators become enamored with numbers and believe that they represent the whole curriculum. Numbers paint incomplete pictures. They indicate "what" and not "why." They are long on description and short on explanation. Too many administrators want more control over teachers and their work, and mapping seems to be the tool to do it. They ignore the human context and have a false idea of how to improve the curriculum.

8. What are the key variables in making sure mapping is successful?

ANSWER: The key variables are the leadership style of the principal or supervisor and his/her relationships with teachers, and the climate prevalent in the work place. We know where mapping has led to important adjustments being made in the curriculum, and where it led to nasty labor confrontations. The key is how it is introduced to teachers and how they perceive it. Great care should be taken in presenting it as a tool to help them solve real problems. Without that approach, it will simply be another paper exercise for teachers and viewed accordingly.

ACTIVITIES FOR PERSONAL AND STAFF DEVELOPMENT

We offer some examples of activities as "starters," but encourage readers to develop their own that will fit their situation.

1. Find the most recent curriculum guide in your school or school district. Which approach appears dominant, the *behaviorist* or the *constructivist?* How do you know?

2. Describe the problems you have faced as a classroom teacher with using a curriculum guide to configure your own teaching. How could such problems be ameliorated?

3. Using the list of possible components of guides listed earlier, have groups of teachers identify what they see as the most desirable ones for guides they'd develop. What are the commonalities among the groups and the differences (e.g., *time* is often a major bone of contention)?

4. Discuss the format for guides. How do you (or your group) feel about three-ring binders vs. flight guide or other formats? Collect some samples of guides from neighboring districts and compare formats.

5. What do you see as the major barriers to implementing some of Deming's ideas in schools? Have any been tried in your own situation? If so, discuss them.

6. Develop a list of the most common teacher complaints about the curriculum in your school system. How many would be solved by using mapping? Explain. Develop a rationale for mapping using these data.

7. Develop your own computerized program to perform the essential arithmetic (or statistical) operations with mapping data. Experiment with different graphic forms for illustrating mapping data.

8. Take a segment of your curriculum and do a Type I or II map. What do the results reveal? Have a group of colleagues do the same for courses they teach in common (e.g., sections of English, math, or history).

Chapter 9

ASSESSING STUDENT LEARNING

Wad-ja-get?

Educators have always been concerned with the assessment of student learning once students have received instruction in the prescribed curriculum. In the United States, *formal* evaluation of such outcomes has its origins in the common school movement in Massachusetts in the mid-1800s where Horace Mann helped develop oral and written means for judging learning and for keeping records of student achievement.

Since that time, educators have continued an ongoing debate about how to assess that learning (Robinson & Carver, 1989, pp. 3–20) and how to represent learning outcomes (Kirschenbaum, Simon, & Napier, 1971).

Central to that debate has been the issue of how such outcomes can be used as *feedback* to the system in order to improve system effectiveness and efficiency. (See the discussion about feedback in the "Quality of Assessment" section of Chapter 3. Also see a helpful book by Herman and Winters (1992), *Tracking Your School's Success* with its assumptions that outcomes can be related to organizational means.)

COMPONENTS OF ASSESSMENT

In this chapter we are concerned primarily with how to *assess* what has been learned (the completed work). We emphasize assessment rather than the traditional word *evaluation* because, as Figure 9.1 depicts, assessment (to estimate, not judge) is now seen by the education profession as the broader concept.

The figure helps outline the overall process. It shows that assessment is comprised of two functions—measurement and evaluation. "Testing"

NOTE: The authors thank Doctor Douglas Harris, Director of Curriculum, National Gardening Association, Burlington, VT, Doctor Herman Meyers, Chair, Department of Education, The University of Vermont, and Doctor Steven Sanborn, Director of Curriculum and Instruction, Chittenden Central Supervisory Union, Essex Junction, VT, for their critiques of this chapter.

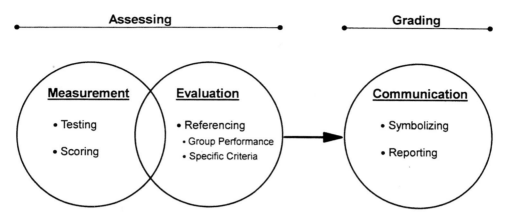

Figure 9.1. Assessing and Grading Student Achievement. From Robinson, G. E., & Craver, J. M. (1989): *Assessing and Grading Student Achievement* (Arlington, VA: Educational Research Service). Used with permission.

in the figure is to be interpreted generically as including norm-referenced tests and criterion-referenced tests for judging what has been learned (the traditional broad categories for classifying tests and other evaluation techniques) (Gronlund & Linn, 1990, pp. 13–17).

In recent years a third category, alternative assessment, has emerged. Because this chapter is not intended to be a primer on testing, it will include sections on only norm-referenced (standardized achievement) tests and alternative assessment which today are at the center of national, state, and local policy debates.

Once "testing" occurs, some kind of judgment (scoring) is made. Then the result(s) is referenced to some group or individual standard. Finally a "grade" is assigned with some indicator of achievement—a letter, a number, description of behavioral frequency, or description of performance based on a rubric. Currently we are in a state of transition from reliance on letters and numbers as indicators of achievement to more emphasis on verbal or written description of performance, often in reference to specific tasks or outcomes (*Educational Leadership*, October 1994). In any case, a report is made to communicate the "grade" to students, parents, school boards, and other appropriate parties (Robinson & Carver, 1989, pp. 2–3). Although the focus of this model and this chapter is on assessing student learning, data from the reporting can be used, combined with other kinds of information, for program evaluation purposes as well.

Ultimately, we believe that "To be useful to society, assessment must advance education, not merely record its status" (National Mathematical Sciences Board, 1993, p. 3). That is a major goal of this chapter, to assist readers in making the process of assessment **useful** to their clients and to society. This is only possible when goals are aligned with the means of assessment and, as Chapter 8 points out, curriculum and assessment are aligned.

> A good testing program should be supplementary not duplicative, usable not confusing, economical not burdensome, comprehensive not sporadic, suggestive not dogmatic, progressive not static. (Lien & Lien, 1980, p. 233)

Considering the accountability environment surrounding education today, it behooves schools to have an assessment plan and program. The Addison Northeast Supervisory Union District in Vermont is an example of a district that has responded to this challenge. Annually it publishes a thirty-page report to educators and the citizenry describing "the variety of assessment indicators used in the Union to understand student progress, determine student needs, and make instructional decisions" (Executive Summary, 1994). In it is information about the composition of the student body, an explanation about the Vermont assessment program results (to be explained later in this chapter), and SAT and CBTS scores.

In terms of curriculum management, work assessment (of learning) must connect with the work design (the prescribed curriculum) and the work (instruction). Attention to all three curricula is necessary in order to answer the question, "What is working?" or "How are we doing?" (Herman & Winter, 1992, pp. 17–20). Figure 9.2, redrawn with some different terms from when the model was introduced in Chapter 4, represents this focus.

TOTAL WORK FLOW

Noted earlier in Chapter 3, there are numerous design/delivery factors that influence the three curricula. A breakdown in any one of them (or a major weakness in one) can have a serious negative effect on student learning.

In addition, there are other causes of breakdowns or weaknesses in the relationships between the curricula such as lack of money, inadequate training of personnel, poor communications, unclear roles and responsibilities, lack of time, and other factors. In essence, all of these factors comprise the **total work flow** of the system including the organizational

Figure 9.2. The Interrelationships of School Work.

structure and the forces impacting decisions relative to that structure. Work flow is connecting means to ends.

Hence, sometimes no matter how well designed the curriculum is and how effectively it is delivered and assessed, it may be impeded from reaching its full potential because of factors within the total work flow. Educators must know how this work flow works if they are to remove other blocks to school improvement that are beyond the reach of curriculum management.

As is the case with other "models" that we have introduced in other chapters, we want to stress that the flow is recursive and not linear. Change is a dynamic, often unpredictable process.

Some of the classic problems in assessing curriculum as it relates to learning are that:

1. only a narrow band of the curriculum is examined
2. only a narrow range of results is examined
3. the range examined becomes a surrogate measure for the entire curriculum
4. work outcomes (assessments) are examined, but not the work and the work flow.

The above can lead to erroneous conclusions about the organization's effectiveness and efficiency. Let us examine these problems in more detail.

Standardized Achievement Tests and the Narrowness Problem

Standardized achievement tests consume an enormous amount of time and resources from schools. The pressures to give them are steady and real. They are "norm referenced," in that local scores are compared against a nationwide sample of scores that emerged from the test being given to students under the same conditions by the publishers. But they are not quality indicators of the status of the local curriculum unless the local system very intentionally finds ways to make that happen. This sample is called a norm group. Results can be reported by student, teacher, grade level, and by school. The emphasis is on **summative** (concluding) evaluation. (It should be noted that there are many kinds of standardized tests that are not "achievement" based, many of which are criterion and not norm-referenced.)

Typically, standardized achievement tests are used to make judgments about the curriculum. However, the extent to which they reflect accurately the real work design (curriculum) of the local area is unknown in most cases unless a district requests item analyses for specific feedback at the teacher and grade level. Even then, the local curriculum itself is not measured: it is only compared to a "hypothetical" common curriculum.

Suppose a test has a "content" match (or alignment) of only 30 percent to a given curriculum. Then the 30 percent is taken as a general indicator of 100 percent of the curriculum. When a school system publishes test results by grade and school, the public (and many professionals) assume that if math, reading, or writing scores are high (or low), the entire curriculum is equally as good (or bad) when this may not be so. This is a narrowness problem at the system level.

But there can be a narrowness problem at the classroom level as well with some teacher-made tests and the concept of "context" alignment. *Context alignment is when the content is taught through a method that facilitates or reinforces the learning.* Here is an example of "mis-alignment" from one of our graduate students.

> Some teacher-made tests at my middle school are suspect because of their contextual flaws. Most middle school students learn best when they are allowed to explore and think through problems. They tend to look at subject matter

globally and learn best when curricula are interrelated and not fragmented into individual departmentalized units. Most of our teachers have worked to bring their teaching in line with this philosophy. Yet last year, when the eighth grade final exams were analyzed, nearly 100 percent of our local tests consisted of multiple-choice questions. Nearly 40 percent of the students failed the exam.

Standardized achievement test batteries (and many teacher-made tests) slant heavily toward the lower end of the cognitive domain of learning (e.g., terminology, facts, conventions; Bloom, 1956) and do not provide data about pupil attitudinal growth. So standardized achievement measures are the most narrow indicator that a school system or school may use to determine the effectiveness of the total work flow. They are not so much inaccurate as inadequate, in that what they measure is only a slice of many other outcomes of curricular and instructional effort. But they have a place in the assessment program of a school/district, provided that they are selected carefully (to assess what the organization has decided *should* be taught—the "frontloading" as discussed in Chapters 4 and 5), and that educators are well aware of the pitfalls to avoid when using them (Worthen & Spandel, 1991). They are a solid predictor of student achievement relative to social economic status (SES) (Schneider & Houston, 1993, p. 8).

Work Outcomes and Suboptimization

Some educator/evaluators advocate concentrating on results, not attending very much to **how** or **why** such outcomes occur. The systems planning movement of the early 1970s, with its emphasis on "goals," "objectives," "targets," or "results" without simultaneously examining variables that affected those results, reinforced this narrow perspective. Arriving at the height of the behavioral objectives mania, the two together were a powerful force (e.g., American Association of School Administrators, 1973; Hostrop, 1973; Immegart & Pilecki, 1973; Odiorne, 1979).

Thus "outcomes" was the cast of the dominant literature of that era and it still has an impact on schools and other organizations— although the current iteration of that process, "strategic planning," has a step relating to an internal organizational analysis (e.g., Cook, 1990; Kaufman & Herman, 1990; McCune, 1986). However, today's "outcomes-based education" movement harkens back to the seventies emphasis:

Outcome-based education (OBE) has an intuitive appeal that hooks people. Simply set the outcomes you expect students to achieve, then teach and reteach in as many different ways and for as long as it takes until everyone meets them. (Evans & King, 1994, p. 12)

Eisner, in his insightful analysis of the evolution of educational evaluation, states that this focus on objectives or outcomes has had a delimiting effect on the practice of evaluation (1985, pp. 29–37).

These "product evaluators" essentially consider schools "black boxes," i.e., "unknown" internal processes, and focus on test scores instead. One way such an approach can be considered legitimate is to assume that: (1) all schools are essentially the same operationally—i.e., the same linkages exist in the same way in all; (2) all schools have sufficient resources to be held accountable for results; and (3) if 1 and 2 are not true, the total effects are trivial anyway.

Suppose that in a school system a single program consumes a large part of the total resources, such as is the case with special education funding in some states, or funding for drug, alcohol, and security systems in some cities (Lindsay, 1995). Since resources are limited, the flow of these resources to these programs enables them to be effective with their clientele. However, the loss of resources to other programs impedes their ability to be as effective or effective at all. The problem is one of **sub-optimization** (Immegart & Pilecki, 1973, p. 8; Juran, 1988, pp. 151–152) where a subunit is successful at the expense of the rest of the organization. This phenomenon is accentuated in decentralized organizations where central authorities lack the authority to deal with suboptimization problems.

Take the case of inner-city magnet schools which have been created to comply with the goal of integration. Integration is the superordinate objective. Learning goals are secondary. These magnet schools require additional resources, resources which might have been allocated to other schools. Magnets may be effective. Non-magnets may not be. As a result, the total school system is less effective. An evaluator looking only at work flow manifested in results might be misled.

Consider another example in which two school systems have installed new reading programs and a common standardized achievement test to assess them. The average test score for District A is higher than for District B, though both are similar socioeconomically.

A results-oriented evaluation might conclude that there are "better" teachers in A than B, when the reason may have little to do with motivation, training, or experience of the two teaching staffs. What if

District A has an aligned curriculum that insures that what is taught is congruent with the testing program, while B does not strive for such congruence? What if District A spends less per child than B, has larger class sizes than B, and fewer modern facilities? A reasonable conclusion might be that teachers are the difference.

"Black box" curriculum evaluators assume that whatever linkages exist for the schools in District A must also exist for District B when that may not be the case. As curriculum thinkers have made the ends of education the primary goal, they have too often ignored total work flow interaction.

The new federal "opportunity-to-learn standards" that are incorporated into the "Goals 2000" legislation speak to the issue of the total work flow and have the potential to counter black box thinking, because these standards address the underlying conditions of education that affect instruction and learning (U.S. Department of Education, May, 1994; Stevens, 1993). These conditions refer to issues such as student access to the core curriculum, time to learn what is taught, and the use of appropriate teaching methods to produce student achievement. "OTL standards seek to ensure that *all* [emphasis in the original] students are provided the learning experiences, conditions, and tools necessary to acquire the knowledge and skills expected of them" (Raugh, 1994, p. 1).

TRADITIONAL TESTING AND CURRENT TRENDS

Here readers may wish to reread the section, "The Impact of Testing" in Chapter 4 for background information on the frequency of standardized testing, money spent on it today, and the impact of tests on policy. A major question raised there is whether we give *too many* and *not too few* of these kinds of tests in schools.

The debate about assessment has accelerated dramatically in recent years. "Assessment" has become the dominant topic in the broad professional literature and in policymaking circles (McDonnell, 1994). It is close to being another "bandwagon" so often prevalent in the profession.

"Assessment" gets linked with terms such as "alternative," "authentic," and "performance," all of which signal a turning away from traditional approaches to "testing" represented by standardized and teacher-made "paper-and-pencil" tests. These terms began to creep into the journals in the mid-1980s, helped along considerably by a ground-breaking monograph published on the subject in 1988 by the National Association of Secondary School Principals (Archibald & Newmann, 1988).

Today, titles such as *A Practical Guide to Alternative Assessment* (Herman, Aschbacher, & Winters, 1992); *Assessing Student Outcomes* (Marzano, Pickering, & McTighe, 1993); *Assessing Student Performance* (Wiggins, 1993); *Classroom Assessment* (Popham, 1995); *Expanding Student Assessment* (Perrone, 1991); *Graduation by Exhibition* (McDonald et al., 1983); *Improving Student Achievement* (Steinberger, 1993); *Making Sense of Testing and Assessment* (American Association of School Administrators, 1993); *Measuring Up* (Rothman, 1995); and *The Changing Face of Testing and Assessment* (Hymes, 1991) pile up on the desks of educators. In addition, as we shall see in this chapter, professional journals such as *Educational Leadership* and *Phi Delta Kappan* have devoted major sections of recent issues to the topic.

What is causing this increased attention to "assessment" as opposed to "testing"? Marzano, Pickering, and McTighe (1993, pp. 9–20) state that three general factors account for the change.

The first is a recognition that education had to shift attention from assessing low-level functional skills and competencies to a broader array of outcomes such as creative thinking, decision making, and problem solving—outcomes which are necessary for all learners in a twenty-first century society (also see Darling-Hammond, 1993). (This shift is symbolized by the learning goals in "Goals 2000.")

The second is the shift away from behavioral theories that emphasize the accumulation of discrete knowledge and skills to "constructivism"—a conception of learning and teaching based on cognitive psychology which emphasizes the broader outcomes listed above. This shift toward constructivist teaching gains credence from the theory of "multiple intelligences" (e.g., Armstrong, 1994; Gardner, 1983; Gardner, 1993) and the notion of "dimensions of thinking" (Marzano, 1992). In the words of a representative of the Educational Testing Service:

> I concur that the standard methods of test theory do not suffice for solving many problems cast in the framework of what we are learning about how people acquire knowledge and competence. (Mislery, 1993, p. 20)

The third reason is the growing recognition that the traditional ways of recording and reporting student achievement (e.g., standardized test scores, letter grades) do not provide informative, diagnostic, and meaningful feedback about and to the learner, given the new emphasis on broader learning outcomes.

In reference to the last reason, a key event occurred in 1988. The "Cannell Report" concluded—after a survey of testing practices in the fifty states—that 90 percent of school districts claim that their standardized achievement test scores exceed the national average, and that about 70 percent of students tested nationwide are told that they are performing above the national average (1987). Since dubbed the "Lake Wobegon effect" after Garrison Keillor's mythical Minnesota town "where all the children are above average," the report symbolized national concerns about traditional testing. As Finn points out:

> So long as one selects the right measures, analyzes the results imaginatively, and interprets them in the most favorable light, one can readily convey the impression that the schools in Kansas or Portland or wherever are doing a respectable job. (Finn, 1991, p. 102)

In other words, it is possible to "backload" the curriculum to the tests so that alignment boosts test scores; hence, everyone can be "above average."

"FairTest," the National Center for Fair and Open Testing, has brought attention to additional concerns about standardized tests—concerns such as the overemphasis on them; the sometimes misuse of SAT and other scores for college admissions; the unfairness of SAT results relative to minority groups; and sex bias in various college admissions tests. Its many analytical reports and presentations at conferences and conventions, plus support from leading foundations, have enabled the organization to become highly influential in the field of assessment practices and policy development.

We see an additional reason, beyond the broad three identified by Marzano, Pickering, and McTighe, for the increased attention to alternative forms of assessment. It is that there is considerable evidence that more "authentic assessment" is a major factor in promoting student "engagement" in the learning process. It is more intrinsically motivating because it is more representative of "real world" tasks—tasks that are relevant to the learner's future. The assessments are connected more to "authentic work" than are standardized and other traditional forms of testing (Newmann, 1992, pp. 23–28).

How did standardized testing become so powerful a force in American education? The infant standardized testing movement began to gain acceptance in the years preceding World War I. The military needed to identify potential officers on the basis of competence rather than social class characteristics (the latter being a commonplace criterion in European nations). Testing was an objective means to achieve this goal while at the same time reflecting the American commitment to equal opportunity. And, as the movement gained credence, it gained more and more support in the general culture.

During the same period, school districts searched for ways to establish "objectively" how they compared to other districts or schools. In addition, the results of standardized tests could be used for program review, hiring and promotion, budgeting, and overall public relations and community support (Resnick, 1981). "By 1960, with the aid of funds available through the National Defense Education Act, it was a rare school district that could not boast its own standardized, norm-referenced testing program" (Madaus, 1985, p. 612).

But during the 1960s, changes were initiated that were to have significant implications for American education. Officials began to use tests to establish and implement state and federal education policy, reflecting a desire to not only inform policymakers about the condition of local education but to insure equality of educational outcomes (Madaus, 1985, p. 613). Gradually, the idea of national assessment gained support, as exemplified by the creation, in 1969, of the National Assessment of Educational Progress, "designed as a voluntary, cooperative program to answer questions such as: Are students learning more today than they did in the past? Is greater progress being made in some subject areas than in others? What education problems exist nationally?" (U.S. Department of Education, June, 1991).

During the 1970s minimal basic competency testing and local use of national standardized tests became the focus of assessment. Then in 1984, spurred by the 1983 publication of *A Nation at Risk* with its strong theme relating to traditional testing, former Secretary of Education Terrel Bell issued a wall chart that focused on state-by-state comparisons of SAT and ACT scores. Although widely criticized regarding the appropriateness of the comparisons, the idea of comparing states was rarely questioned (Salganik, 1985). Clearly, the political climate was shifting from the days when local control and local analysis dominated education.

This radical shift, given the traditions of state rights and local control, is exemplified by President Clinton's signing of the "Goals 2000: Educate America Act" in April 1994. This law, rooted in the "America 2000" strategy of the Bush administration, for the first time in the nation's history codifies eight national goals for public elementary and second-ary schools, including establishing voluntary national content standards and achievement tests (Pitsch, 1994). (However, with the change in the composition of the Congress as of November 1994 to a Republican majority in the House and the Senate, considerable opposition has emerged to the Act on the grounds that it represents additional federal interference in state and local control of education [Pitsch, 1995].)

So, while there has been an explosion of interest in, publications about, and training in the use of alternative forms of assessment, there is also a strong national push to increase the use of standardized achievement testing, a push that may now be countered by a new political reality.

> Here we have the major paradox of the reform movement of the eighties: significant improvements in the quality of schooling are impossible without structural changes, but increased dependence on mass administered tests at all levels has had the effect of strengthening existing structures and forms of control. (Berlak, 1992, p. 7)

These opposing forces demonstrate how the educational system often is pulled in opposite directions, thus insuring a recursive rather than linear pattern to the total work flow discussed earlier. The result is that public schools are on a possible "collision course," squeezed between traditional and emerging forms of testing (Darling-Hammond, 1993).

This clash is likely to be with us for the foreseeable future. Even if the economy continues to slowly but steadily improve, the current budget-reducing and tax-cutting modes of both major parties and President Clinton virtually insures that less and less money will be available to schools from the federal government. The "Improving America's Schools Act" with its infusion of $60 billion of federal funds into public school coffers over the next five years will fuel federal motivation to influence state and local education toward the direction articulated in "Goals 2000." But if there is successful opposition to the program and its impact is reduced, there could well be a move to renege on the $60 billion itself. Then more of the control will flow back to the states.

Oregon is a state that demonstrates this trend toward state control. In 1990 voters passed Measure 5 that limited local property taxes and shifted the bulk of financing of local schools to the state. As a result, "Measure 5 also effectively shifted control of Oregon's nearly 300 school districts to the state level. With funding comes control" (Conley, 1994, p. 3).

STANDARDS AND HIGH-STAKES TESTING

In concert with these trends—and gaining force—are those who advocate raising standards for grade promotion and high school graduation and creating "high-stakes" tests.

What is a standard? We like Wiggins' definition.

> A standard offers an objective ideal, serving as a worthy and tangible goal for *everyone* (emphasis in original)—even if, at this point in time, for whatever reason, some cannot (yet!) reach it. (1993, p. 286)

A key point is that standards are always out of reach; they are not met easily.

Good schools have always had high standards without state mandates. In some states mandates become part or all of the standards. In New York, for example, students have the option of earning a Regents diploma provided they demonstrate competency by passing Regents Examinations based on state courses of study (Bureau of Elementary and Secondary Testing Programs, January 1993).

What is new is the thrust at the *federal* level to raise standards, which began with the creation of the National Education Goals Panel that monitors the nation's progress toward the six national goals established through the America 2000 program of the Bush administration (U.S. Department of Education, April 1991), and now the eight goals of "Goals 2000." The second step was through the Goals 2000 legislation which includes a National Education Standards and Improvement Council that will "examine and certify voluntary national standards; state standards for content, student performance, and opportunities to learn; student assessment systems"; and a National Skill Standards Board which will "stimulate the development of a voluntary national system of occupational standards and certification" (U.S. Department of Education, May 1994). However, to date no appointments have been made to the council, and there is considerable congressional and state opposition to it (Diegmueller, 1995, p. 8). The board is in operation. Noteworthy is that achievement tests play a central role in the legislation.

What is also new is the accompanying effort of national professional organizations to develop standards in separate subject fields. The initiating organization was the National Council of Teachers of Mathematics which, in 1989, issued its landmark publication, *Curriculum and Evaluation Standards for School Mathematics.* The document has become a model for other such associations that are working to develop standards in their fields (Diegmueller, 1994).

Here are examples of standards. In mathematics:

> NCTM Standard 3: Mathematics as Reasoning. In grades 9–12, the study of mathematics should include numerous and varied experiences that reinforce and extend logical reasoning skills so that all students can make and test conjectures; formulate counterexamples; follow logical arguments;....(National Council of Teachers of Mathematics, 1989, p. 143)

In social studies (proposed):

> National Council for the Social Studies V: Individuals, Groups, and Institutions (early grades): (a) identify roles as learned behavior patterns in group situations such as student, family member, peer play group member, or club member; (b) give examples of and explain group and institutional influences such as religious beliefs, laws, and peer pressure, on people, events, and elements of culture....(Diegmueller, 1994, p. 14)

States, too, are getting into the act. A recent 50-state survey revealed that 31 have begun work on content standards (Diegmueller, 1995, p. 15).

Finally, a major private venture into the standards endeavor is the New Standards Project, a joint venture of the Learning Research and Development Center at the University of Pittsburgh and the National Center on Education and the Economy. Funded by foundations, the project aims to develop performance standards, authentic assessments, and strategies for professional development that can be used by states and national professional organizations that are engaged in similar ventures (Simmons & Resnick, 1993). The project intends "to make thinking, problem-solving, and communicating skills 'count' by creating and fostering assessments designed to elicit them" (Viadero, 1994, p. 22).

The standards train is on the track and steaming ahead. It is generating intense national debate on issues such as whether we need national standards at all, or whether standards should be established mostly locally in keeping with the history of American education, yet compared to the template of some national or maybe even international benchmarks. It is also generating debate on the issue of whether to raise standards first and then pull students up to them or whether, given the inequalities of educational opportunity across the nation's schools and systems, more resources should be allocated first in order to enhance their learning opportunities and hence meet the standards.

Some analysts are beginning to point out that a standards-based or proficiency-based system is a minefield of unanswered questions. How many standards and accompanying benchmarks should there be? How can proficiency in meeting a standard be determined? What are the elements of adequate proficiency? How much detailed "proof" is needed to assess a desired level of performance? Each level of detail leaves more "questions, ambiguities, and inferred meanings" because there is an "inherent arbitrariness" to the process (Conley, 1993, p. 32).

Clearly, all of these questions and their potential answers contain significant implications for the assessment of learning. To make sense out of the plethora of standards pouring into schools—and recognizing that most districts and schools do not have the time and capacity to "wade through" them for local application—the Mid-Continent Regional Educational Laboratory has distilled the standards from all the national subject area associations into a single "user-friendly" document (Kendall & Marzano, 1994).

The many questions and concerns have propelled the standards movement to the top of the political agenda of the Republican majority in Congress. Never friendly to the idea of national standards, the more conservative wing of the party has raised additional questions and issues that have led a national education newspaper to state:

> The movement to set national academic standards, in which several years of work and several millions of taxpayer dollars have been invested, is in danger of falling victim to a political backlash. (Diegmueller, 1995a, p. 1)

Accompanying this possible backlash is the lack of support for implementing the National Education Standards and Improvement Council. Clearly, the pace of the national standards movement has slowed sharply with responsibility reverting to the states.

Paralleling the standards movement is what is commonly referred to as "high stakes testing, . . . the use of test results to make important decisions about the test taker" (Mehrens, 1994, p. v). Just as we have always had high standards, we have always had high-stakes tests. What is new is to deny students a high school diploma or not recommend them for a college based on **test results**, not transcript grades. Tests of this kind, connected to the standards movement, evaluate what students know and are able to do based on their education. Much of the evaluation depends on the professional **judgment** of educators, grounded in performance criteria and quantitative or qualitative rating scales (Herman, Aschbacher, & Winters, 1992, pp. 44–79).

A prime example of such stakes is the development of a "Certificate of

Initial Mastery" by the New Standards Project. The intent is that one day it could "supercede the high school diploma as the basic educational credential sought by employers and by colleges" (Viadero, 1994, p. 23). "The idea is that all students are expected to meet the certificate standard and that it is the same for all students" (Tucker, 1993, p. 11).

The CIM generates additional questions relative to assessment. If a diploma is a "property right," will its denial—based on a test—withstand a challenge in court? If tests can be used for such a purpose, then what test quality will meet such a challenge? And, in keeping with traditions of local education, to what degree can local districts, with available resources, develop such "litigious proof" tests? Or can states and even national projects produce such tests?

The most notable response to some of these questions comes from recent events in the Littleton, Colorado school system, where Littleton High School, with board approval, had implemented a "high-stakes" program which required graduates (starting with the class of 1995) to pass nineteen outcomes-based competencies. For example, the communications competency required a student to "speak and write articulately and effectively" and "read and listen actively." In mathematics, a student "effectively applies mathematical principles and operations to solve a range of problems." Carnegie units or credits were no longer to be the base of graduation criteria (Westerberg & Westerberg, 1992, p. 36).

But in the winter of 1994, community opposition to the policy led to the ouster of several board members and their replacement with a majority of "back-to-the-basics" members who proceeded to "repeal the performance-based graduation requirements. Board members restored traditional requirements under which students must take certain courses to earn a diploma" (Bingham, 1994).

Reasons for the restoration included the community feeling that academics were being neglected in favor of less demanding and ill-defined subjects; that teachers were more concerned about shaping students' attitudes and beliefs than they were in insuring that they knew "the basics"; and a feeling that many graduation requirements were too vague and that the assessments were not technically sound enough to prevent someone from graduating. The performance-based system was allowed to remain as an option for classroom assignments (see Bradley, 1994 and David & Felknor, 1994).

Littleton may not be an aberration on the educational landscape. In 1991, Oregon passed a massive school-reform law, "The Oregon Educational Act for the Twenty-First Century." It contained provisions for promotion and graduation similar to those of Littleton High School. Currently, considerable opposition has emerged, most of it revolving around the promotion and graduation requirements. A strong effort is being mounted to either repeal major parts of the law or to repeal it altogether (Lively, 1995).

The demise of this system in Littleton, which had been crafted carefully beginning in 1987 with the infusion of significant local funds and about $300,000 in outside contributions (used mainly to pay for substitute teachers and after-hours time for teachers to write assessments and work on the standards) (Rothman, 1992, p. 23), supports McLaughlin's conclusion about "going slow" with high-stakes testing. After reviewing the work of several national experts on the subject of testing "as a reform strategy," she pointed out that this movement does not "fiddle at the margins of the classroom" but rather "reaches into the heart of the undertaking" (1991, p. 251).

But, as a recent survey of national and state policymakers' views toward assessment demonstrates, "going slow" will be extremely difficult in the present political climate. The survey showed that policymakers are not restrained from policy implementation because of technical questions or feasibility issues.

> They see an extraordinary window of opportunity in which a broad spectrum of constituents has endorsed the idea of national standards and a system of linked assessments. But they recognize that this policy window could close just as quickly as it opened, as new issues in education and other policy areas crowd assessment off the national agenda. (McDonnell, 1994, pp. vii–viii)

Here we have another example of the total work flow being affected by environmental forces.

Confusing isn't it? Just a few months after this national survey we hear the report that the national standards movement may "fall victim to a political backlash." The best advice we can offer within this swirl of shifting political sands is that it behooves local districts to formulate their own assessment policies if they want to establish some sense of control over this critical component of curriculum management.

ALTERNATIVE ASSESSMENT

"New" forms of assessment, "alternative," "authentic," or "performance," are, like standards and high stakes, not really new at all. Good teachers have always used them to evaluate the outcomes of student work, to get at the heart of real learning. Oral examinations, science fairs, writing portfolios, performances in the arts and in athletics, and making products in industrial arts and vocational subjects are just a few examples of such creative assessments. Today they are grouped under headings such as "portfolios," "demonstrations," "exhibits," and "profiles." These kinds of assessments have attracted increased attention in recent years because of the powerful trends described previously.

What do these umbrella terms mean? "Alternative" means options to traditional testing. "Authentic" means tests that are given under conditions representing closely a real-life context *as perceived by the learner.* "Performance" means that the learner has completed or demonstrated behavior that the assessor wants to measure—but may measure in a contrived situation (Meyer, 1992).

Wiggins contends that there is an important difference between an **assessment** and a **test.** He says that, "An assessment is a comprehensive, multifaceted analysis of performance; it must be judgement-based and personal" (1993, p. 13). A test, on the other hand, is an "instrument," a measuring device that is one component of the assessment process. Typically the notion of standardization is associated with tests, and the role of judgment is minimalized (and sometimes eliminated). Assessments are usually rooted in a **context,** whereas tests are usually **decontextualized** (pp. 206–236).

There are two other unusual aspects of alternative assessment. The first is that it is woven integrally into instruction. It measures key classroom objectives and the results should represent student performance. This process encourages **formative** feedback to the teacher and the learner so that each benefits through the process (Herman, Aschbacher, & Winters, 1992, pp. 2–5).

Finally, it is much more difficult to attain reliability with alternative assessments than with standardized tests. Raters need considerable training to insure scoring consistency because judgment is at the heart of alternative assessment. The possibilities of scorer or rater bias and even capriciousness are very real (Herman, Aschbacher, & Winters, 1992, pp. 80–94).

Also, to ensure validity, teachers must put similar effort into creating interesting, challenging, and meaningful assignment tasks, directly linked to desired student outcomes (Herman, Aschbacher, & Winters, 1992, pp. 33–43). Wiggins refers to the concept of "authenticity" as akin to validity but not equal to it. Designing an authentic assessment requires the educator to tackle tough issues such as identifying an engaging and worthy task that fits the context facing the learner; identifying specific and public evaluation criteria; and identifying ways for the assessor and assessee to interact around the task (Wiggins, 1993, pp. 229–230). Hence, designing valid and reliable authentic assessments requires considerable knowledge, skill, and time.

In states that have launched into the authentic assessment movement, **reliability** — not validity — issues have sparked initial debate, but validity issues will soon come to the fore. For example, in 1991 the Vermont State Board of Education endorsed and recommended (but did not mandate) a portfolio-based program.

> The program employs both standardized assessments and portfolios to collect information about the performance of Vermont students in grades 4 and 8 in the areas of writing and mathematics. Last April, the Uniform Assessment was administered to all students in participating schools and a sample of portfolios was requested from every supervisory union. The statewide sample of portfolios was scored in June by a group of teachers who had completed a special scoring qualification exercise and special training to assure consistency in their judgements. (Vermont Assessment Program, 1993–94). (N.B.: As of the 1994–1995 school year, writing assessments were moved to grade five, and as of September 1995, mathematics portfolios and a uniform test were added for grade 10.)

Writing portfolios are judged on the criteria of purpose, organization, details, voice or tone, and grammar/usage/mechanics. Mathematics portfolios are judged on the criteria of communication (language, representation, and presentation) and problem solving (understanding the problem, how it was solved, "why," and "so what"). The writing assessment also contains a uniform writing prompt and the selection of a "best piece." The mathematics assessment also contains a uniform assessment of two 40-item multiple-choice tests and a single on-demand task. The multiple-choice outcomes are compared with a national sample of mathematics outcomes from the National Assessment of Educational Progress mathematics test.

Though not mandated, fifty-nine of sixty districts participate in the program. When it was implemented, the State Department of Education stressed that assessment outcomes would not relate to the "normal curve"; students were not to be divided into quarters or quartiles; and outcomes were not intended to compare districts or schools. However, in the fall of

1994, the department did publish comparative data by district, a move that generated considerable negative reaction from some educational quarters (Geggis, 1994c, pp. 1B, 2B; Burke, 1994, p. 2).

Until the results of the third year were processed (1993–1994), researchers found that reliability of scoring was quite low, especially in writing (Koretz, Klein, McCaffrey, & Stecher, 1993). However, reliability increased in writing for 1993–1994 and remained stable in mathematics (Mappus, 1994). "This shows that the whole profile of performance is moving up," said the Commissioner (Geggis, 1994c).

Because of the success of the alternative assessment program, the State Board of Education is making plans to implement a three-year comprehensive statewide assessment system that will build on components of the portfolio process and uniform assessments currently in place (Mills, 1994a). Thus, while this system is not a mandate from the state, clearly most schools will soon use it. Peer pressure alone will entice lagging schools to implement it, just as they did with the initial portfolio process. Few schools, even if they wanted to, could stand up to the pressure of constituents and the media by failing to adopt a centrally driven innovation that is linked to a popular national trend. Also, money is tight in Vermont, too, so demonstrating accountability of a very real expectation. What is happening in Vermont is an example of more centralization of control over local schools (as we discussed earlier in regard to high-stakes testing and increased state and federal financial support). It is also an example of the "top-down, bottom-up" strategy for effecting change that Fullan describes. "The more that top-down and bottom-up forces are coordinated, the more likely that complex systems will move toward greater effectiveness" (1994, p. 201).

Vermont is a state that has "put performance assessment to the test." Many teachers and administrators support the contention that alternative assessment is driving change in writing and mathematics curricula, materials, and methods. Classroom practice is decidedly different in the fourth and eighth grades in most schools, and where it is not (content and context alignment at work), portfolio and uniform assessment results are lower than in schools where there is alignment. Anecdotal evidence also provides strong evidence that "good schools" are moving to implement alternative assessment practices in all grades in order to support and reinforce fourth and eighth grade learnings; failure to do so would cause considerable disruption in the learning process if students are forced to experience abrupt changes in assessment practices from grade to grade. As English pointed out in 1987, "When one changes tests, and when tests are important indicators of what happens in schools, one *changes* schools" (English, 1987, p. 92). Recently, the Commissioner of Education wrote, "There were hundreds of such meetings last year (on portfolios), and they represent a quiet revolution" (Mills, 1994b, p. 13).

The Future of Alternative Assessment

What does the future hold for alternative assessment? Will the movement become institutionalized to the degree that standardized testing is integral to educational practice? Or will many districts and schools adopt the practices and even implement them only to see them disappear? Will the movement prove to be another bandwagon? Or will policymakers force alternative assessment on districts and schools that are unprepared to implement it with the result that there will be a backlash (such as in Littleton and in Oregon) against the practices? Alternative assessment—because of its roots in the classroom and the fact that it engages teachers and students—will "stick around" to become a permanent fixture in schools.

However, whether it will become a powerful force to truly change instruction and how students learn or whether it will become just another appendage to existing practices hinges largely on how several issues are dealt with at the site level. Some of the key issues are: not burning out teachers because performance assessments are very time consuming to develop and conduct; finding the resources to educate and reeducate teachers in the technology of assessing; not sacrificing key "basics" in favor of depth of coverage; and finding shortcuts to insure validity and reliability (Hymes, 1991, pp. 49–50).

In addition, the long-term success of the movement is also dependent upon meeting successfully the challenge of other issues. Some of these are: nailing down the conceptual clarity that now is often hidden within a labyrinth of terms and concepts; developing mechanisms for feedback and criticism; developing more effective and less time-consuming ways to assess critical and complex thinking; resolving the daunting issues surrounding the standardization of evaluation criteria and performance so they can support necessary comparisons but not at the expense of the richness and power possible with individual assessments; and convincing key stakeholders—students, parents, school boards, and legislators—

that alternative assessments are valid, reliable, and respectable means to evaluate learning (Worthen, 1993, pp. 447–454).

The findings of Newmann and Archibald (1992) add to the mix of challenges. Following the spread of alternative assessment practices from a policy perspective, these researchers point out that at least four conditions are essential to future acceptance, and their conditions have a major impact on instruction and scheduling. The first is the need for students to have consistent opportunities for collaboration with peers in order to stimulate learning and construct knowledge. The second is the need to provide students with access to knowledge bases through modern technology. The third is the need for students to have scheduling flexibility and influence over the pace and procedures of learning so that they can truly invest themselves in alternative assessments. The fourth is the need to provide students with more flexible time than is available within the traditional fifty minute class period (1992, pp. 78–79).

Lastly, Newmann and Wehlage have identified five "standards" that can help educators determine the quality of assessments. Do the assessments: (1) emphasize higher-order thinking on the cognitive taxonomy?; (2) push students to work on depth rather than breadth of knowledge?; (3) connect learning to the "real" world and not just the classroom?; (4) provide opportunities for students to engage in frequent and sustained "conversation" with peers and teachers?; and (5) convey high expectations for all students in a supportive classroom learning environment? They see these standards as assisting schools to determine how implementation of alternative assessments is affected by organizational factors, curricular content, leadership, and the culture of the school and the community (1993). All of the above questions and needs present formidable challenges for schools considering or embarking on the journey of alternative assessment.

Few in-depth, on-site studies have been done of organizations actually implementing these new practices and attempting to meet most of these standards. Maeroff has conducted such a study in Rhode Island where the state department of education supports an alternative assessment system for elementary schools. He concluded that, "For all its attractiveness, alternative assessment is fraught with complications and difficulties, not unlike having to endure life with a teenager as the price for the joys of parenthood" (1991, p. 274). He also concluded that assessment was causing important changes in classrooms.

All of the above issues relating to alternative assessment send a clear message to districts and schools to—as McLaughlin stated earlier—"go slow" in their implementation of these practices, provided that they can resist hastily conceived practices forced on them by policymakers. It is far better to "think big and start small" in order to be successful than to implement grandiose programs that could fail to meet their potential. A strategy of "small wins" makes great sense with an innovation that is so complex and yet so promising to truly change education (Larson, 1992a). As Fullan states after his comprehensive review of the change literature, in some instances "It may be necessary to start on a small scale and use this as leverage for further action" (1991, p. 64).

Alternative assessment is such a case. The caution is particularly appropriate where alternative assessment is being turned into another form of high-stakes testing. Administrators and teachers together should determine the degree to which proposed practices meet Fullan's criteria relating to the nature of an innovation—namely, relevance, readiness, resources, need, clarity, complexity (in terms of being understandable and manageable), and quality/practicality (1991, pp. 63–64, 68–73).

THE ROLE OF STANDARDIZED TESTING IN MEASURING WORK

In addition to those educational reasons for standardized testing (discussed earlier), for *political* reasons alone schools cannot afford *not* to use them, since many citizens believe "the only credible indicator of improved educational performance is improved performance on standardized tests" (Berlak, 1992, p. 6). Among the lay public, the 1994 Annual Phi Delta Kappa Gallup Poll on public education found that 73 percent of respondents thought that some kind of national standardized examinations were "very important" or "quite important" as a means to improve the schools, recognizing that in the eyes of the public "examinations" may be different than "tests," the more common term (1994, p. 48). A nationwide survey of standardized testing at the district level showed that 95 percent administered such tests and that 86 percent consider them an important part of their "accountability program" (Hymes, 1991, p. 10).

These survey results reinforce the fact that standardized tests have been part of the ethoes of American education since the turn of this century and have been so for a variety of legitimate reasons that go beyond sheer accountability. They are readily available, well-developed, relatively inexpensive, administratively simple to arrange, have considerable strengths in validity and reliability (especially the latter), and can measure a broad range of outcomes in a timely, cost-effective manner (Hymes, 1991, p. 11; Madaus, 1985, p. 614). They can also be a stimulus to examine equity issues because low test scores typically elicit concerns about who is or is not achieving and why. Performance on reading and mathematics achievement tests was at the heart of the effective schools movement of the 1970s. Edmunds and others used such tests to focus on the institutional characteristics of urban schools that, despite formidable obstacles, managed to provide an effective education to children from low-income families (Edmunds, 1978, 1979).

However, these tests have several limitations and weaknesses which have already been outlined, not the least of which is their low alignment to the local curriculum and their high alignment to SES. Too many districts and schools, reacting to the political realities, give these tests indiscriminately grade by grade and file the results—but fail to think about the negative ramifications of such practices, ramifications such as disenchanted students, cynical teachers, skeptical parents, boards, and laypeople, and negative public fallout. We can report that in graduate course after graduate course that we have taught for a decade where students have been asked, "Does your district give standardized tests, and, if so, how are the results used and have you ever seen them?", the overwhelming response is, "Yes, we give them but I have never seen any results and know nothing about their use." This is inexcusable, given the time and money allocated to giving the tests.

Here are some ideas for districts and schools that are committed to the *educational* uses of standardized tests:

- Decide (through a collaborative process between educators and the board) at what grade levels it is most appropriate to use them (e.g., 3, 6, and 9).
- Decide how the tests fit into the overall district assessment plan and program.
- Determine the degree of alignment with the prescribed curriculum and correlation with textbook series (if there are such).
- If the test does not align because certain content has been intentionally excluded from the curriculum, and yet the test will be given on that content, ensure that there is an explanation about the low scores for that material.

- Decide how the outcomes will be reported and how they are to be explained to the readers of the reports.
- Plan to pay for planned periodic item analyses by student, by teacher, by grade level, and by school.
- Hold principals responsible for teachers using the item analyses and for principals doing the same for their school.
- Ensure that there is someone on staff (an administrator, teacher, or counselor) who knows about the pros and cons of standardized testing, the interpretation of results, and strategies for local use. (The same recommendation holds for alternative assessment.)
- Assume that if the test is given, it is sensible to "teach to it"; otherwise results could be highly detrimental to the district and schools. Then pay for the administrators, teachers, counselors, and other staff to be educated about the nature of the test, its format, types of questions asked, and how to interpret outcomes. (Most test companies provide this service.)

Schools with this commitment must also be able to respond to many criticisms about standardized testing, criticisms that are tough to answer. Those with a plan such as the one developed by the Addison Northeast District, discussed earlier, will be much more able to respond. Critics claim that these tests emphasize multiple-choice formats; that they encourage cheating; that they are biased and discriminatory; that some children do not test well and hence testing is basically unfair; that comparisons are odious; and that testing of this kind takes too much time for the benefits accrued (Finn, 1991, pp. 166–173).

TEACHING TO THE TEST

One of the most controversial and misunderstood issues in education is that of "teaching the test" or "teaching to it." Clearly, it is unethical to "teach the test," but to give tests and not teach "to them" in terms of their nature (objective, authentic, etc.), their format, and their general content is foolhardy at best. The tests we administer should be a clear indicator of what is valued in the curriculum and what it is that we want students "to be good at" (Wiggins, 1989, p. 41). Chester Finn, the former Under Secretary of Education, concluded after his analysis of our public school system that:

> So long as we look to test results for information on learning outcomes and consider them the basis for accountability at the several levels of the educa-

tional system, it stands to reason that the nature and content of the particular test we use are quite important. It should be a test *worth* [emphasis in the original] teaching to. That's what gives it a catalytic quality and transforms it into a participant in education reform, instead of being an exercise in monitoring and bean counting. (Finn, 1991, p. 165)

But obviously there are many dangers in advocating for this position. Excessive time can be spent preparing for the test if drill and practice learning activities predominate over richer learning activities, and if local teacher and school autonomy and professionalism become undermined. There are few formal guidelines available to steer educators through this thicket of possible dysfunctional results from allowing standardized tests to *frontload* the curriculum. Local dialogue is a must.

THE NEED FOR LOCAL POLICY

The high-octane testing environment surrounding districts and schools today requires that they attend to *their* policies on the matter. Without thoughtful policies, schools and educators will be buffeted around by the forces described in this chapter and hence will convey to their constituents that they are mindlessly reacting to the latest fad. What needs to be acknowledged is that assessment is for school improvement *and* accountability. Rather than a fad, we believe that a new paradigm of assessment is emerging, one that is moving from the dominance of the scientific, psychometric paradigm to a partnership with the qualitative, contextual paradigm (Berlak, 1992, pp. 11–13).

Such a partnership will mean that various forms of assessment have a place in the educational arena and that a mix of practices to create a balanced testing program is the need for the future. (For a helpful publication on the subject see Hymes, 1991.) Herman and Winters call this "sensible, school-based evaluation" (1992, pp. 10–12).

Districts need policies such as this one from the Chittenden Central Supervisory Union in Vermont. Wiggins, after conducting research for his treatise on alternative assessment, concluded: "I know of only a handful of school districts that have testing and assessment policies" (1993, p. 25).

The Chittenden Central Supervisory Union believes that assessment is an integral part of the teaching and learning process. We view assessment as the gathering of information to recognize each student's uniqueness, and to encourage self-evaluation, reflection and self-directed learning. We further believe that assessment supports the curriculum and provides information to students, staff, and the community. Therefore, assessment is an on-going, developmentally appropriate process which uses a variety of strategies to accommodate individual learners. (1993)

Effective curriculum management hinges on this kind of district level commitment to this key leg of the management triangle.

ASSESSMENT OF WORK DESIGN

Curriculum can be assessed on the following criteria that implicitly relate to student learning: clarity; scope; sequence; depth; flexibility; validity; and balance.

Pick up a curriculum guide. If it does not contain descriptors which connect it to testing or to instruction, it can still be evaluated independently. Does it include objectives? Are such objectives clear? Are content sections sufficiently specific so they can be translated in an unambiguous manner to teaching situations or test selection?

Behavioral objectives are not easily translated into what the teacher does; that is, they stress what happens after the work and are not really statements of the work. For example: Given one hour, the student will identify and describe in writing at least five methods for organizing messages as they are presented in the textbook.

Eisner has postulated an alternative method of stating objectives as *expressive* rather than *behavioral.* Expressive objectives identify the type of *encounter* the student is to have and do not specify beforehand what the student is to learn. Outcomes emerge from the encounter. Outlining the encounter or the situation is more easily translated into work teachers do in shaping an instructional environment including fitting their own behavior into that environment (Eisner, 1985, pp. 69–70). The field of teaching is replete with books about methods, yet there is a paucity of texts that examine how teacher actions leading to "encounters" are demonstrably more appropriate in some contexts than others in order to attain certain results.

The **clarity** of curriculum should be much like opening any do-it-yourself kit and trying to follow the directions. Whether or not the outcome is achieveable or important can be left aside for the moment. The real question is, "Are the directions clear enough so that the desired result can be attained?"

Quite another matter is whether or not the outcome *can* be specified ahead of time. Suppose that the result desired is an innovative response. What then? In that case an expressive objective seems to be ideally suited. The work design focuses on how to set up a situation so that an innovative response is triggered.

All of these indices can and are used to examine curriculum apart from the *results* it obtains. *Results* can be examined from the perspective of the learner (work measurement) or the impact within the system (articulation and coordination) which is a partial assessment of work flow. The design of work is, in technical terms, an engineering problem. Curriculum design, in the words of Beauchamp, is "the substance and organization of goals and culture content so arranged as to reveal potential progression for learners through levels of schooling" (Beauchamp, 1975, p. 196).

The design of work has to be compatible with the physical structure of the places where teaching and learning occur (discussed in Chapter 2). Ideally, the structure should be built around the functions or the design of work (the curriculum). Practically speaking, the single classroom structure of most schools continues to exercise a profound influence on curriculum design. Curriculum design "fits" this definition of teacher work. It is highly unlikely that dramatic breakthroughs in the restructuring of curriculum or learning will occur until this structure, which has decapitated some promising curricular ideas, is fundamentally altered.

ASSESSMENT OF THE WORK PERFORMED

Evaluation of the work performed that affects learning means an evaluation of **teaching** (or better yet, **instruction**) if the teaching is connected to the curriculum. Perhaps no subject has been so emotionally charged as teacher evaluation. There are models of teaching (Joyce & Weil, 1986) and models for the evaluation of teaching (Stanley & Popham, 1988). As we have pointed out in other sections, teaching has and continues to be examined by many in isolation from the definition of the work to be performed as specified within a curriculum.

In our experience, it is rare for a school district's teacher evaluation policy and process to refer at all to teacher responsibilities for implementing and teaching to the prescribed curriculum. Districts need policies such as the one from South Burlington, Vermont described in the section on "Monitoring" in Chapter 4. The absence of such a policy sends a signal that reinforces the practice of near totally autonomous professionals going about their work bounded largely by individual rather than system boundaries.

Many of the reform proposals that emerged in the 1980s also ignored the necessity for a sound curriculum developed **prior** to the time teaching is conceptualized and then evaluated. Rather, it was believed that removing organizational constraints and "freeing" teachers would automatically usher in a new level of improved work design. How this was to occur was never quite explained. It is as though each teacher carries around in her or his head the proper definition of work, and how it must be connected to reinforce what has been taught/learned before, and how it is to be carried into the future within the confines of a new organizational structure. Ignored was the power of the thousands of hours of observing classroom instruction that students are exposed to as they progress from kindergarten through high school, instruction that overall takes place in single classrooms. This model of teaching dominates over any of the alternatives described by Joyce and Weil.

Prior to the time of the wide acceptance of the graded school, it was possible for a teacher to know the entire curriculum because the teacher was expected to teach all students and at all grade levels. Within this work place, given enough materials of suitable utility and a reasonable class size, a teacher *could* deliver the entire elementary-secondary curriculum. In this work setting, articulation and coordination were minor if nonexistent problems.

That changed when schools divided the one-room school into graded level classes. As we have seen in previous chapters, records show that once separate graded classes became prevalent, courses of study (curriculum) became necessary to: (1) show teachers what part of the curriculum they were responsible for and (2) ensure connections in the work flow between the separate grades. It is not an accident that there were no curriculum books until 1900, though schools existed in great numbers prior to that time (Schubert, 1980). Curriculum rose in importance when age-grading became common practice in school systems; it fundamentally altered the work of the teacher, reducing the scope of things taught and thereby making work more manageable. The trade-off was that *continuity,* once more easily assured in a non-graded structure, was sacrificed.

Hence, to enhance organizational effectiveness, personnel supervision or monitoring became necessary in order to coordinate the activities of employees. As Glickman et al. put it, "We can think of supervision as the *glue* [emphasis in original] of a successful school" (1995, p. 5). It is the function that draws together discrete elements into whole-school action. By so doing, structure was added to the work flow at the "micro" level of the school to counter the pull toward the separate cells (classrooms). Unfortunately, as we discussed the situation in the section on "monitoring" in Chapter 4, there are (to quote Glickman again) "more 'glueless' than 'glued' schools" (p. 5). Such conditions have a tremendous negative impact on student outcomes.

Finally, supervision in itself, if defined primarily as teacher and school development (per Glickman), is not adequate to assess the work performed. Integral to that organizational function is an effective process of teacher evaluation (and, we want to emphasize, one for evaluating administrators and other personnel). As is the case for curriculum development, library shelves are chock-full of books and other materials relative to teacher evaluation. Experts keep searching for the most effective approaches, with many highly useful approaches developed and, in many instances, implemented across the country. Stanley and Popham's book (1988) is one example of an excellent compendium of "best practices." Unfortunately, the situation with teacher evaluation is similar to that of supervision in too many of our schools, along with the aforementioned need to tie more closely the work of the teacher to the prescribed curriculum.

USING RESULTS AS AN INDICATOR OF SCHOOL QUALITY

Work results are important, but only *after* one has determined that elements of quality control are present and interactive and that suboptimization is not a problem. This means that total work flow is functional and linked through the different levels of the system. It means that the evaluator, whether administrator or teacher, *knows* what ought to be going on within the school and understands the context of the work place. When results are examined the evaluator is reasonably assured that using data as feedback will not perpetuate a problem but assist in its alleviation.

If a school system is not behaving *as a system*, then arguing that raising test scores will produce improved pupil performance is likewise specious because a test score is an implicit composite of linked instruction and learning, i.e., "a system." If there are no interacting relationships between work content, work measurement, and the actual work, raising the calibration for examining the work done simply narrows the range of tolerance for judging the work. The result is a higher rejection rate (student failure) of the work completed rather than an improvement in the work.

Improving calibration resulting in narrowing the tolerance for the work done as a strategy to improve the work rests ultimately on there being a connection between the two. If that relationship is not present, only the rate of rejection goes up, not the quality of the work nor any change in the outcome. The work is unaffected. Improved inspection (supervision) alone will not change anything of substance either.

One of the critical connections is between work measurement (the assessment of the results of the work) and work tasks. The extent to which it is known what work tasks (teaching behaviors) impact the attainment of work outcomes is the extent to which data can be useful in modifying the work tasks.

Teachers often ask, "What should I do differently to improve pupil learning?" The more immediate the feedback, the more relevant the response. That is one reason why follow-up studies of graduates are usually not a useful means to alter curriculum and instruction. Too much has been forgotten, staff has changed, the curriculum is not static, and data collected are at too "macro" a level to be useful to teachers.

There are at least seven basic work changes or combinations of the seven that *may* result in work modification on the part of the teacher. These are shown in Table 6. One can study the table through the lens of a behaviorist or constructivist. The table can generate analysis and further meaning for a teacher.

No doubt more changes could be identified that would lead to improved quality control. For example, the teacher may modify work organization via changes in pupil grouping practices, or by matching teaching style with learning style, or by other changes in the work place. Still another solution may be improved supervision or monitoring which is really improved work performance by ensuring greater adherence to valid work design.

Improving the work means systematically installing good quality control in design and, when results are not forthcoming, striving to weed out possible breakdowns via a process of elimination. In such a situation, the procedure is diagnostic. Part of the process must include questions about what the results are, what kinds of values they represent, and how

Table 6
SEVEN BASIC DIRECTIONS THAT CHANGE WORK IN SCHOOLS

Type of Direction	Possible Cause	Type of Decision Required	Probable Data Source(s)
1. *"Teach this Instead of that"*	• improper content selection	• inclusion/exclusion	• lack of test alignment • lack of content to be taught to time available • lack of adherence to guide • incorrect/vague guide
2. *"Change the test"*	• improper work measurement or too narrow	• match of curricula to test (proper validation and alignment to test)	• alignment data show mismatch • consistent inability to improve scores due to poor alignment
3. *"Teach more/less of this"*	• lack of pupil mastery	• change stress or pacing	• poor test results where content has been taught but inadequate time spent to teach it

4. *"Teach this before (or after) that"*	• lack of identified sequence
	• incorrect sequence
		• change content/time ordination	• poor results (test scores) reveal content taught but no cumulative strength across grade levels due to:
			  • inadequate guides
			  • inadequate sequential teaching
			  • inadequate monitoring

5. *"Teach it within this situation"*	• no content match between test and classroom situation	• proper contextual reference in the classroom	• contextual alignment data between testing protocols and classroom learning environment
6. *"Change test calibration"*	• test calibration does not match alignment-content-context match	• change calibration	• passing scores exceed capability of alignment to deliver • high failure rates
7. *"Change the work structure"*	• ineffective student grouping practices • improper student assignment to a course or grade	• re-grouping of students on criteria that impact achievement • change grading practices • change scheduling practices • change work place structure	• test achievement dispersion too large • discipline problems • chronic student failure rates

educators have determined their propriety within the constellation of values which could be selected.

The evaluator should always be concerned about the *translation* of purpose into work design (curriculum). Work purposes are both overt and covert, and both are legitimate foci of the evaluator's scrutiny. Evaluators who bypass these questions become merely technicians who assume the work design is correct and look only for how it is linked to work and work measurement. Too often they fail to ask, "How does the system *know* if this is the 'right work' or 'What is right?'" These are the larger domains of questioning purpose and dealing with means/ends dilemmas.

"What is right" involves selecting an orientation to not only the work but the role of the person doing the work and value orientations which reveal how much control a teacher should possess over the total work to be done. A school not concerned with a coordinated work design because of the lack of concern for work results (or the lack of external assessment and visibility) will develop quite a different work climate and procedures than one which is concerned with *design and results*.

SUMMARY

Curriculum assessment must be placed in the context and structure of **the total work flow** of the organization, because numerous internal and external forces can either enhance or impede the organization's ability to affect student learning. Educators assessing learning must look beyond the narrow indicators of effectiveness that come from standardized achievement tests. However, these tests still have an important place in the assessment programs of schools.

Today, there are many changes occurring in assessment that have the potential to alter, in fundamental ways, traditional approaches to evaluating student performance. Several forces push education in that direction, forces such as more emphasis on teaching creative thinking, decision making, and problem solving to all students. Such outcomes cannot be assessed by reliance on traditional objective-type tests.

Hence, educators have focused increased attention on the development of alternative assessments such as portfolios, performances, and exhibitions. Alternative assessments are judgment based, embedded in a learning context, and integrally woven into instruction. They are time consuming to develop and have numerous reliability and validity issues connected to them.

The current local, state, and national attention being given to assessment requires that schools and districts develop their own assessment policies if they are not to be buffeted about by the shifting sands of policymaking.

In addition to using assessment methods to assess learning, schools can also use some indirect measures such as the work design (guides) and the quality of instruction. Finally, teachers can make at least seven basic changes in their work that may affect learning outcomes.

DIALOGUE

These are the questions most often asked of the authors about the content in this chapter:

1. Why is "teaching to the test" such an anathema in our schools?

ANSWER: Because of the long history of the dominance of standardized achievement testing we (understandably) feel that test results will be "invalidated" if students have an understanding as to the nature and the content of the test before they take it. We want to be sure that we know *objectively* how our children compare to the national norms, and "teaching to the test" will destroy that certainty.

2. Why don't more schools have local policies and clear practices regarding the use of tests and other assessments?

ANSWER: Administrator and teacher preparation programs give little attention to traditional testing no less all the newer forms of alternative assessments. Assessment has never been seen as an important component of the curriculum in most professional programs and still isn't as we discussed in Chapter 2. "Testing" in the form of standardized test results has always been seen as somewhat of a mysterious and arcane activity that is the responsibility of "someone else" in the system. Guidance personnel often have a traditional testing background that is adequate for the interpretation of individual test scores but not for assistance in school and district policymaking regarding testing and assessment.

3. What is the most common information used for curricular evaluation?

ANSWER: Unfortunately, the most common information is standardized achievement test scores as a measure of the efficacy of a curriculum. This can lead to some serious errors about what constitutes an effective curriculum as we discussed earlier in the section on these tests. The reason is that these tests are based on the assumption of random events, i.e., the bell-shaped curve. That is contrary to the function of a curriculum which is to produce, to the greatest degree possible, planned learning outcomes for students. The two are simply incompatible. Alignment attempts to resolve the dilemma by either "frontloading" or "backloading" the curriculum.

4. Are "result-free" evaluations desirable or possible?

ANSWER: An evaluator may examine a work situation only for processes or relationships and not be concerned about whether such processes produce different, better, or the same results. In most cases such evaluators believe that the processes (or actions) they are reviewing are the ends or ought to be. For example, if one believes that "thinking skills" are what is "good," then one doesn't care if math facts are acquired. The process of thinking is more important than the acquisition of facts or results. In these cases the means are substituted for the ends.

ACTIVITIES FOR PERSONAL AND STAFF DEVELOPMENT

We offer some examples of activities as "starters" but encourage readers to develop their own for their situations.

1. Examine your school's or district's policy on testing and assessment. If there is one, how adequate is it for the era we are now in? If there is none, why not? What steps would have to be taken to design and implement one?

2. How do educators in your system feel about "teaching to the test?" Do they recognize a time when doing so might be quite appropriate or even necessary? What kind of staff development activity could be designed around this question?

3. What standardized achievement tests are given in your school and district? How are the outcomes disseminated and to whom? How are they used? How do parents and educators feel about their use currently, and do they see needs to change practices?

4. To what degree are educators in your system knowledgeable about alternative forms of assessment? What practices already are used by some teachers? What aids and impedes their use now and what resources, training, etc., would be needed to make their use more common? What is the degree of interest and receptivity among other staff to begin examining these forms? What strategy(s) would work to begin to move the system in this direction? What role would administrators need to assume for alternative assessments to become more common?

5. Have your colleagues select some starter books/monographs on

alternative assessment listed in that section of this chapter. Map out a reading plan that will lead to some dialogue aimed at moving the system toward more use of the practices.

Chapter 10

CURRICULUM AUDITING

It began as an idea. It is growing as a practice. The idea was to examine the records of a school system, its rationale and objectives, compare them to its activities, determine if the results obtained were appropriate, and then issue an objective public report (Griffin & Bryce, 1995, p. 17). Auditing differs from accreditation in many respects. The most obvious is that the audit's scope is the *school system,* while accreditation deals with individual *schools* (see English, 1992, pp. 116–117).

Auditing differs from curriculum management in that the scope and focus of curriculum management, as with accreditation, is also the *school,* but in addition its *classrooms.* Auditing evolved in tandem with curriculum management. It is a logical extension of the assessment theme that runs through curriculum management, but the extension hones in on administrative, economic, and political support factors that are crucial to the effectiveness of schools through their teachers in classrooms. Knowledge of auditing without knowledge or curriculum management and vice versa severely impedes the implementation of each.

Originally the brainchild of Leon Lessinger (1970) in his best-selling book *Every Kid A Winner,* the curriculum audit has established itself as cutting-edge practice in American education. The first audit was completed in Columbus, Ohio in 1979 (English, 1992, p. 92). By 1995, over one hundred audits had been realized, including two in foreign countries (Steffy, 1989; Poston, 1992; English, Vertiz & Bates, 1995).

Every idea has a kind of *infrastructure,* an internal scaffolding that enables it to construct and link a series of concepts into practice. Auditing the curriculum was not an exception to this process. After Lessinger, there came a series of concepts which have buttressed the curriculum audit (English, 1978, 1979a, 1979b; English & Steffy, 1982, 1983). These pertained to applications of the concept of quality control and linked it to school management practices and assessment results (English, 1986, 1988). The audit provided the public with a view of how inputs, in the form of taxpayer resources, were linked from board policy to the classroom and reflected in assessment outcomes (Downey, 1992; English & Steffy, 1992; Frase, 1992; Green, 1992). What the audit has accomplished is to sketch out the details of what Chapter 9 described as the "black box" model of school effectiveness. The "black box" model is silent about how inputs become outputs in schools. The audit has succeeded in constructing a persuasive scaffolding of how this should occur (Streshly, 1992). In the process it also challenges the present structure of school system organization (Griffin & Bryce, 1995).

As we discussed in the Introduction, most school systems are organized in a "layer cake" model, i.e., each layer (board, superintendent, assistant superintendent, supervisors, principals, assistant principals, counselors and teachers) lies on top of each hierarchically and is connected at the edges. However, there are no vertical linkages between the layers that actually connect the operations of one to the operations of the other. This has resulted in what Weick (1976) has referred to as "loosely coupled" systems. Within and between the layers of organization lie pockets of "no-person's land" in which ambiguity protects autonomy. The command structure of educational organizations is not "tight." It is not always clear who is responsible for what, especially when things go wrong. It also means that activities at one layer do not necessarily impact another except perhaps incidentally or obliquely (Coble, 1992; Livingston, 1992). The adoption of board policies may not ever impact the operations of teachers in classrooms. In this sense there may be no policy control of curriculum by the board of education, something that nearly all state law assumes should occur and is possible (Downey, 1995).

The Five Standards of the Curriculum Audit

The standards of the curriculum audit are embodied in the concept of quality control (Vertiz, 1992; Griffin, 1995). They are:

(1) **Control: The School System is in Control of Itself.** The very first audit standard centers on the idea that the system, *as a system,* is in control and can direct its internal operations. This doesn't mean that control isn't shared, or that the system can shut off or ignore key constituencies in the larger community. It does mean that there is internal connectivity from the policymaking level to the classroom, from school board to teachers (see Downey, 1992). Without this capability the whole notion of accountability becomes suspect. If a system cannot direct and

change its functions, it cannot be responsible for what it does or doesn't accomplish.

(2) *Direction: The School System Knows Where It's Going.* The second audit standard deals with purposive behavior. Organizational activities are given meaning by what they are supposed to accomplish. In order to comprehend whether any part of an organization, or the entire organization itself, is performing well or poorly, one has to have some idea of what it is supposed to accomplish. Organizations provide services or products. They incorporate important social symbols, narratives and myths.

This audit standard assumes that school systems are *rational.* By that is meant that they attempt to accomplish goals or purposes by clustering and directing their resources towards attaining them (Silver, 1983, p. 77; English, 1988, p. 329). But, as we saw in Chapter 2, their "organized anarchy" characteristics make it difficult for them to be managed and led as neat, tight bureaucracies.

If school systems aren't rational they can't be accountable and they can't be governed, at least not in the way the public believes they should be controlled. The central notion is that via the public electorate, representatives are chosen to direct the operations of the schools. The "will" of the public is translated through the board of education via its executive staff (the superintendency team) and ultimately to the classroom. The direction should be purposive, i.e., *goal directed.* All notions of planning and budgeting for school systems rest on the idea that they can and are *rational.* Feedback from auditing can help systems to operate more rationally.

(3) **Connectivity and Equity: The Marble Cake:** A school system meeting this audit standard has constructed the internal linkages between hierarchical layers to connect them operationally. Instead of the layer cake, the system has become a marble cake as portrayed in the Introduction. A "loosely coupled" system has become more tightly connected. In so doing it can be changed more quickly, directed more purposefully, and ultimately become more economical, i.e., *efficient,* using as few resources as possible to attain goals. At this point, the audit deals with the distribution of resources, with the notion that those areas of the system requiring more resources should receive them. That is the concept of *equity.* It is the *unequal* allocation of money, staff, time, and materials to those with the greatest needs.

Budgeting by formulae flies against the concept of equity, unless the equations take into account need differentiation among the clientele being served by the system.

(4) **Feedback: The System Adjusts Future Performance Based on Past Performance.** It is assumed that an effective organization can discover or assess its own operations and, based upon that source of feedback, adjust its operations so that it attains a greater share of its goals or objectives. This is the feedback loop (see Streshly, 1992).

Paramount in this idea is the *connectivity* among and between its operational levels/layers. Control and connectivity are central to making feedback work. The audit standards are interdependent.

(5) **Productivity: Ultimately Cost Is Important.** When an organization is rational and reaching its goals (a determination of its effectiveness), calculations can be made to determine if there are more efficient (cheaper) ways of doing the same job. However, it makes no sense to discuss cost or engage in cost-benefit analyses until and unless it is determined that the organization is effective (reaching its goals in the first place). And in no case should cost be the determining factor, because that pollutes the idea of effectiveness.

The audit searches for the ways a school system has engaged in cost-benefit studies and how it relates its budgetary increases and/or decreases to the attainment of purposes/goals. Typically, no such determinations are developed (see Vertiz & Bates, 1995).

Format of the Curriculum Audit

The format and structure of the curriculum management are as follows:

  I. **INTRODUCTION Background, History, District, Finances, Scope of Work**
  II. **METHODOLOGY The Model for the Audit, Standards for the Auditors, Data Sources of the Audit, Standards for the Audit**
 III. **FINDINGS (listed by audit standard with exhibits)**
 IV. **RECOMMENDATIONS (in priority order)**
  V. **SUMMARY**

The *Introductory* part of an audit discusses the history of the school system, its operations, numbers of schools, any recent controversies and extant finances. This part of the audit establishes the geopolitical *context* in which the school district functions on a day-to-day basis.

The *methodology* of the audit presents *how* the audit team was selected, the generic data sources used and presents a quantification table for use of such terms as "nearly all" or "many." Standards for selecting the auditors include technical expertise and the principles of independence, objectivity, materiality and full disclosure.

Materiality means that implicit in the contract between the auditors and the entity being audited, the audit team has the authority to select the most important and relevant facets of operations to study and report. *Full disclosure* means that anything which is *material* must be fully explicated without compromise in the audit report.

The data sources for the audit are those common to nearly all reports: documents, observation (site visitation), and interviews. These are configured differently depending upon whether a finding is a *design problem* (i.e., conceptual or definitional) or a *delivery problem* (implementational or operational). The major data sources for *design problems* are documents followed by interviews and observation. The major data sources for *delivery problems* are observation, interviews and documents.

The section in the audit dealing with findings presents gaps or deficiencies (positive or negative) of the documented situation in the school system compared to an *audit standard* (see English, Vertiz & Bates, 1995). The typical documents which pertain to each of the five audit standards are listed below:

Curriculum Management Audit Standard 1: Control

- federal law and regulations
- state law and regulations
- board policies
- strategic or long-range plans
- annual goals and objectives
- annual reports
- table of organization (TO)
- outside evaluations of district functions/operations
- annual CPA report of the finances
- annual budget requests or reviews
- facility plans and enrollment projections

Curriculum Management Audit Standard Two: Direction

- strategic or long-range plans
- board policies
- system-wide curriculum goals/objectives

- curriculum long-range plans
- curriculum development plans
- curriculum guides
- curriculum reports
- school course catalogues
- state-mandated course offerings

Curriculum Management Audit Standard Three: Connectivity and Equity

- budget documents
- enrollment reports by sex and race by school, grade level
- personnel descriptions by job level, race and sex
- OCR (Office of Civil Rights) reports
- program reviews and/or accreditation reports
- required state reports
- annual reports by the district and/or schools
- dropout and/or graduate follow-up studies
- climate studies or annual plans
- federal/state project applications/reports
- monitoring plans/reports

Curriculum Management Audit Standard Four: Feedback

- board policies on test adoption/purpose of testing
- annual testing reports/plans
- monitoring reports based on test/assessment scores
- general public/board reports on testing
- state reports on testing/assessment
- federal/state reports where test data are reported or projected
- graduate follow-up studies, college placement records
- dropout reports
- Census data regarding SES, typical homes, other key variables
- accreditation reports/reviews

Curriculum Management Audit Standard Five: Productivity

- economic forecasts, local Chamber of Commerce studies
- state economic forecasts
- long- and short-range budgetary details, tax rates, growth of the tax base, assessments, collections
- long/short-range facility plans, bond issues

- school budgetary forecasts, projections, budget reports
- accreditation reports

Audit *recommendations* are based on a priority of high to low. The most important recommendations come first, followed by the least important recommendations. Here is a set of recommendations from a mid-sized school system in Texas audited in the winter of 1995 (AASA, 1995):

Recommendation 1: Develop, adopt, and implement a usable mission statement and set of district-wide achievement objectives (p. 176);

Recommendation 2: Revisit and reconsider a comprehensive strategic and long-range plan to establish and sustain constancy of purpose (p. 178);

Recommendation 3: Develop, adopt and implement a comprehensive set of board policies to direct curriculum management and ensure quality control (p. 180);

Recommendation 4: Establish an Office of Educational Accountability (OEA) and a central curriculum council (p. 182);

Recommendation 5: Refine and enlarge the unique school concept as a vehicle for addressing inequities in the system (p. 183);

Recommendation 6: Refine and clarify the relationship between campus improvement plans and board-approved achievement targets (p. 185);

Recommendation 7: Implement a systematic leadership development program which ensures a high-quality leadership cadre (p. 186);

Recommendation 8: Develop and implement a philosophy which reflects more accurately the concept of the middle school (p. 187);

Recommendation 9: Reorganize central office personnel involved in training and development into a single integrated operation (p. 189);

Recommendation 10: Develop and implement a formal process for receiving and acting upon district-generated reports (p. 190);

Recommendation 11: Revise and expand job descriptions to conform to the restructured table of organization (p. 191);

Recommendation 12: Establish and implement equitable curriculum/instruction and personnel hiring practices (p. 192);

Recommendation 13: Revise the budgeting process and the budget to a more programmatic format to permit wider involvement and cost-benefit analysis (p. 194);

Recommendation 14: Develop a comprehensive student assessment program which includes advanced placement exams (p. 197);

Recommendation 15: Engage in programmatic adjustments to the school curriculum (p. 199);

The curriculum management audit is completed with a summary statement which attempts to place the audit into perspective for action. Here is an actual audit *Summary* from the Newport News, Virginia, *Curriculum Management Audit,* completed in March 1993:

> Without much fanfare, the Newport News Public Schools, Virginia, has joined the company of many other urban school systems by becoming a *minority majority* entity. Minorities now comprise over 52 percent of the division's 30,000+ students.
>
> Even as this event has transpired, the division has not faced up adequately to this *reality*. The school division has not been completely desegregated. Vestiges of all African-American and all white schools remain. African-American pupil achievement lags behind white achievement throughout the system. There are no promising signs it will be ameliorated soon. A tracking plan used in the schools isolates, stigmatizes, and reduces learning expectations for minority students. The result is an insidious form of re-segregation of the schools, even as busing is used to desegregate them.
>
> The major problem facing the Newport News Public Schools is the lack of an equal educational opportunity for its minority majority children. The problem is not only policy and managerial in nature. It is a profoundly moral one.
>
> There are no quick fixes or easy victories in sight. To address the issues surrounding the *achievement gap* will require deep, systemic change, and involve attitudinal mind-sets more so than those of a technical nature.
>
> To resolve the *achievement gap* will mean ALL of the following:
>
> * abandoning the practice of tracking and permanent grouping that isolates, stigmatizes, and lower achievement expectations for minority children;
> * designing and delivering more developmentally appropriate curricula and testing;
> * terminating any practice or procedure that perpetuates racial segregation in any form;
> * effectively recruiting larger numbers of minority teachers.
>
> The audit team has recommended that the *strategic mission* of the Newport News Public Schools be the total elimination of the *achievement gap* between races in 13 years, beginning with next year's kindergarten classes. This would mean that by the year 2006 this gap, rooted in false assumptions and limited instructional practices and procedures, will have disappeared completely in the school division. It is an ambitious project. (AASA pp. 94-5)

Two years later the Newport News Public Schools had a success story to tell about the way it had begun to turn the corner on the problems identified in the curriculum management audit (see *Video Journal of Education,* 1995).

The Power of the Curriculum Management Audit

Increasingly, school administrators, boards and the public want to be reassured that everything that is possible to do to improve the educational program is being done. They also face some internal political problems that make it difficult to bring about change. Part of the problem may be that the school system is reluctant to admit there are problems.

Based on the hundred or so audits completed to date (English, Vertiz, & Bates, 1995) and two doctoral dissertations ascertaining impact (Menchhofer, 1993; Kemen & Gallagher, 1995), the following generalizations appear supportable.

(1) **Audits are Usually Initiated by Those In Top Positions.** Audits are usually initiated by superintendents or boards of education who are not satisfied with some level of the curricular operations. By bringing in an outside team, a third-party look can be obtained. What is emerging is that the concept of the audit and *quality* are recognized as compatible (Downey, 1992).

(2) **Objectivity is a Prerequisite to Dealing with Touchy Political Problems.** There are few purely technical problems in school systems without political overtones. The objectivity brought by a third party to the school system is a critical component for credibility and resolution of such problems.

(3) **The Audit Provides the Leverage to Engage in Change.** Experience has amply demonstrated that audits provide boards and superintendents with considerable leverage to change curriculum, introduce improvements in control, and provide support for the necessary budgetary additions (Griffin, 1995; Vertiz, 1995).

(4) *Audits "Cool Off" Power Plays and Personality Conflicts.* Audits depersonalize the "hot" fallout of internal organizational power plays and shifts. By examining data, interviewing, and visiting sites, the curriculum auditor places the good of the entire organization above the politics of the day and can create the grounds for new coalitions and consensus towards instructional improvements.

(5) **Audits Reassure the Public Even If They Contain Negative Results.** One astute superintendent who presented the findings of a curriculum audit began his news conference by confessing, "We didn't bring this guy 2000 miles to give us a slap on the back. We wanted to get better and, therefore, we had to know where we had to improve. Now we know."

Strangely, negative results are reassuring. They can become the political base upon which to engage in refinement and reform. They can become the basis for improved support and funding. The public relations "sugar coating" technique has not worked in restoring public confidence in public education. In the long run, bad news can become good news.

Common Mistakes In Undertaking a Curriculum Audit

Enough time has passed and enough curriculum audits have been completed to offer some advice about undertaking a curriculum audit.

(1) **Select the Auditors on Expertise and Experience: Ask to See Examples of Past Work and Talk to Former Clients.** If cost is the only variable that will determine who does your curriculum audit, you most likely will find one short on experience if not expertise.

When considering an auditor, require references for past work. Talk to superintendents, board members, and community officials about the auditor's past. Ask to see copies of completed audits. If audits were paid for by public funds, they belong in the public domain and cannot be copyrighted. Share the audits with other officials in your school system. Imagine yourself and your district in those audits. Ask candidly if you and your staff can "take the heat." If not, look to alternatives other than auditing (see Bower & Russell, 1995).

(2) **Avoid Audits that are Shotgun Treatments Rather than Focused Examinations.** Some school systems have decided to elicit the help of businesses by asking for volunteers to study the schools. Few businesses know much about the core educational functions in schools. Fewer still face the demands for equity and access that have been thrust upon the schools by the courts. So, most businesses are politically naive about educational politics.

Asking for hordes of volunteers to examine the Chicago Public Schools, for example, produced a report with 253 recommendations that overwhelmed the district (Ayers, Bacon, & Perkins, 1981). The potpourri of findings and solutions did not emanate from a coherent theoretical base, nor a common set of standards.

Meaningful audits and organizational reviews are conducted by smaller, more cohesive teams using tighter and explicit criteria which ensures consistency of treatment and manageable recommendations. Not more than two-dozen recommendations should be contained in the final report. The reason is that change requires energy and often from the same people. Too many recommendations overwhelm the key people in the organizational hierarchy at the apex.

(3) **Everything of Importance and Value May Not Be Quantifiable.** Certain dimensions of doing audits are quantifiable. Documents exist or they do not. They include certain criteria or they do not. They are utilized by the staff or they are not. They lead to results or they do not. Most of that data are quantifiable.

Some data are not quantifiable. For example, a climate of despair or danger in schools may only be indirectly quantifiable by failure rates or dropout rates of students. The attitude of teachers and administrators who harbor deep prejudices that minority children are not capable may not be visible except perhaps in very low expectations for achievement. Secretaries who put children down, counselors who demean the potential of females, or teachers who refuse to give homework because they don't want to correct the papers may have to be experienced and recorded anecdotally. Curriculum audits are examples of quantitative and qualitative methods working in tandem.

(4) **Curriculum Audits are Not Research Reports.** The difference between auditing and research is that the latter is testing a theory, the former is applying one. Both use *research methods*, i.e., techniques of data gathering and interpretation.

A researcher never becomes part of the research. At some point an auditor intervenes in the organization with a set of recommendations. At this point the auditor is no longer objective or neutral since all organizations are governed by political coalitions. Inevitably, an auditor has to take sides with some faction(s) in an organization. Even if an audit begins as neutral, in the end it becomes part of the machinery. If it does not, then it has not been effective.

Summary

Curriculum audits have been conducted since 1979. Over one hundred audits have been performed nationally and internationally. A powerful new data base is being gathered about school system strengths and weaknesses based on the auditing standards and data-gathering methods.

Audits have been shown to be able to confront some of the most difficult political problems in American education. The standards of the audit are centered in the notion of *quality control.*

Audits are neither public relations ploys nor research studies. Rather, they are examples of applied data gathering which ultimately end with recommendations designed to change the operations of the entity being audited. So audits are interested in more than descriptions or hypotheses testing. The ultimate determination of the audit process is an improved organization, one that is focused and connected, equitable, effective and finally efficient.

DIALOGUE FOR IMPLEMENTATION

These are the questions most commonly asked of the authors about the ideas in this chapter:

1. What has been the major impetus for the growth of the curriculum management audit in education?

ANSWER: We believe it is attributed to high-risk state testing programs, the inability of school systems to deal with the political problems involved in the desegregation of schools, and the inability to link resource acquisition to improved levels of pupil achievement.

2. What are the weakest arguments for the audit?

ANSWER: The audit deals with context, but it does not see the schools as an active agent of political change in the larger society. Some would argue that it is therefore a process to reinforce the political status quo in which schools reinforce socioeconomic hegemony and domination.

3. Some of the documents are listed more than once under the audit standards. Isn't this duplicative?

ANSWER: Some documents are sources for many functions and activities in organizations. The budget, for example, touches nearly all aspects of school systems and other organizations. This is reflected in the audit data base.

4. Are there times when it isn't a good idea to think about a curriculum management audit?

ANSWER: If the superintendent and the board are fearful they have not done their jobs and know that an audit will reveal it, they shouldn't undertake an audit. Those afraid of an audit usually have good reasons to be.

5. When is the best time for an audit?

ANSWER: In the first or second year of a superintendency. The audit is a wonderful way to establish past history and sketch out "ground zero," i.e., what the district was like prior to the new incumbent taking over. If a superintendent or a board waits too long, they become identified with the problems because they did not take steps to divorce themselves from their origination, propagation, or prolongation.

ACTIVITIES FOR PERSONAL AND STAFF DEVELOPMENT

We offer some examples of activities as "starters," but encourage readers to develop their own that will fit their situation.

1. Compare a past accreditation report to the audit standards listed in this chapter. Where do they merge and where are they distinct? What do you think are the reasons?
2. Collect the following documents: several curriculum guides; current board policies; past system budgets; testing reports; any short- or long-range plans. Do these documents reflect a layer or a marble cake? Provide specific examples of your determination.
3. Explain five problems your school or school district has recently encountered. Which ones rest on the idea that the school or school system is rational? Do you believe in rationality? Why or why not?
4. Prepare a proposal for your own board of education to undertake a curriculum management audit. What do you anticipate their reactions to be? How would you speak to their objections?
5. In some ways, *A Nation at Risk: The Imperative for Educational Reform,* published in 1983, was a national curriculum audit of the country's schools. Analyze this report compared to the five standards and data sources listed in this chapter. What observations could you make about that report?

EPILOGUE

In the Introduction, we stated that the overarching aim of this book was to provide readers with effective and efficient processes and practices of curriculum management. In delivering on this aim, we mixed theory and practice throughout the pages. To cite Kurt Lewin's dictum, "There is nothing so practical as good theory." We believe that the feedback we have received over these last ten years from students in our courses and in in-service programs about the "powerful" nature of curriculum management is testimony to the fit of Lewin's dictum as a buttressing theme for this book. And the content we have presented is relevant to a variety of organizations within the broad field of education and human services, and also to other organizations, because, as we pointed out in Chapter 1, "nearly all complex organizations have a curriculum."

As we approach the end of the twentieth century, virtually all of those organizations are facing formidable challenges of survival or at least viability. The challenges come from a host of political, economic, social, technological and other trends that seem to be accelerating in complexity and confoundedness. We are in "permanent white water," which could lead to institutional paralysis rather than action. As professionals, we cannot let that happen. We have a responsibility to exert leadership so that our organizations will not only survive these turbulent times but will be ready to enter the twenty-first century as strong and vital societal institutions. All of us must be leaders, because the challenges are too complex and confounding for single leaders to meet them. It is almost analogous to 1776 when Benjamin Franklin said to John Hancock upon the signing of the Declaration of Independence, "We must all hang together, else we shall all hang separately."

In the case of the public school, the focus of the text, working together as a professional team will be essential if schools are to emerge from the current decade into the year 2000 as critical instruments for societal improvement. The enemies of schools dot the landscape and are gaining strength. Legitimate criticisms, combined with a calculated "manufactured crisis," orchestrated since the early 1980s by identifiable conservative critics, have led to the creation of policy alternatives to the public school, alternatives in the form of charter schools and schools of choice, with vouchers waiting in the wings for the next election. Privitization is with us and moving rapidly into the mainstream of acceptance. We concur with the conclusion of Berliner and Biddle:

> To the best of our knowledge, no campaign of this sort has ever before appeared in American history. Never before had an American government been so critical of the public schools, and never had so many false claims been made about education in the name of "evidence." (1995, p. 4)

The result of all these alternatives is that increasing tight resources are being diverted away from the masses who attend school toward the benefit of a select few of that population.

This is not to say that educators themselves, in too many instances, are not also responsible for the perceived crisis. Years of curriculum auditing across the United States, combined with our other experiences working in and with schools, have revealed the best and the worst about them. There is much good news across school system after school system in these United States. That good news, the results of the highly professional and dedicated work of countless unsung educators, too often gets ignored in the maelstrom of everyday problems and those that are sometimes "manufactured."

But the research results from a sample of fifty-nine audits also uncovered "educational malpractice" in too many places where outmoded, unthinking, and plain stupid practices by educators (often aided and abetted by school boards and local politicians) are not benefiting students and, in the process, undermining belief and confidence in our schools and providing ammunition to the critics (English, 1988; Frase, English, & Poston, 1995; Vertiz & Bates, 1995). In these situations, the conditions are also often magnified because of lack of interest in and support for schools by the community. We must and we can do better.

In a provocative new book analyzing a century of public school reform, Tyack and Cuban conclude that the major aim of reform is to improve *learning* "generously construed as rich intellectual, civic, and social development, not simply as impressive test scores" (1995, p. 136). This is the central message of our book. Curriculum management concepts, practices, and processes can be of considerable help to educators on the front lines of school improvement, improvement aimed at the crux of what schooling is all about: learning. But applying what we have discussed will not bring about near instant transformation. All social organizations, as we have stressed throughout this text, are complex and slow to change radically. But they can and do improve, often through gradual and incremental innovation. In tandem with it, improvement comes also through professionals embodying "the dirty fingernails tradition—hard work in the service of worthy causes" (Oliphant, 1995).

> It may be fashionable to decry such change as piecemeal and inadequate, but over long periods of time such revisions of practice, adapted to local contexts, can substantially improve schools. (Tyack & Cuban, 1995, p. 5)

We must continue on this journey to make our schools better, but we must make every effort, given the seriousness of the problems we face in education, to speed up the process of reform. The journey will be a challenging, frustrating, exhilarating, tiring, but most vital endeavor for our nation's future.

BIBLIOGRAPHY

Addison Northeast Supervisory Union. (1994). ANESCU assessment report. Bristol, VT.

Adler, M. J. (1982). *The Paideia proposal.* New York: Macmillan Publishing Co., Inc.

American Association of School Administrators. (1973). *Management by objectives and results.* Arlington, VA.

American Association of School Administrators. (1982). *Time on task.* Arlington, VA.

American Association of School Administrators. (1993). *Making sense of testing and achievement.* Arlington, VA.

American Association of School Administrators. (1993, March). A curriculum management audit of the Newport News public schools, Virginia. Arlington, VA, 100 pp.

American Association of School Administrators. (1995, July). A curriculum management audit of the Round Rock independent school district. Arlington, VA, 207 pp.

Apple, M. W. (1986). *Teachers and texts: A political economy of class and gender relations in education.* New York: Routledge, Chapman, and Hall.

Apple, M. W. (1970). *Ideology and curriculum.* London: Routledge, Chapman, and Hall.

Aram, J. D. (1976). *Dilemmas of administrative behavior.* Englewood Cliffs, NJ: Prentice-Hall.

Archbald, D. (1993, October). Restructuring in the eyes of practitioners: An analysis of "next century" school restructuring proposals. *International Journal of Educational Reform, 2*(4), 384–398.

Archibald, D. A., & Newmann, F. M. (1988). *Beyond standardized testing.* Reston, VA: National Association of Secondary School Principals.

Armstrong, T. (1994). *Multiple intelligences in the classroom.* Alexandria, VA: Association for Supervision and Curriculum Development.

Associated Press. (1986, July 29). Shuttle tape shows pilot knew of trouble. *Courier-Post*, p. 1.

Atkinson, C. (1983). *Making sense of Piaget: The philosophical roots.* London: Routledge, Chapman, and Hall.

Avenoso, K. (1996, January 18). School chief likely to scrap MAT exam. *The Boston Globe*, p. 31.

Ayers, T. G., Bacon, W. H., & Perkins, D. S. (1981). *Special task force on education Chicago school reform: Recommended actions.* Chicago, Illinois.

249

Bailey, T. (1991, March). Jobs of the future and the education they will require: Evidence from occupational forecasts. *Educational Researcher, 20*(2), 11–20.

Baker, D. P. (1992, April). Compared to Japan, the U.S. is a low achiever . . . really. *Educational Researcher, 22*(3), 18–20.

Banks, J. R. (1991). *Selecting a Thinking Skills Program.* Lancaster, PA: Technomic.

Battistich, V., Solomon, D., Kim, D., Watson, K. M., & Schaps, E. (1995, Fall). Schools as communities, poverty levels of student populations, and students' attitudes, motives, and performance: A multilevel analysis. *American Educational Research Journal, 32*(3), 627–658.

Beauchamp, G. (1975). *Curriculum theory.* Wilmette, IL: The Kagg Press.

Beck, L. G. (1994). *Reclaiming educational administration as a caring profession.* New York: Teachers College Press.

Bellah, R. N. (1970). *Beyond belief.* As cited in W. F. O'Neill, *Educational ideologies* (p. 119). Santa Monica, CA: Goodyear Publishing Company.

Bennett, A. (1994, September 6). U.S. Marxists thrive despite communism's demise. *The Wall Street Journal,* pp. B1–B6.

Bennett, W. J. (1989). James Madison high school. In J. J. Lane & H. J. Walberg (Eds.), *Organizing for learning toward the 21st century.* Reston, VA: NASSP, pp. 9–15.

Bennett, W. J. (1988). *James Madison elementary school.* Washington, DC: U. S. Department of Education.

Bennett, W. J. (1987). *James Madison high school.* Washington, DC: U. S. Department of Education.

Berkak, H. (1992). The need for a new science of assessment. In H. Berack et al. (Eds.), *Toward a New Science of Educational Testing and Assessment.* Albany: State University of New York Press, pp. 1–21.

Berliner, D. C., & Biddle, B. J. (1995). *The manufactured crisis: Myths, fraud, and the attack on America's public schools.* Reading, MA: Addison-Wesley.

Berliner, D. C. (1984). The half-full glass: A review of research on teaching. In P. O. Hosford (Ed.), *Using what we know about teaching.* Alexandria, VA: Association for Supervision and Curriculum Development, pp. 51–75.

Bestor, A. (1956). *The restoration of learning.* New York: Alfred A. Knopf.

Beyer, B. K. (1987). *Practical strategies for the teaching of thinking.* Boston: Allyn and Bacon.

Bidwell, C. W. (1965). The school as a formal organization. In J. G. March (Ed.), *Handbook of organizations.* Chicago: Rand McNally, pp. 972–1022.

Bingham, J. (1994, February 7). Chavez out in Littleton. *The Denver Post,* pp. 1, 7A.

Bleakley, F. R. (1993, July 6). Many companies try management fads, only to see them flop. *The Wall Street Journal,* pp. A1, A8.

Block, J. H. (Ed.). (1971). *Mastery learning: Theory and practice.* New York: Holt, Rinehart and Winston.

Block, J. H. (1971). *Mastery learning.* New York: Holt, Rinehart, and Winston.

Bloom, A. (1987). *The closing of the American mind.* New York: Simon and Schuster.

Bloom, B. S. (Ed.). (1956). *Taxonomy of educational objectives: Handbook I: Cognitive domain.* New York: David McKay.

Bloom, B. S. (1964). *Stability and change in human characteristics.* New York: John Wiley.

Bloom, B. S. (1981). *All our children learning.* New York: McGraw-Hill.

Bobbitt, F. (1929). Problems involved in adapting schools. In G. M. Whipple (Ed.), *Adapting the Schools to Individual Differences.* Bloomington, IL: Public School Publishing Co., pp. 224–230.

Bolman, L. G., & Deal, T. E. (1991). *Reframing organizations.* San Francisco: Jossey-Bass.

Bode, B. H. (1930). *Modern educational theories.* New York: Macmillan.

Bonner, S. F. (1977). *Education in ancient Rome.* Berkeley: University of California Press.

Bonstingl, J. J. (1992). *Schools of quality.* Alexandria, VA: Association for Supervision and Curriculum Development.

Bower, N., & Russell, M. (1995, Fall). One district's journey. *Insight,* Journal of the Texas Association of School Administrators, *9*(3), 24–28.

Bowles, S., & Gintis, H. (1976). *Schooling in capitalist America.* New York: Basic Books.

Bradley, A. (1994, June 1). Requiem for a reform. *Education Week, 13*(36), 21–25.

Bradley, L. (1993). *Total quality management for schools.* Lancaster, PA: Technomic.

Briggs, T. H., Leonard, J. P., & Justman, J. (1950). *Secondary education.* New York: Macmillan.

Brooks, J. C., & Brooks, M. G. (1993). *In search of understanding: The case for constructivist classrooms.* Alexandria, VA: Association for Supervision and Curriculum Development.

Bruner, J. S. (1961). *The process of education.* Cambridge: Harvard University Press.

Bureau of Elementary and Secondary Testing Programs. (January 1993 Edition). *Regents examinations, regents competency tests, and proficiency examinations: School administrators manual.* Albany, NY: The State Education Department.

Burke, M. (1994, December). Broken promises: Portfolios become political. *Vermont-NEA Today, 61*(5), 2.

Burr, I. W. (1976). *Statistical quality control methods.* New York: Marcel Dekker, Inc.

Burron, A. (1994, October). Traditionalist Christians and OBE: What's the problem? *Educational Leadership, 51*(6), 73–75.

Canady, R. L., & Rettig, M. D. (1993, December). Unlocking the lockstep high school schedule. *Phi Delta Kappan, 75*(4), 310–314.

Cannell, J. J. (1987). *Nationally normed elementary achievement testing in America's public schools: How all fifty states are above the national average.* Daniels, W VA: Friends for Education.

Callahan, R. E. (1962). *Education and the cult of efficiency.* Chicago: The University of Chicago Press.

Carlson, D. (1982). Updating individualism and the work ethic: Corporate logic in the classroom. *Curriculum Inquiry, 12*(2), 125–160.

Carlson, R. O. (1964). Environmental constraints and organizational consequences: The public school and its clients. In D. G. Griffiths (Ed.), *Behavioral Science and Educational Administration.* Chicago: The University of Chicago Press, pp. 262–276.

Carnegie Council on Adolescent Development. (1989). *Turning points in preparing American youth for the 21st century.* New York: Carnegie Corporation.

Carr, J. F., & Harris, D. E. (1993). *Getting it together: A process handbook for K–12 curriculum development, implementation, and assessment.* Boston: Allyn and Bacon.

Carroll, J. (1989). *The Copernician plan: Restructuring the American high school.* Andover, MA: The Regional Laboratory for Educational Improvement of the Northeast and Islands.

Carroll, J. M. (1994, October). The Copernician plan evaluation: The evolution of a revolution. *Phi Delta Kappan, 76*(2), 105–113.

Carroll, J. J. (1994). *The Copernician plan evaluated: The evaluation of a revolution.* Topsfield, MA: Copernician Associates.

Carter, D. G. (1993, January). Structural change and curriculum reform in an Australian education system. *International Journal of Educational Reform, 2*(1), 56–67.

Cartwright, D. (1965). Influence, leadership, and control. In J. March (Ed.), *Handbook of organizations.* Chicago: Rand McNally, pp. 1–47.

Castetter, W. B. (1986). *The personnel function in educational administration* (4th ed.). New York: Macmillan.

Chandler, D. (1995, July 5). Shuttle makes graceful exit. *The Boston Globe,* p. 3.

Chion-Kennedy, L. (1994, September). Negotiating the challenge of outcome-based education. *The School Administrator, 8*(51), 9–19.

Chion-Kenney, L. (1994, September). Responding to the backlash: The key is involving the whole community. *The AASA School Administrator, 8*(51), 10–19.

Christian-Smith, L. K. (1987, Winter). Gender, popular culture, and curriculum: Adolescent romance novels as gender text. *Curriculum Inquiry, 17*(4), 365–406.

Chittenden Central Supervisory Union. (1994). *Guide for student assessment.* Essex Junction, VT.

Chittenden Central Supervisory Union. (1993). *Curriculum implementation and management policy.* Essex Junction, VT.

Chubb, J. E., & Moe, T. M. (1990). *Politics, markets, and America's schools.* Washington, DC: The Brookings Institute.

Clark, J., & Agne, R. (1996). *Integrated learning: Strategies for interdisciplinary high school teaching.* Boston: Allyn and Bacon.

Coble, L. (1992, Winter). A district's response to its audit report. *Education,* 113.2, 190–4.

Cohen, M. D., March, J. G., & Olsen, J. P. (1979). People, problems, solutions, and the ambiguity of relevance. In J. G. March and J. P. Olsen (Eds.), *Ambiguity and choice in organizations.* Bergen, Norway: Universitetsforlaget, pp. 24–37.

Cohen, M. D., & March, J. G. (1974). *Leadership and ambiguity.* New York: McGraw-Hill.

Coleman, J. E. et al. (1966). *Equality of educational opportunity.* Washington, DC: U. S. Government Printing Office, pp. 20–23.

Conley, D. T. (1993). *Roadmap to restructuring.* Eugene, OR: ERIC Clearinghouse on Educational Management, University of Oregon.

Conley, D. T. (January 28, 1994). Proficiency-based admission standards study (PASS). Eugene, OR: Office of Academic Affairs, Oregon State System for Higher Education.

Cook, B. (1990). *Strategic Planning for America's Schools* (2nd ed.). Arlington, VA: American Association of School Administrators.

Council of Chief State School Officers. (1994). *School-to-Work Opportunities Act: Summary of the Act.* Washington, DC.

Cremin, L. A. (1961). *The transformation of the school.* New York: Vintage Books.

Cubberly, E. P. (1929). *Public school administration.* Boston: Houghton Mifflin.

Cubberly, E. P. (1948). *The history of education.* Boston: Houghton Mifflin.

Darling-Hammond, L. (1993, October). Reframing the school reform agenda. *Phi Delta Kappan, 74*(10), 753–761.

Davis, A., & Felknor, C. (1994, March). The demise of performance-based graduation in Littleton. *Educational Leadership, 51*(6), 64–65.

Deming, W. E. (1993). *The new economics.* Cambridge, MA: MIT Press.

Deming, W. E. (1986). *Out of the crisis.* Cambridge, MA: MIT Center for Advanced Engineering Study.

Dewey, J. (1902). *The child and the curriculum.* Chicago: University of Chicago Press.

Diegmueller, K. (1995, April 12). Struggling for standards. An *Education Week* Special Report, pp. 1–70.

Diegmueller, K. (1995a, January 11). Backlash puts standards work in harm's way. *Education Week, 14*(16), 1, 14–15.

Diegmueller, K. (1995b, April 12). Running out of steam. An *Education Week* Special Report, pp. 1–70.

Diegmueller, K. (1994, September 28). Standards-setters hoping to publish best sellers. *Education Week, 14*(16), 1, 12–13.

Dowdy, Z. R. (1994, June 23). School pact reached, seen as "new era." *The Boston Globe,* pp. 1, 18.

Downey, C. J. (1992, Winter). Applying the quality fit framework to the curriculum management audit. *Education, 113*(2), 203–209.

Downey, C. J. (1995, Fall). Power policies. *Insight,* Journal of the Texas Association of School Administrators, *9*(3), 19–23.

Drucker, P. F. (1973). *Management.* New York: Harper and Row.

Dunn, R., & Dunn, K. (1979). Using learning style data to develop student prescriptions. In *Student Learning Styles.* Reston, VA: National Association of Secondary School Principals, pp. 109–122.

Dunn, R., & Griggs, S. A. (1988). *Learning styles: Quiet revolution in American secondary schools.* Reston, VA: National Association of Secondary School Principals.

Durkin, M. C. (1993). *Thinking through class discussion.* Lancaster, PA: Technomic.

Earley, M. (1992). Can we move writing across the curriculum? In J. M. Jenkins and D. Tanner (Eds.), *Restructuring for an interdisciplinary curriculum.* Reston, VA: National Association of Secondary Principals.

Edmunds, R. (1978). *A discussion of the literature and issues related to effective schooling.* A paper presented to the National Conference on Urban Education, St. Louis, MO, July 10–14.

Edmunds, R. (1979, October). Effective schools for the urban poor. *Educational Leadership, 37*(1), 15–24.

Educational Leadership. (October, 1985). *43*(2), 4–76. (Several articles devoted to testing.)

Educational Leadership. (1994, October). 52.2. (The entire issue is devoted to grading and reporting.)

Eisner, E. W., & Vallence, E. (Eds.). (1974). *Conflicting conceptions of curriculum.* Berkeley, CA: McCutchan Publishing.

Eisner, E. W. (1985). *The art of educational evaluation.* Philadelphia: The Falmer Press.

Elam, S. M., Rose, L. C., & Gallup, A. M. (1994, September). The 26th annual Phi Delta Kappan Gallup poll of the public's attitudes toward the public schools. *Phi Delta Kappan, 76*(1), 41–56.

English, F. W., & Kaufman, R. A. (1975). *Needs assessment: A focus for curriculum development.* Washington, DC: Association of Supervision and Curriculum Development.

English, F. W. (1978). *Quality control in curriculum development.* Arlington, VA: American Association of School Administrators.

English, F. W. (1979a, March). Management practice as a key to curriculum leadership. *Educational Leadership, 36*(6), 7–13.

English, F. W. (1979b, May). Re-tooling curriculum within on-going school systems. *Educational Technology, 19*(5), 7–13.

English, F. W. (1980, April). Curriculum mapping. *Educational Leadership, 37*(7), 558–559.

English, F. W. (1980). Curriculum development within the school system. In A. W. Forshay (Ed.), *Considered Action for Curriculum Improvement.* Alexandria, VA: Association for Supervision and Curriculum Development.

English, F. W., & Steffy, B. E. (1982, January). Curriculum as a strategic management tool. *Educational Leadership,* 276–278.

English, F. W., & Steffy, B. E. (1983, February). Differentiating between design and delivery problems in achieving quality control in school curriculum management. *Educational Technology,* 29–32.

English, F. W., & Steffy, B. E. (1983, Fall). Curriculum mapping: An aid to school curriculum management. *Spectrum, Journal of School Research and Information, 1*(3), 24–25.

English, F. W. (1986, March). Developing total curriculum quality control: Responding to the challenge of the HSPT. Trenton, NJ: New Jersey Department of Education.

English, F. W. (1987). *Curriculum management for schools, colleges, business.* Springfield, IL: Charles C Thomas.

English, F. W. (1988). *Curriculum auditing.* Lancaster, PA: Technomic.

English, F. W. (1991). Visual traces in schools and the reproduction of social inequities. In K. M. Borman (Ed.), *Contemporary issues in U.S. education.* Norwood, New Jersey: Ablex Publishing Corporation, pp. 84–104.

English, F. W., & Steffy, B. E. (1992, Winter). Promise and problems of the curriculum audit. *Education, 113*(2), 168–171.

English, F. W. (1992). *Deciding what to teach and test.* Newbury Park, CA: Corwin Press.

English, F. W. (1994). *Theory in educational administration.* New York: Harper Collins.

English, F. W., & Hill, J. C. (1994). *Total quality education: Transforming schools into learning places.* Thousand Oaks, CA: Corwin Press.

English, F. W. (1995, Fall). The curriculum management audit: Uncorking the genie from the bottle. *Insight,* Journal of the Texas Association of School Administrators, *9*(3), 12–14.

English, F. W., Vertiz, V., & Bates, G. (1995, Fall). Gauging the impact of the curriculum management audit. *Catalyst for Change, 25*(1), 13–15.

Evans, K. M., & King, J. A. (1994, March). Research on OBE: What we know and don't know. *Educational Leadership, 51*(6), 12–17.

FairTest. The National Center for Fair and Open Testing, 342 Broadway, Cambridge, MA 02139-1802.

Farrel, J. A. (1994, October 21). An old school rally for Kennedy. *The Boston Globe,* pp. 1, 32.

Ferguson, L. C. (1994, August). *The art and science of holistic alignment.* Scottsdale, Arizona: Evans Newton.

Filley, A. C., & House, R. J. (1969). *Managerial processes and organizational behavior.* Glenview, IL: Scott, Foresman.

Finn, C. E., Jr. (1991). *We must take charge.* New York: The Free Press.

Fisher, C. W., Berliner, D. G., Filly, N. N., Marliave, R., Cahen, L. S., & Dishaw, M. M. (1980). Teaching behaviors, academic learning time, and student achievement: An overview. In C. Denham & A. Lieberman (Eds.), *Time to learn.* Washington, DC: National Institute of Education.

Fitzgerald, F. (1979). *America revised.* Boston: Little, Brown.

Foose, L. O. (1881). *Report of the superintendent of public instruction, commonwealth of Pennsylvania.* Harrisburg: Lanes Hart, State Printer.

Foster, W. P. (1980). Administration and the crisis of legitimacy: A review of Habermasian thought. *Harvard Educational Review, 39*(2), 243–260.

Freeland, K. (1991). *Managing the Social Studies Curriculum.* Lancaster, PA: Technomic.

Frase, L. E. (1992, Winter). Constructive feedback on teaching is missing. *Education, 113*(2), 176–181.

Frase, L. E., English, F. W., & Poston, W. K., Jr. (Eds.). (1995). *The curriculum management audit.* Lancaster, PA: Technomic.

Freire, P. (1970). *Pedagogy of the Oppressed.* New York: The Seabury Press.

Fuchsberg, G. (1994, January 7). Visioning missions becomes its own mission. *The Wall Street Journal,* pp. B1–B4.

Fullan, M. G. (with S. Stiegelbauer). (1991). *The new meaning of educational change* (2nd ed.). New York: Teachers College Press.

Fullan, M. G. (1993). *Change forces.* New York: The Falmer Press.

Fullan, M. G. (1994). Coordinating top-down and bottom-up strategies for educational reform. In R. F. Elmore & S. H. Fuhrman (Eds.), *The governance of curriculum.* Alexandria, VA: Association for Supervision and Curriculum Development, pp. 186–202.

Gaffield, C. (1994, February). Children's lives and academic achievement in Canada and the United States. *Comparative Education Review, 38*(1), 36–64.

Galbraith, J. R. (1977). *Organization design.* Reading, MA: Addison-Wesley.

Gardner, H. (1983). *Frames of mind: The theory of multiple intelligences.* New York: Basic Books.

Gardner, H. (1991). *The unchecked mind.* New York: Basic Books.

Gardner, H. (1993). *Multiple intelligences: The theory in practice.* New York: Basic Books.

Gardner, H. (1995, November). Reflections on multiple intelligences: Myths and messages. *Phi Delta Kappan, 77*(3), 200–209.

Geggis, A. (1994, October 27). State's student portfolios pass tests of reliability. *The Burlington Free Press,* pp. 1B, 2B.

Giroux, H. A. (1994). *Disturbing pleasures.* New York: Routledge, Chapman and Hall.

Giroux, H., & McLaren, P. (1992, April). American 2000 and the politics of erasure: Democracy and cultural differences under siege. *International Journal of Educational Reform, 1*(2), 99–110.

Giroux, H. A. (1988). *Schooling and the struggle for public life.* Minneapolis: University of Minnesota Press.

Glatthorn, A. A. (1994, October). Constructivism: Implications for curriculum. *International Journal of Educational Reform, 3*(4), 449–455.

Glegg, A. R. L. (1995, January). Inquest on a failure: The dual entry kindergarten experiment in British Columbia. *International Journal of Educational Reform, 4*(1), 25–28.

Glickman, C. E. (Ed.). (1992). *Supervision in transition.* Alexandria, VA: Association for Supervision and Curriculum Development.

Glickman, C. D., Gordon, S. P., & Ross-Gordon, J. M. (1995). *Supervision of instruction: A developmental approach* (3rd ed.). Boston: Allyn & Bacon.

Gonzalez, R. D. (1994, October). Race and the politics of educational failure: A plan for advocacy and reform. *International Journal of Educational Reform, 3*(4) 427–36.

Good, T. L., & Brophy, J. E. (1978). *Looking in classrooms.* New York: Harper & Row.

Goodlad, J. I. (1984). *A place called school.* New York: McGraw-Hill.

Goodlad, J. I. (1990). *Teachers for our nation's schools.* San Francisco: Jossey-Bass.

Goodlad, J. I. (1994). *Educational renewal: Better teachers, better schools.* San Francisco: Jossey-Bass.

Gordon, R. (1994, January 31). A lasting legacy for managers. *The Wall Street Journal,* p. A12.

Gotwals, J. (1881). *Report of the superintendent of public instruction, commonwealth of Pennsylvania.* Harrisburg: Lanes Hart, State Printer.

Gould, S. J. (1981). *The mismeasure of man.* New York: Norton.

Grannis, J. C. (1972). The school as a model of society. In D. E. Purpel & M. Belanger (Eds.), *Curriculum and the cultural revolution.* Berkeley, CA: McCutchan, pp. 146–165.

Graver, L. (1954). *A history of the first Pennsylvania state normal school.* Millersville, PA: Nazareth Publishing Co.

Green, T. F. (1969). Schools and communities: A look forward. *Harvard Educational Review, 39*(2), 243–260.

Greene, S. (1992, Winter). Productivity: Improving the educational system over time. *Education, 113*(2), 187–189.

Gregorc, A. F. (1979). Learning/teaching styles: Potent forces behind them. *Educational Leadership, 36,* 234–236.

Greer, C. (1972). *The great school legend.* New York: The Viking Press.

Griffin, A., & Bryce, C. (1995, Fall). Step up to the audit. *Insight,* Journal of the Texas Association of School Administrators, *9*(3), 15–18.

Griffin, E. (1995, December). Jump starting reform through a curriculum audit. *AASA School Administrator, 11*(52), 18–24.

Gronlund, N. E., & Linn, R. L. (1990). *Measurement and evaluation in teaching* (6th ed.). New York: Macmillan.

Guskey, T. R. (1985). *Implementing mastery learning.* Belmont, CA: Wadsworth.

Haladyna, T. M., Nolen, S. B., & Haas, N. S. (1991). Raising standardized achievement test scores and the origins of test score pollution. *Educational Researcher, 20*(5), 2–7.

Hall, E. T. (1977). *Beyond culture.* New York: Anchor Books.

Hall, G. E., & Hord, S. M. (1987). *Change in schools.* Albany, NY: SUNY Press.

Halverson, P. M. (1961). The meaning of balance. In *Balance in the curriculum.* Washington, DC: Association for Supervision and Curriculum Development.

Hansenfeld, Y. (Ed.). (1992). *Human services as complex organizations.* Newbury Park, CA: SAGE Publications.

Harp, L. (1993, September 22). PA Parent becomes mother of "outcomes" revolt. *Education Week, 13*(3), 1, 20–21.

Harp, L. (1994, June 15). Pass or fail. *Education Week, 13*(38), 18–23.

Harrow, A. J. (1972). *A taxonomy of the psychomotor domain.* New York: David McKay.

Hendery, D. (1992, February). Outcomes-driven or outcomes-drivel? The answer is alignment. *Quality Outcomes-Driven Education,* 9–15.

Herman, J. L., Ansbacher, P. R., & Winters, L. (1992). *A practical guide to alternative assessment.* Alexandria, VA: Association for Supervision and Curriculum Development.

Herman, J. L., & Winters, L. (1992). *Tracking your school's success.* Newbury Park, CA: Corwin Press.

Herrnstein, R. J., & Murray, C. (1994). *The bell curve.* New York: Free Press.

Hersey, P., & Blanchard, K. H. (1993). *Management of organizational behavior: Utilizing human resources* (6th ed.). Englewood Cliffs, NJ: Prentice-Hall.

Hess, Jr., G. A. (1992, July). Midway through school reform in Chicago. *International Journal of Educational Reform, 1*(3), 270–284.

Hill, J. (1992). *The new American school.* Lancaster, PA: Technomic.

Hirsch, Jr., E. D. (1987). *Cultural literacy: What every American needs to know.* Boston: Houghton Mifflin.

Hoffman, C. M. (1987). *Curriculum gone astray: When push came to shove.* Lancaster, PA: Technomic.

Hostrop, R. W. (1973). *Managing education for results.* Homewood, IL: ETC Publications.

Howard, J. (1984). *Margaret Mead: A life.* New York: Simon & Schuster.

Hoyle, J. R., English, F. W., & Steffy, B. E. (1990). *Skills for successful school leaders* (2nd ed.). Alexandria, VA: American Association of School Administrators.

Huberman, M. (1983). Recipes for busy kitchens. *Knowledge: Creation, Diffusion, Utilization, 4*(4), 478–511.

Hunkins, F. P. (1980). *Curriculum development.* Columbus: Charles E. Merrill.

Hunter, M. (1982). *Mastery teaching.* El Segundo, CA: TIP Publications.

Hutchins, R. M. (1953). *The conflict in education.* New York: Harper & Row.

Hymes, D. L. with Chafin, A. E., & Gonder, P. (1991). *The changing face of testing and assessment.* Arlington, VA: American Association of School Administrators.

Illich, I. (1970). *Deschooling society.* New York: Harper & Row.

Immegart, G. L., & Pilecki, F. J. (1973). *An introduction to systems for the educational administrator.* Reading, MA: Addison-Wesley.

Jencks, C. et al. (1972). *Inequality.* New York: Basic Books.

Jenkins, J. M. (1992). Some common threads of the interdisciplinary curriculum. In J. M. Jenkins & D. Tanner (Eds.), *Restructuring for an interdisciplinary curriculum.* Reston, VA: National Association of Secondary School Principals, 101–104.

Johnson, S. M. (1990). Redesigning teachers work. In R. F. Elmore and Associates, *Restructuring schools: The next generation of educational reform.* San Francisco: Jossey-Bass, pp. 125–151.

Jones, A. J., Grizzell, E. D., & Grinstead, W. J. (1939). *Principles of unit construction.* New York: McGraw-Hill.

Jones, Beau Fly et al. (1987). *Strategic teaching and learning: Cognitive instruction in the content areas.* Alexandria, VA: ASCD.

Joyce, B., & Weil, M. (1986). *Models of teaching* (4th ed.). Englewood Cliffs, NJ: Prentice-Hall.

Judson, G. (1995, December 7). For education company, a shift in vision. *New York Times,* p. A13.

Juran, J. M. (1988). *Juran on planning for quality control.* New York: The Free Press.

Kahn, S. D. (1977). The numbers game: How the testing industry operates. In P. L. Houts (Ed.), *The myth of measurability.* New York: Hart Publishing.

Katz, M. B. (1987). *Class, bureaucracy, and schools.* New York: Praeger.

Katz, D., & Kahn, R. L. (1978). *The social psychology of organizations* (2nd ed.). New York: John Wiley & Sons.

Kaufman, R. (1988). *Planning educational systems.* Lancaster, PA: Technomic.

Kaufman, R. A., & English, F. W. (1979). *Needs assessment: Concept and application.* Englewood Cliffs, NJ: Educational Technology Publications.

Kaufman, R., Herman, J., & Watters, K. (1995). *Educational planning: Strategic, tactical, operational.* Lancaster, PA: Technomic.

Kaufman, R., & Herman, J. (1990). *Strategic planning in education.* Lancaster, PA: Technomic.

Kaufman, R. A. (1983). Needs assessment. In F. W. English (Ed.), *Fundamental Curriculum Decisions.* Alexandria, VA: Association for Supervision and Curriculum Development, pp. 53–67.

Keefe, J. F. (1979). Learning style: An overview. In *Student learning styles: Diagnosing and prescribing programs.* Reston, VA: National Association of Secondary School Principals.

Keefe, J. F. (1987). *Learning style: Theory and practice.* Reston, VA: National Association of Secondary School Principals.

Kelly, W. R. (1881). *Report of the superintendent of public instruction, commonwealth of Pennsylvania.* Harrisburg: Lanes Hart, State Printer.

Kemen, H. J., & Gallagher, K. S. (1995). A follow-up study of three school districts. In L. E. Frase, F. W. English, & W. K. Poston, Jr. (Eds.), *The curriculum management audit.* Lancaster, PA: Technomic, pp. 277–295.

Kendall, J., & Marzano, R. (1994). *The systematic identification and articulation of content standards and benchmarks.* Aurora, CO: Mid-Continent Regional Educational Laboratory.

Kirschembaum, H., Simon, S. B., and Napier, R. W. (1971). *Wad-ja-get?: The grading game in American education.* New York: Hart Publishing.

Kliebard, H. M. (1982, January). Education at the turn of the century: A crucible for curriculum change. *Educational Researcher, 11*(1), 16–24.

Koretz, D., Klein, S., McCaffrey, D., & Stecher, B. (1993, October 18). *Interim report: The reliability of Vermont portfolio scores in the 1992-93 school year.* Santa Monica, CA: Rand Institute on Education and Training.

Kozol, J. (1967). *Death at an early age.* New York: Bantam Books.

Krathwohl, D. R., Bloom, B. S., & Masia, B. B. (1964). *Taxonomy of educational objectives: Handbook II: Affective domain.* New York: David McKay.

Krug, E. A. (1964). *The shaping of the American high school.* New York: Harper & Row.

Kuhn, A., & Beam, R. D. (1982). *The logic of organizations.* San Francisco: Jossey-Bass.

Kuhn, T. S. (1962). *The structure of scientific revolutions.* Chicago: The University of Chicago Press.

Larson, R. (1992, January). Can the frog become a prince? Context and change in the 1990's. *International Journal of Educational Reform, 1*(1), 59–68.

Larson, R. L. (1992a). *Changing schools from the inside out.* Lancaster, PA: Technomic.

Larson, R. L. (1993). Making sense of change: What we know from research and practice. In J. R. Hoyle & D. M. Estes (Eds.), *NCPEA: In a New Voice,* Lancaster, PA: Technomic, pp. 276–290.

Lehner, U. C. (1995, October 20). Is the vaunted "Asian miracle" really just an illusion? *The Wall Street Journal,* p. A10.

Lessinger, L. (1970). *Every kind a winner.* New York: Simon & Schuster.

Lieberman, M. (1989). *Privatization and education choice.* New York: St. Martin's Press.

Lieberman, M. (1993). *Public education: An autopsy.* Cambridge, MA: Harvard University Press.

Livingston, G. A. (1992, Winter). Curriculum control: After an educational performance audit, are you really finished? *Education, 113*(2), 199–201.

LeTendre, G. K. (1994, April). Distribution tables and private tests: The failure of middle school reform in Japan. *International Journal of Educational Reform, 3*(2), 126–136.

Letteri, C. A. (1980, March/April). Cognitive profile: Basic determinant of academic achievement. *Journal of Educational Research,* 195–199.

Levin, D. (1993, October 4). Robert Eaton thinks "vision" is overrated and he's not alone. *The Wall Street Journal,* pp. A-1, A-6.

Lien, A. J., & Lien, H. S. (1980). *Measurement and evaluation of learning* (4th ed.). Dubuque, IA: W. C. Brown.

Lindsey, D. (1995, November 22). Report contests huge boost in school dollars. *Education Week, 15*(12), 1, 7.

Lively, K. (1995, April 28). Rocky road to reform. *The Chronicle of Higher Education, 41*(33), 54–55, 59.

Lortie, D. E. (1975). *Schoolteacher: A sociological study.* Chicago: The University of Chicago Press.

Madaus, G. F., & Tan, A. G. (1993). The growth of assessment. In G. Cawelti (Ed.), *Challenges and achievements of American education.* Alexandria, VA: Association for Supervision and Curriculum Development.

Madaus, G. F. (1985, May). Test scores as administrative mechanisms in educational policy. *Phi Delta Kappan, 66*(9), 611–617.

Maeroff, G. I. (1988). *The empowerment of teachers.* New York: Teachers College Press.

Maeroff, G. I. (1991). Assessing alternative assessment. *Phi Delta Kappan, 73*(4), 272–281.

Mager, R. F. (1962). *Preparing objectives for programmed instruction.* San Francisco, CA: Fearon Publishers.

Manatt, R. (1994, April). Seeking a middle ground for school reform—meeting the challenge of the conservatives and evangelicals. *International Journal of Educational Reform, 3*(2), 226–241.

Manatt, R. P. (1988). Teacher performance evaluation: A total systems approach. In S. J. Stanley and W. J. Popham (Eds.), *Teacher evaluation: Six prescriptions for success.* Alexandria, VA: Association for Supervision and Curriculum Development, pp. 79–109.

Manatt, R. P. (1995). *When right is wrong.* Lancaster, PA: Technomic.

Mappus, L. L. (1994, September 23). Letter to commissioner of education Richard P. Mills reporting on Vermont's assessment needs and status. Columbia, SC: Insite, Inc.

March, J. G., & Olsen, J. P. (Eds.). (1979). *Ambiguity and choice in organizations.* Bergen, Norway: Universitetsforlaget.

Marzano, R. J., Brandt, R. S., Hughes, C. S., Jones, B. F., Presseissen, B. Z., Rankin, S. C., & Suhor, C. (1988). *Dimensions of thinking: A framework for curriculum and instruction.* Alexandria, VA: ASCD.

Marzano, R. J. (1992). *A different kind of classroom: Teaching with dimensions of learning.* Alexandria, VA: Association for Supervision and Curriculum Development.

Marzano, R. J. (1992). A rationale and framework for teaching thinking tactics. In J. W. Keefe & H. J. Walberg (Eds.), *Teaching for thinking.* Reston, VA: National Association of Secondary School Principals, pp. 15–26.

Marzano, R. J., Pickering, D., & McTighe, J. (1993). *Assessing student outcomes.* Alexandria, VA: Association for Supervision and Curriculum Development.

McCune, S. D. (1986). *Guide to strategic planning for educators.* Alexandria, VA: Association for Supervision and Curriculum Development.

McDonald, J. P., et al. (1993). *Graduation by exhibition.* Alexandria, VA: Association for Supervision and Curriculum Development.

McDonnell, L. M. (1994, June). Policymakers' views of student assessment. CSE

Technical Report 378. Los Angeles: National Center for Research on Evaluation, Standards, and Student Testing.

McGregor, D. (1960). *The human side of enterprise.* New York: McGraw-Hill.

McGuffy's Second Eclectic Reader. (1879). New York: American Book Co.

McQuown, M. L. (1881). *Report of the superintendent of public instruction, commonwealth of Pennsylvania.* Harrisburg: Lanes Hart, State Printer.

McLaren, P. (1986). *Schooling as a ritual performance.* London: Routledge, Chapman, and Hall.

McLaughlin, M. W. (1991, November). Test-based accountability as a reform strategy. *Phi Delta Kappan, 73*(3), 248–251.

McNeil, J. D. (1996). *Curriculum.* New York: Harper Collins.

Meeker, M. N. (1969). *The structure of intellect.* Columbus, OH: Charles E. Merrill.

Mehrens, W. A. (1994). *Issues and recommendations regarding implementation of high school graduation tests.* Oak Brook, IL: North Central Regional Educational Laboratory.

Menchhofer, M. P. (1993). *A case study exploring the impact of a curriculum audit conducted in the Ladue school district.* Unpublished doctoral dissertation, University of Denver, Denver, CO.

Messick, S., & Associates. (1976). *Individuality in learning.* San Francisco: Jossey-Bass.

Meyer, C. A. (1992, May). What's the difference between *Authentic* and *Performance* Assessment? *Educational Leadership, 49*(8), 39–40.

Mills, R. P. (1994a, November 1). Proposed assessment activities [Letter to Vermont education leaders]. Montpelier: Department of Education.

Mills, R. P. (1994b, March 1994). Vermont's student assessment works. In *From the board room.* Montpelier: Vermont School Boards Association.

Mintzberg, H. (1994). *The rise and fall of strategic planning.* New York: The Free Press.

Mislery, R. J. (1993). Foundations of a new test theory. In N. Frederiksen, R. J. Misher, & I. I. Bejar (Eds.), *Text theory for a new generation of tests.* Hillsdale, NJ: Lawrence Erlbaum Associates.

Murphy, J. (1992). Restructuring America's schools: An overview. In C. E. Finn, Jr., & T. Rebarber (Eds.), *Education reform in the nineties.* New York: Macmillan.

Nasaw, D. (1979). *Schooled to order.* New York: Oxford University Press.

National Center on Education and the Economy. (1990, June). *America's choice: High skills or low wages!* Rochester, New York.

National Commission on Excellence in Education. (1993). *A nation at risk: The imperative for educational reform.* Washington, DC: U.S. Government Printing Office.

National Council of Teachers of Mathematics. (1989). *Curriculum and evaluation standards for school mathematics.* Reston, VA.

National Education Association. (1993). *It's about time.* Washington, DC.

National Mathematical Sciences Education Board. (1993). *Measuring counts: A policy brief.* Washington, DC: National Academy Press (for the National Research Council).

Neill, A. S. (1960). *Summerhill: A radical approach to child rearing.* New York: Hart Publishing.

Neill, D. M., & Medina, N. J. (1989, May). Standardized Testing: Harmful to Educational Health. *Phi Delta Kappan, 70*(9), 688–697.

Newmann, F. M., & Wehlage, G. G. (1995). *Successful school restructuring.* Madison, Wisconsin: Center on Organization and Restructuring of Schools. University of Wisconsin.

Newmann, F. M. (Ed.). (1992). *Student engagement and achievement in American secondary schools.* New York: Teachers College Press.

Newmann, F. M., & Archibald, D. A. (1992). The nature of authentic academic achievement. In H. Berlak et al., *Toward a new science of educational testing and assessment.* Albany: State University of New York Press, pp. 71–83.

Numbers, R. L. (1992). *The creationists.* Berkeley: University of California Press.

Oakes, J. (1992). Can tracking research inform practice? Technical, normative, and political considerations. *Educational Researcher, 21*(4), 12–21.

Odiorne, G. S. (1979). *MBO II.* Belmont, CA: Fearon Pitman.

O'Donoghue, T., & O'Brien, S. (1995, October). Teachers' perceptions of parental involvement. *International Journal of Educational Reform, 4*(4), 404–414.

Oliphant, T. (1995, August 22). Kennedy's dirty fingernails tradition. *The Boston Globe,* p. 15.

O'Neil, J. (1994, October). Aiming for new outcomes: The promise and the reality. *Educational Leadership, 51*(6), 6–10.

Owens, R. G. (1995). *Organizational behavior in education* (5th ed.). Englewood Cliffs, NJ: Prentice-Hall.

Pankratz, R. S. (1992, April). Political realities in setting state educational standards. *International Journal of Educational Reform, 1*(2), 139–148.

Parenti, M. (1974). *Democracy for the few.* New York: St. Martin's Press.

Peddiwell, G. (1939). *The saber-tooth curriculum.* New York: McGraw-Hill.

Perrone, V. (Ed.). (1991). *Expanding student assessment.* Alexandria, VA: Association for Supervision and Curriculum Development.

Peters, T. J., & Waterman, R. H. (1982). *In search of excellence.* New York: Harper & Row.

Phenix, P. H. (1964). *Realms of meaning.* New York: McGraw-Hill.

Phi Delta Kappan. (1981, May). *62*(9), 623–641. (Most of the issue is devoted to testing.)

Piaget, J. (1971). *The psychology of intelligence.* London: Routledge & Kegan Paul.

Piaget, J. (1973). *To understand is to invent.* New York: Grossman Publishers.

Piaget, J. (1977). *The development of thought.* New York: The Viking Press.

Piaget, J. (1970). *Structuralism.* New York: Basic Books, Inc.

Pierpoint, J. (1981). *Modern educational measurement.* Englewood Cliffs, NJ: Prentice-Hall.

Pinar, W. (1978). Currere: Toward reconceptualization. In J. R. Gress & D. E. Purpel (Eds.), *Curriculum: An introduction to the field.* Berkeley: McCutchan, pp. 526–545.

Piner, W. F., & Grumet, M. R. (1976). *Toward a poor curriculum.* Dubuque, IA: Kendall/Hunt.

Pitsch, M. (1994, April 6). With students' aid, Clinton signs goals 2000. *Education Week, 13*(28), 1, 21.

Pitsch, M. (1995, June 7). Goals 2000 fails to gain firm foothold. *Education Week, 13*(28), 1, 21.

Popham, J. W. (1981). *Modern educational measurement.* Englewood Cliffs, NJ: Prentice-Hall.

Popham, W. J. (1995). *Classroom assessment: What teachers need to know.* Boston: Allyn & Bacon.

Popkewitz, T. S., Tabachnick, B. R., & Wehlage, G. (1982). *The myth of educational reform.* Madison: University of Wisconsin Press.

Poston, Jr., W. K. (1992, Winter). Curriculum auditing: Effects upon school improvement in international schools. *Education, 113*(2), 195–197.

Pounds, R. L. (1968). *The development of education in Western culture.* New York: Appleton-Century-Crofts.

Powell, A. G., Farrar, E., & Cohen, D. C. (1985). *The shopping mall high school.* Boston: Houghton Mifflin.

Prather, S. H. (1881). *Report of the superintendent of public instruction, commonwealth of Pennsylvania.* Harrisburg: Lanes Hart, State Printer.

Raugh, M. (1994, October). *Opportunity to learn standards: Questions and answers.* Andover, MA: The Regional Laboratory for Educational Improvement of the Northeast and Islands.

Reimer, E. (1971). *School is dead.* New York: Anchor Books.

Resnick, D. P. (1981, May). Testing in America: A supportive environment. *Phi Delta Kappan, 62*(9), 625–628.

Rippa, S. A. (1992). *Education in a free society.* New York: Longman.

Robinson, G. E., & Carver, J. M. (1989). *Assessing and grading student achievement.* Arlington, VA: Education Research Service.

Robinson, G. E., & Brandon, D. P. (1994). *NAEP test scores: Should they be used to compare and rank state educational quality?* Reston, VA: Educational Research Service.

Rogers, D. (1968). *110 Livingston street.* New York: Random House.

Rohlen, Thomas P. (1983). *Japan's high schools.* Berkeley, CA: University of California Press.

Rothman, R. (1992, April 22). Testing shifts from memorization to investigation in Littleton, Colorado. *Education Week, 11*(31), 1, 22–23.

Rothman, R. (1995). *Measuring up: Standards, assessment, and school reform.* San Francisco: Jossey-Bass.

Salganik, L. H. (1985, May). Why testing reforms are so popular and how they are changing education. *Phi Delta Kappan, 66*(9), 607–610.

Sapon-Shevin, M. (1994). *Playing favorites: Gifted education and the disruption of community.* Albany: SUNY Press.

Sarason, S. B. (1982). *The culture of school and the problem of change.* (2nd ed.). Boston: Allyn & Bacon, Inc.

Sergiovanni, T. J. (1993). *Moral leadership.* San Francisco: Jossey-Bass.

Schlesinger, J. M., William, F., & Forman, C. (1993, September 29). Japan inc., wracked by recession, takes stock of its methods. *The Wall Street Journal,* pp. A1–A4.

Schneider, J., & Houston, P. (1993). *Exploding the myths.* Arlington, VA: American Association of Educational Service Agencies.

Schonberger, R. J. (1982). *Japanese manufacturing techniques.* New York: The Free Press.

Schubert, W. (1980). *Curriculum books: The first eighty years.* Washington, DC: University Press of America.

Scriven, M. (1988). Evaluating teachers as professionals: The Duties-based approach. In S. J. Stanley & W. J. Popham (Eds.), *Teacher Evaluation: Six Prescriptions for Success.* Alexandria, VA: Association for Supervision and Curriculum Development, pp. 110–144.

Senge, P. (1990). *The fifth discipline.* New York: Doubleday/Currency.

Settle, J. C. (1995). *An exploratory case study of professional development and other critical elements in the implementation of primary programs in eight public Kentucky elementary schools.* Unpublished doctoral dissertation, University of Kentucky, Lexington, Kentucky.

Sharpe, R. (1994, May 10). Efforts to promote teaching of values in schools are sparking heated debate among lawmakers. *The Wall Street Journal,* p. A20.

Shepard, L. A. (1991, October). Psychometricians' beliefs about learning. *Educational Researcher, 20*(7), 2–16.

Silver, P. (1983). *Educational administration.* New York: Harper and Row.

Simmons, W., & Resnick, L. (1993, February). Assessment as the catalyst of school reform. *Educational Leadership, 50*(5), 11–15.

Singham, M. (1995, December). Race and intelligence: What are the issues? *Phi Delta Kappan, 77*(4), 271–278.

Sizer, T. R. (1992). *Horace's school: Redesigning the American high school.* Boston: Houghton-Mifflin.

Sizer, T. R. (1984). *Horace's compromise: The dilemma of the American high school.* Boston: Houghton Mifflin.

Skinner, B. F. (1948). *Walden two.* New York: Macmillan.

Smith, B. O., Stanley, W. O., & Shores, J. H. (1950). *Fundamentals of curriculum development.* New York: World Book Co.

Smith, P. (1910). *Report of the state superintendent of public schools of the state of Maine.* Waterville, ME: Sentinel Publishing Co.

South Burlington School District. (1993–1994). *Evaluation and Supervision Guidelines.* South Burlington, VT.

Spady, W. (1994, October). Choosing outcomes of significance. *Educational Leadership, 51*(6), 18–22.

Spady, W. (1995). *Outcome-based education: Critical issues and answers.* Arlington, VA: American Association of School Administrators.

Spring, J. (1988). *Conflict of interests.* New York: Longman.

Springer, S. P., & Deutsch, G. (1981). *Learning.* San Diego, CA: Harcourt, Brace, Jovanovich.

Staddon, J. E. R., & Ettinger, R. H. (1989). *Learning.* San Diego, CA: Harcourt, Brace, Jovanovich.

Stanley, S. J., & Popham, W. J. (Eds.). (1988). *Teacher evaluation: Six prescriptions for success.* Alexandria, VA: Association for Supervision and Curriculum Development.

State of Vermont. (1990). Act (#)230. An Act Relating to Reforms in Special Education. Montpelier, Vermont: General Assembly of the State of Vermont.

Steeves, F. L., & English, F. W. (1978). *Secondary curriculum for a changing world.* Columbus, OH: Charles E. Merrill.

Steffy, B. E. (1989). Curriculum auditing as a state agency tool in takeovers. *National Forum of Applied Educational Research, 3*(1), 5–16.

Steffy, B. E. (1992, January). Assault on the bureaucracy: Restructuring the Kentucky department of education. *International Journal of Educational Reform, 1*(1), 16–31.

Steffy, B. E. (1993). *The Kentucky education reform: Lessons for America.* Lancaster, PA: Technomic Publishing Co.

Steffy, B. E. (1995). *Authentic assessment and curriculum alignment: Meeting the challenge of national standards.* Rockport, MA: Pro-Active Publications.

Stefkovich, J. A., & Guba, G. J. (1995, April). School reform in Chicago: A study of structures and symbols. *International Journal of Educational Reform, 4*(2), 131–142.

Steinberger, E. D. (1993). *Improving student achievement.* Arlington, VA: American Association of School Administrators.

Stephen, J. (1881). *Report of the superintendent of public instruction, commonwealth of Pennsylvania.* Harrisburg: Lanes Hart, State Printer.

Sternberg, R. J. (1993). *Beyond I.Q.* Victoria, Australia: Cambridge University Press.

Streshly, W. (1992, Winter). The feedback loop. *Education, 113*(2), 182–6.

Stevens, F. I. (assisted by J. Grykmes). (1993). *Opportunity to learn: Issues of equity for poor and minority students.* Washington, DC: National Center for Education Statistics.

Supplee, A. P. (1881). *Report of the superintendent of public instruction, commonwealth of Pennsylvania.* Harrisburg: Lanes Hart, State Printer.

Sykes, G. (1990). Fostering teacher professionalism in schools. In R. F. Elmore and Associates, *Restructuring schools: The next generation of educational reform.* San Francisco: Jossey-Bass.

Tanner, D., & Tanner, L. (1975). *Curriculum development: Theory into practice.* New York: Macmillan.

Tanner, D., & Tanner, L. N. (1980). *Curriculum development.* New York: Macmillan.

Tanner, D. (1986). Are reforms like swinging pendulums? In H. J. Walberg & J. W. Keefe (Eds.), *Rethinking reform: The principal's dilemma.* Reston, VA: National Association of Secondary School Principals, pp. 5–17.

Tanner, D. (1992). Synthesis versus fragmentation: The way out of curriculum confusion. In J. M. Jenkins & D. Tanner (Eds.), *Restructuring for an interdisciplinary curriculum.* Reston, VA: National Association of Secondary School Principals, pp. 1–14.

Taylor, F. W. (1911). *The principles of scientific management.* New York: Harper and Row.

Terman, L. M. (1916). *The measurement of intelligence.* Boston: Houghton Mifflin Company.

The Holmes Group. (1956). *Tomorrow's teachers.* East Lansing, MI: Michigan State University.

The New McGuffey Second Reader. (1901). New York: American Book Company.

The Outing of Outsourcing. (1995, November 25). *The Economist,* pp. 57–58.

The Regional Laboratory for Education Improvement of the Northeast and Islands. (October 1994). *Status report on voluntary national standards in education* (2nd ed.). Andover, MA.

Thomas, C. (1995, December 8). History report indicts education. *The Journal Gazette,* p. 13A.

Thomson, S. D. (Ed.). (1993). *Principals for our changing schools.* Fairfax, VA: National Policy Board for Educational Administration.

Thorndike, E. L. (1924). Mental discipline in high school studies. *Journal of Educational Psychology, 15,* 83–98.

Toch, T. (1991). *In the name of excellence.* New York: Oxford University Press.

Treat, J. E. (1995, December 11). A weapon for the corporate battlefield. *The Wall Street Journal,* p. A12.

Troutman, B. I. (1994, July). Leadership by design: The anatomy of a reorganization. *International Journal of Educational Reform, 3*(3), 311–319.

Trump, J. L. (1977). *A school for everyone.* Reston, VA: National Association for Secondary School Principals.

Tucker, M. (1993, November). Designing the new American high school. Rochester, NY: The National Alliance for Restructuring Education.

Tuckman, B. W. (1985). *Evaluating instructional programs.* Boston: Allyn and Bacon.

Tyack, D. B. (1974). *The one best system.* Cambridge: Harvard University Press.

Tyack, D., & Cuban, L. (1995). *Tinkering toward utopia: A century of public school reform.* Cambridge, MA: Harvard University Press.

Tyler, R. (1936). Defining and measuring objectives of progressive education. *Education Research Bulletin, 15,* 67–71.

Tyler, R. (1949). *Basic principles of curriculum and instruction.* Chicago: University of Chicago Press.

Tyree, A. K., Jr. (1993, Spring). Examining the evidence: Have states reduced local control of curriculum? *Educational Evaluation and Policy Analysis, 15*(1), 34–50.

U.S. Department of Education. (1991, April). *America 2000: An education strategy.*

U.S. Department of Education. (1991, June). *National assessment of educational progress.* Washington, DC.

U.S. Department of Education. (1994, May). *Community update: Goals 2000.* (No. 13.) Washington, DC.

U.S. Department of Labor. (1991, May). *What work requires of schools: A SCANS report for America 2000.* The Secretary's Commission on Achieving Necessary Skills.

U.S. Government Printing Office. (1994). *Prisoners of time.* Washington, DC.

Vaill, P.B. (1984). Process wisdom for a new age. In J. D. Adams (Ed.), *Transforming work.* Alexandria, VA: Miles River Press, pp. 18–34.

Vaill, P. B. (1989). *Managing as a performing art: New ideas for a world of chaotic change.* San Francisco: Jossey-Bass.

Vermont Assessment Program: Summary of Assessment Results, 1992–1993. (November 2, 1993). Montpelier: Department of Education.

Vermont Assessment Program. (1993–1994). Montpelier: Department of Education.

The Vermont Middle Grades Task Force. (1991, December). *The middle matters:*

Transforming education for Vermont's young adolescents. Montpelier: Department of Education.

Vertiz, V. (1992, Winter). The curriculum audit: A quality control vehicle to school reform. *Education, 113*(2), 165–167.

Vertiz, V. (1995, Fall). What the curriculum audit reveals about schools. *AASA School Administrator, 11*(52), 25–27.

Vertiz, V., & Bates, G. (1995, February 11). *The curriculum management audit: Revelations about our schools.* Unpublished paper presented to the American Association of School Administrators Annual Convention, New Orleans, LA.

Video Journal of Education. (1995, Issue 501). Developing aligning, and auditing curriculum. Salt Lake City, UT.

Walberg, H. (1993). Productive use of time. In L. W. Anderson & H. J. Walberg (Eds.), *Timepiece: Extending and enhancing learning time.* Reston, VA: National Association of Secondary School Principals, pp. 1–8.

Wallace, K. M. (1995, April). The contribution of the mass media to the education policy process. *International Journal of Educational Reform, 4*(2), 124–130.

Waller, W. (1965). *The sociology of teaching.* New York: John Wiley and Sons.

Walton, M. (1986). *The Deming management method.* New York: Perigee/Putnam.

Walton, M. (1990). *Deming management at work.* New York: Perigee/Putnam.

Wang, M. C., Haertel, G. D., & Walberg, H. J. (1993, December/1994, January). What helps students learn? *Educational Leadership, 51*(4), 74–79.

Watts, G. D., & Castle, S. (1993, December). The time dilemma in school restructuring. *Phi Delta Kappan, 75*(4), 306–310.

Weick, K. (1976). Educational organizations as loosely coupled systems. *Administrative Science Quarterly, 23* (December), pp. 1–19.

Weinstein, D. F. (1986). *Administrator's guide to curriculum mapping.* Englewood Cliffs, NJ: Prentice-Hall.

Westbury, I. (1992). Comparing American and Japanese achievement: Is the United States really a low achiever? *Educational Researcher, 21*(5), 18–24.

Westerberg, J., & Westerberg, T. (1992, October 14). Base graduation on performance and not seat time. *Education Week, 12*(6), 36.

Wickersham, J. P. (1881). *Report of the superintendent of public instruction, commonwealth of Pennsylvania.* Harrisburg: Lanes Hart, State Printer.

Wiggins, G. (1989, April). Teaching to the (Authentic) test. *Educational Leadership, 46*(7), 41–47.

Wiggins, G. P. (1993). *Assessing student performance.* San Francisco: Jossey-Bass.

Wikeley, F., & Hughes, M. (1995, July). Parents and educational reform in the UK. *International Journal of Educational Reform, 4*(3), 301–309.

Williams, M., & Kanabakyashi, M. (1994, April 29). Some maverick firms in Japan are changing its business climate. *The Wall Street Journal,* pp. A1–A5.

Wise, A. E. (1979). *Legislated learning.* Berkeley: University of California Press.

Wise, A. E. (1988). Legislated learning revisited. *Phi Delta Kappan, 69*(5), 329–333.

Worthen, B. R., & Spandel, V. (1991, February). Putting the standardized test debate in perspective. *Educational Leadership, 48*(5), 65–69.

Zais, R. S. (1976). *Curriculum: Principles and foundations.* New York: Thomas Y. Crowell.

AUTHOR INDEX

SUBJECT INDEX